HENRI ROCHEFORT

BOOKS BY ROGER L. WILLIAMS

Henri Rochefort, Prince of the Gutter Press

Modern Europe 1660–1945

Gaslight and Shadow, The World of Napoleon III

Henri Rochefort

PRINCE OF THE GUTTER PRESS

ROGER L. WILLIAMS

Charles Scribner's Sons · New York

To my good friend Helen S. Tordt

The Greeks used to paint pictures of gods on their pots;
we, probably, cannot do as much, but we may put some
pictures of insects on them, and reptiles;—butterflies,
and frogs, if nothing better.

JOHN RUSKIN
Fors Clavigera

Acknowledgments

In the Bibliography, I have indicated my obligation to many published works and to collections of public and private papers still unpublished. I should like, however, to extend more specific thanks to Mme. Tulard, the Director of the Archives de la Préfecture de Police in Paris, and to her associates, who gave me every help and kindness during my months of research among them. My thanks also go to Mme. Olivier Ziegel, whose preliminary researches on my behalf enabled me to employ my months of research in Paris with great efficiency. This preliminary research was made possible by a grant from the Antioch College Faculty Fund, and a further grant-in-aid was provided by the American Philosophical Society to cover travel expenses. Perhaps these were small sums, by present-day foundational standards, but they are gratefully acknowledged as making individual research and writing still possible.

Several people gave me particular aid or encouragement, for which my thanks: To Mme. Maurice Joron for permission to use personal letters in her possession; to M. Adrien Dansette for encouraging me in the direction my views of Rochefort were leading me; to Helen S. Tordt, Michael J. Kraus, and Shirley P. Katzev, who gave generously of their time helping make the manuscript more readable. Without much doubt I held out too stubbornly against some of their suggestions for improvement, but the book is the better for those I accepted.

The illustrations are reprinted by permission of Roger Viollet, Documentation Générale Photographique, 6 rue de Seine, Paris.

ROGER L. WILLIAMS

Santa Barbara, California
February 15, 1966

Contents

List of Illustrations

Introduction

Midway in the nineteenth century, the French accepted a virtual dictatorship as the latest answer to the political and social instability that had plagued the nation for sixty years. Napoleon III's Second Empire, founded in 1852, had required a *coup d'état* the previous year for its impetus, and the illegitimacy of its birth haunted the Empire, and the Emperor, for the next eighteen years.

Henri Rochefort, bent on a literary career, was two years out of secondary school when Napoleon III seized power. To have radical political views was a commonplace among the Parisian youth, and the Emperor was hardly their idol. By 1868, Rochefort blossomed into the most notorious of the imperial enemies—not the most dangerous of them certainly, but the noisiest. His journal, *La Lanterne*, really a pamphlet, became the rage of the boulevards, and some of his quips are still remembered today in Paris.

Two years later the Empire succumbed to war, to be succeeded by a provisional government republican in form. Since the days of the Great Revolution, French republicanism had been tinged with puritanism, the special republican virtues presumably being sobriety and decency. Rochefort continually advanced himself under the Republic as the steadfast symbol of high principle, but in truth he fell remarkably short of his assertions, just as the French discovered that the Republic had not overwhelmed them with virtue upon the exit of Napoleon III and Offenbach.

We know that historically men have advanced a variety of justifications as qualifying them for dictatorial power or for the special privilege of conserving the constitution and defending the liberties of the governed. The claim may be based on ability, on talent, the origin of an aristocracy; it may be based on tradition, an hereditary right to govern; it may be based on priestly function by those who serve as the link between men and God; it may be crassly based on a utilitarian principle to appeal to a society devoted above all else to sanitation and punctuality. But the claim that modern men —that is to say, the descendants of Machiavelli—have found most difficult to accept is the claim of virtue. For better or for worse, the philosopher-king is felt to be out-of-place in smoke-filled rooms.

For the French in particular, the man of virtue passing as politician, whether he raises the vision of a headhunter à la Robespierre or a vision of a holy savior, implies full-scale political naïveté. In the case of Rochefort, they were right. He never knew himself to be wrong or meanly-inspired; even his friends knew his political ineptitude.

Why study him then? If he was not a leading politician or statesman, Rochefort was a well-known polemicist in his own day, and that day lasted for over thirty years. He had something to say about every regime, every scandal, and most leading politicians through those turbulent years—rarely anything flattering. One can, therefore, trace the course of French political history from the late Second Empire through the Dreyfus affair by surveying the vehemence and viciousness of Rochefort's journalistic frays.

More than political history emerges in the telling. Rochefort was of impoverished noble origin, and behind the façade of egalitarian utterances lurked the temperament of a frivolous, irresponsible aristocrat. The conversion of the silk purse was incomplete. To this aspect of social history one must add the psychological aspect. For Rochefort's radical extremism does not appear to have been simply a political or social matter. Had he lived in the post-Freudian world, a variety of unpleasant medical terms might have been applied to him. We have, in brief, that personality which is equally at home on the extreme Left or on the extreme Right, and, indeed, inhabited both in a life rich in equivocation.

CHAPTER I

The Early Years

1831-1868

One can say of him, tritely, that he spent his whole life in the hope of making himself interesting.

JULES RENARD

IF THE publication of one's memoirs is indication of self-esteem, that Henri Rochefort's ran to five volumes may be taken as his own measure of his place in history. Even the title, *Les Aventures de ma vie*, gave his daily incidents a dramatic tone beyond the humdrum confines of humbler memorialists. When the fifth volume appeared in the autumn of 1896, Rochefort was so well known as a polemicist that none but the blindly devoted could believe that his memoirs would be gospel truth, a fact that did not erase their importance. For here one finds warmed over the polemics of a passionate life, a vast *apologia* for a life of ceaseless virtue amidst the corrupt and self-seeking. A newspaper moderately friendly to Rochefort, in reviewing the final volume, frankly raised objections

1

about his interpretation of recent events, yet insisted that "Rochefort's good faith is beyond question." [1] Not everyone in France, by any means, would have agreed.

Most everyone did know, on the other hand, that Henri Rochefort was really the Marquis Henri de Rochefort-Luçay and that the Rochefort name was an ancient and distinguished one. Of Burgundian origin and what we have come to call *noblesse d'épée,* the Rochefort family ultimately had four branches, the Luçay branch being distinct before the end of the fifteenth century. Several members of the family served as chancellors and marshals of France from the fifteenth to the eighteenth centuries. Luçay was a barony in Berri, near Valençay. Though the family had other domains too, the chief residence until 1790 was the Château de Luçay-le-Mâle. Henri Rochefort's grandfather was the last member of the family to reside in the château. A lieutenant-colonel in the Royal Army, he followed the King's brothers into exile and lived in Coblenz. Apparently anticipating the confiscation decrees of the Revolutionary government, he sold most of the family properties; but his foresight proved in vain as he received payment in the new revolutionary paper money which quickly lost its value. The lands had been legally sold, however, so that after the Revolution the family had no hope of indemnification and was regarded as impoverished nobility.

Rochefort's paternal grandmother did not follow her husband into exile, but remained in Paris with her newborn son. She was arrested toward the end of 1792 and held for trial before the Revolutionary Tribunal. Her family believed that she was still alive at the end of the Terror in 1794 only because her jailers had been reluctant to send her to trial and certain execution when she had an infant son. [2] Named Claude-Louis-Marie, he became the first head of the family to live the life of a Parisian bourgeois.

The fluidity of French society in the nineteenth century has long been of interest to social historians and caricaturists. The confusion of social lines grew partly from rapid economic development and change in Western Europe as well as from the social and political upheavals following 1789. Not surprisingly, then, we find it an era of extraordinary *arrivisme* and of uncertainty about social position. As for the aristocrats in particular, after 1815 they showed doubt about their future. We have from one of their number, Chateaubriand, the observation that an aristocracy has three stages: that of ability, that of privilege, and that of vanity. By that reckoning, there was not much doubt about where the French aristocracy stood in the nineteenth century: new creations were comparatively few, but the acquisition of false titles by aspirant bourgeois flourished as never before, a self-congratulatory traffic that has never ceased in France.

Poverty-stricken though he was, the Marquis Claude-Louis-Marie de Rochefort-Luçay (1790–1871) remained a Legitimist and was unreconciled to the new order all his life. His bitterness over the Revolution and Napoleon won him a position on a Legitimist journal after 1815, the *Drapeau Blanc* (which the liberals of the day called the *Crapaud Blanc*); and he later wrote for an even more extreme Legitimist publication, the *Quotidienne,* although he did not share the paper's enthusiasm for bloody reprisals against former revolutionaries. He increasingly turned his literary attention to writing for the theater, turning out a number of light works by himself as well as in collaboration with others. His Legitimist loyalty was recognized when Louis XVIII appointed him Secretary-General for the colony of Ile de Bourbon (now Reunion), a post he occupied for nearly three years. But he was happiest as a playwright as indicated in the title of his *Mémoires d'un Vaudevilliste* (1863).[3]

Aristocratic Legitimist he may have been, but he married a commoner, Nicole Morel, whose father had been a staunch Republican soldier during the Revolution. They had three daughters, Caroline-Françoise, Emilie, and Palmyre; Henri was the fourth and last child, born in Paris on January 31, 1831. The reader of *Les Aventures de ma vie,* knowing that Henri Rochefort came to share his mother's political views rather than his father's, should be struck by the ambiguity of his childhood recollections. His mother's given name does not appear, and her relatives are scarcely mentioned. The name-dropping flatters only the aristocratic side of the family,

3

and the relatives mentioned are sometimes so distant that they have nothing significant to do with his story. Yet, these same pages are shot through with bits of information that Rochefort cited as proof of an infantile anticlericalism and love of liberty, as if his later republicanism had been firmly rooted in the sound principles of his maternal birthright. We learn, for instance, that at the age of six he was sent for an extended visit with two aunts near Orléans, Madame de Saint-Maur and the Baronne d'Almais de Curnieux. To avoid being taken to mass he would disappear into the fields and meadows, where he befriended a thirteen-year-old cowherd named Caroline. She taught him his favorite game, grabbing a cow's tail and letting himself be pulled around the meadow. He did not see that this favorite game assumed various political forms in his later career.

Primary school produced few notable memories. Rochefort remembered that he had been treated kindly by his teachers, possibly because of his father's custom of sending them good tickets for theaters that were not making money. Secondary school was a more serious matter, since the impoverished family could not afford the financial burden. Fortunately, Rochefort père had friends in the Ministry of Public Instruction, and the government provided assistance that enabled Henri to enroll in the Collège Saint-Louis in 1843. Rochefort remembered the school, in the rue de la Harpe, as the worst prison of his life. Long after graduation he could still smell the "sour odor of the old goats, corridors, and stairs. . . . In prison the body alone is detained . . . and your mind at least is allowed to pass freely through the bars." [4]

Rochefort won no honors at school, although he was thought to have a good memory and intelligence. But he was also frail, pale, and anemic, and was regarded as overly timid and nervous. During his fourth year, a professor asked the students to write compositions commemorating the marriage of the Duc de Montpensier, son of King Louis-Philippe. Rochefort wrote his in verse, which the self-seeking instructor forwarded to the Tuileries. Back came a pencil case lettered in gold, a reward that earned considerable disapproval for Rochefort from most of the faculty and many of the students, as the regime enjoyed little popularity by 1847. Accused of crawling at the feet of the great, he angrily smashed the pencil case and later called the incident his debut into politics. As a compensation, he wrote a poem in honor of the Republican poet Béranger.

> What ink has moistened your pen,
> To mix so well the gall of bitterness
>   With Anacreon's smile,
> You who adorn your palette with a hundred colors
> And reveal the portrait of Napoleon
>   With the portrait of Lisette?
>
> You who, for twenty years, in peaceful times,
> As in the stormy days of political crimes,
>   Have been the apostle of liberty!
> And have with genius alone worn the chain
> And know how to unite Roman pride
>   And Roman simplicity?
>
> A noble victim of the hatred of kings,
> Nothing has silenced your sublime voice:
>   A prisoner, you have sung!
> And now as the kings are forgiven by your lyre,
> Pass the peaceful fall weaving the laurels
>   Gathered in summer!
>
> But whether my skiff unfurls its sails
> Under a bright sun or a starless sky,
>   In calm or in danger,
> Whether to taste happiness or find a tempest,
> I shall invoke the echo of my heart
>   Which gives back the beloved name of Béranger.[5]

The aging poet replied: "Is it true that you are only fifteen years old? Oh, if at that age I had written verses as well turned, as poetic, I should have believed myself called to a high destiny. I, at fifteen, hardly knew ortography [sic]."[6]

The February Revolution of 1848, which overthrew the July Monarchy and established the Second Republic, engendered immense excitement among the schoolboys, although most of them were unaware of the political issues at stake. Nevertheless, it was an opportunity to take part in the uproar and too good to miss. A student delegation called on the headmaster for permission to go into the streets, but he refused on the grounds that he was responsible to their families for their safety. Within several days, discipline at the school collapsed and a gate was found unlocked. Out poured the students, meeting head-on a mob armed with swords and firearms and shouting, "To the Panthéon." Once they got to the Panthéon, a new shout, "To the Tuileries," sent them all off in that direction. After a busy day of revolution, Rochefort went to his own home to go to bed and woke up next morning to find that he had been expelled from school. The expulsion order was reversed, however, by the new Republican Minister of Public Instruction, who congratulated the schoolboys for their Republican heroism.

Politics had taken on a new reality for the students, and arguments and squabbles among them were common. Radicalism became fashionable for the majority, and when the frightful insurrection known as the June Days broke out, the majority favored the rebels. To his great pleasure Rochefort had not long to remain in school after the revolutionary excitement: he received the Bachelier ès Lettres on July 30, 1849.[7]

Although his education had not prepared him for any particular profession, Rochefort knew that he had to earn a living because of his family's financial state. He thought that his future lay in writing, but he was undecided about *what* he would write. Meanwhile, he secured through a family friend a tutoring position at the home of the Comtesse de Montbrun, who had two children, nine and ten. He found the position intolerably humiliating. His fondness for children quickly won him the affection of his pupils—and, according to him, their mother's jealousy. She began attending the lessons to supervise his Latin instruction and, worse, began inviting him to her dinner parties, introducing him as M. le comte de Rochefort-Luçay, "who has been good enough to give my two children Latin lessons."[8] He was uncertain whether she meant to reveal his impoverished state or to use his name to lend luster to her own blazon, which merely dated from the First Empire. This tutorial episode of a few weeks destroyed all notions of a teaching career and drove him to write his first play.

This first attempt was the juvenile and hackneyed plot that one might expect from an eighteen-year-old. Rochefort took the manuscript to the disorderly apartment of Henri Murger, whose *Scènes de la Vie de Bohème* then enjoyed a success in the theater. The reception was unfriendly, and Rochefort was taunted about it by his sisters, who had always made fun of his timidity and fragility. He then began medical school as a sure route to greater financial rewards, but proved to be far too delicate to endure the sights and odors of a medical education.

At the age of twenty, Rochefort finally obtained a salaried position. A family friend, Paul Merruau, offered to get him a job at the Hôtel de Ville where a brother, Charles Merruau, was Secretary-General. As no regular position was vacant, Rochefort found himself, midsummer of 1851, attached to the municipal Department of Patents, where he interviewed "several inventors and ten madmen" each day. He claimed that the most favored projects in that era were perpetual-motion devices, invariably powered by something that was not perpetually moving, and devices to direct the flight of balloons, invariable sponsored by men unable to afford balloons to test their devices.[9]

On December 2, 1851, after nearly six months of this tedium, Rochefort read on his way to work the proclamation of President Bonaparte's *coup d'état*. Stunned by this threat to the Republic and overwhelmed by a feeling of helplessness, he avoided his office and sought out friends in the Latin Quarter. On December 4, he and several of these friends joined a small group of workers who were raising a barricade near the Porte Saint-Martin. Fortunately, they were not attacked by troops; indeed, Rochefort was not even armed. Next day he returned to his office, making no mention of the fact that he had opposed the successful *coup*.

In the subsequent review of personnel, he was given a more

permanent position in the Department of Architecture and a raise from 100 to 125 francs a month. Here his principal colleague was Drumont, father of the journalist Édouard Drumont and a man considerably interested in literature. They spent their lunch hours discussing literary matters, and with Drumont's encouragement Rochefort spent most of his office hours experimenting with plots. It is hardly surprising that Rochefort soon had a reputation for idleness; but he was also known for his wit, as a result of which he was popular with his fellows and usually indulged.[10] The Secretary-General did, however, shift him once again in the hope of greater industry, this time to the Municipal Archives, which had a funereal atmosphere for one who was interested in the vaudeville stage. Rochefort tells us that the archivist's job centered around watching the dossiers and documents sleep in their containers.[11] When Baron Haussmann became Prefect of the Seine in 1853, there were further shake-ups in the civic departments. Rochefort found himself transferred to the office that checked the municipal accounts, where the personnel was a bit less mummified, and where his salary was increased to 300 francs. Since he had absolutely no ability in accounting, he got into the habit of approving every paper that passed over his desk.

After his graduation from Saint-Louis, Rochefort had begun to spend as many afternoons as possible in the Louvre and soon discovered that he had a taste for painting and art objects. At the Hôtel Drouot, the state-financed center for art sales, he gained much experience about art values and some insight into the sophistication of many art experts. He noted for sale once a portrait of Louis XV, said to be by Velasquez, but his fondest recollection was a "Head of Christ" claimed to be the work of the well-known painter of the Bologna school, Salvator Mundi. During those early years of civil service penury, Rochefort was occasionally able to turn this new knowledge to needed profit, acting as an adviser to purchasers until such time when he became a collector himself.

During his lifetime, Rochefort was often called a pamphleteer. His debut as such came in 1853 at the time of the imperial marriage.

8

The new Emperor, Napoleon III, required an heir to perpetuate his dynasty. The royal houses of Europe, however, displeased by the reappearance of a Bonaparte and, thus, the rupture of the 1815 peace settlement, were disinclined to provide a royal princess for the French throne. Nor could the Emperor, forty-four at his accession, afford to tarry while royal dispositions softened. Aristocratic Paris alternated between shock and amusement as it watched the Spanish Montijo family push its beautiful daughter Eugénie into the Emperor's path. (Rarely has a hopeful mother-in-law campaigned so openly for such high position—and won.) The boulevard wits soon exchanged unflattering jokes, songs, and poems honoring the situation, one sample of which should suffice:

> Montijo, more beautiful than wise,
> Heaps vows upon the Emperor.
> This evening, if he finds a maidenhead,
> It will mean that she had two of them.[12]

Despite the public opposition to a nonroyal marriage, Napoleon III went before Parliament to speak about "the woman of his choice," promising that she would have the virtues of the Empress Josephine, qualities about which no one seemed very clear. The situation was made worse by the Emperor's own sexual reputation, leading one of the outstanding snobs of the day, Nestor Roqueplan, to say of the Empress that "she will simply be the best kept woman in France."[13] Rochefort's contribution was a song entitled *Madame César,* which speculated about which of Madrid's many bachelors had been responsible for Eugénie's birth. He published it anonymously in Brussels and was well advised to do so, considering the press laws of the Second Empire.

By 1854, Rochefort's father had become aware of Henri's literary ambitions, and he introduced him to his friend Alexandre Dumas, then about to found a journal, *le Mousquetaire.* Dumas was kind enough to allow the young Rochefort to join the staff despite his lack of experience, and Rochefort produced several articles to which he could sign his name. The collaboration ended when Rochefort realized that he was not going to be paid for his articles. Shortly after, he finished a one-act play in which couplets alternated with puns. He sent it off to Jean Commerson, the chief editor of *Le Tintamarre* and a man known to have opposed the *coup* of 1851. Founded in 1843, *Le Tintamarre* (meaning The Racket) was a satirical weekly regarded as the most original of its kind in that day: "Our aim! to nose out self-advertisement, to unmask charlatanism, to track down quack Puff in all its treacherous disguises, under its philanthropical masks, that is the main thought which has inspired the creation of this paper!" [14]

One can imagine Rochefort's delight when Commerson invited him to call and told him that his play was amusing and well done, and, more, that Commerson had taken the liberty of sending it on to the director of the Folies-Dramatiques. Months went by and the director of the Folies-Dramatiques failed to put the play on the bill, until a disenchanted Rochefort realized that Commerson had not taken him seriously and had probably not even taken the trouble to read the manuscript. Ultimately the play got into the promised hands, and Rochefort had his theatrical debut with *Un Monsieur bien mis* in March of 1856. This was the first of his eighteen light comedies to be produced. [15]

In his memoirs, Rochefort was never more vague than when mentioning his mistresses and wives. He seems to have taken his first mistress about 1855, when he was about twenty-four, and it was evidently a short-lived affair. The following year his first child was born, to another woman, Marie Renauld, a twenty-two-year-old domestic, who also is nameless in the memoirs. He named the child Noémie, born April 2, 1856, at the Maison et École d'Accouchement in Paris. [16] Being irreligious and anticlerical, he refused to have her baptized. Ernest Blum, a friend of Rochefort, wrote that Rochefort took care of Noémie in his tiny single room as soon as she was taken from the wet nurse, implying that Marie Renauld did not live with them. [17]

With a child to support, Rochefort was the more driven to augment his civil service salary. In 1857 he met a man named

Kugelmann, publisher of a small journal called *La Presse théâtrale,* who had just lost his drama critic. Kugelmann offered the position to Rochefort, who remained with the journal until early 1859, when he resigned on finding that Kugelmann used favorable review notices to extort extra subscriptions from those favored and threatened them with ruinous reviews unless they complied. There would come a time in Rochefort's life when he would be less delicate about subscription-increasing techniques.

A new opportunity appeared almost at once, however, after Rochefort had appraised an art collection against which the owner wished to borrow money. As the man obtained the loan that saved him from catastrophe, he wanted to reward the appraiser; and when Rochefort discovered that the man was a stockholder in *Le Charivari,* a satirical journal just then being reorganized, he asked for assistance in obtaining a position with the paper. Thus began, in 1859, a collaboration that lasted until 1864. The journal was run by a triumvirate: Louis Huart, Clément Caraguel, and Taxile Delord; and its staff included Pierre Véron, Albert Wolff, and Louis Leroy. Cham and Daumier contributed the cartoons. As the press laws made it advisable to shy away from political topics, Rochefort was urged to devote his column to theatrical and social notices.[18]

Writers cannot be expected to be enthusiastic about censorship of the press, and censorship was heavier under the Second Empire than it had been under the previous regime. But the unpopularity of the Second Empire with journalists has usually obscured the fact that they had not, as a group, given much support to the Second Republic either. Their political dissatisfaction reflected the fact that the Republic of 1848 had been a compromise of necessity pleasing to few; and the President of the Republic, Louis-Napoleon Bonaparte, as the symbol of that compromise, became the target of journalistic frustration. A further aggravating factor was the fact that the President enjoyed considerable personal popularity throughout the country, enabling him to overwhelm fractious political party chiefs and their newspaper allies.

After the *coup d'état* of 1851, the Minister of the Interior,

Morny, ordered his prefects to prevent unfavorable press comments on the *coup,* and in Paris the government suspended the most notable opposition papers. Other papers continued to appear by omitting all comment on the *coup.* Ten days later, the suspended papers were allowed to publish, but they were under close supervision, and a harsh censorship law was anticipated.[19] Such was the expectation when one editor wrote to his readers on February 1, 1852: "Events which seem enormous for us are really only moments in the totality of time. . . . More than ever life has become a pilgrimage and this world a place of passage."[20]

The Press Law of February 17, 1852, summed up most of the restrictive legislation dating from 1814: Every newspaper dealing with "politics or social economy" was required to have a government license, to be renewed with every staff change. Even foreign journals sold in France needed government authorization. Each journal had to deposit a sum of money wtih the government, "caution money," the amount somewhat higher than it had been under the Second Republic; and the stamp tax for newspapers was raised from five to six centimes. The law included some novel features: It became illegal to publish false news, whether in good or bad faith; parliamentary debates could not be reported except as supplied from official releases; anyone deprived by law of his civil rights could not publish an article; press offenses were no longer to be heard in the assize courts with a jury, but in "correctional courts" without jury; and one felony or two misdemeanors within a two-year period led to automatic suppression of the paper. The law also gave government officials discretionary power to punish journalists for words displeasing to the government, but which technically could not be described as breaches of the law. This meant that the Minister of the Interior and his prefects in particular could issue warnings. After three such warnings, a paper could be suppressed for two months. The President of the Republic was also armed with broad suppressive powers in the name of public safety.

With the restoration of Empire on December 2, 1852, this new press law was retained for the next sixteen years. It was clearly despotic on paper and infuriated the literary world. Yet its most arbitrary clauses were, in fact, the least abusive in practice. The biggest problem was getting a license to publish in the first place, and that was largely a matter of red tape rather than a governmental ruse to prevent publication of newspapers. By the time Rochefort became associated with *Le Charivari,* the Empire was shifting to a more liberal position, making it easier to obtain licenses; and a more liberal press law was generally expected by 1860—although it did not actually come forth until 1868. The closest student of the censorship has concluded that the actual censorship was far less than was provided for by the letter of the law, but that the possibility of censorship was a continual annoyance which made editors uneasy and led them to assume that the government was both better informed and more malevolent than was the case.[21]

One might, therefore, further characterize the press law as impolitic, for if in fact the regime was more liberal than its laws, those laws only fomented unnecessary hatred and opposition for the regime. Worse, the laws had to be implemented by civil servants, and the plodding variety of these often applied the letter of the law more strictly than the government had intended. This led to both arbitrariness, which is more often the quality of the petty rather than the great, and to ridiculousness, which earned the contempt of that dangerous enemy, the intelligentsia. Even Rochefort, for all his later hatred of the Second Empire, which he called an Asiatic despotism, avowed that the subordinate despots went far beyond the despot-in-chief, especially in matters censorial. He recalled a vaudeville manuscript submitted to the censors by Paul Siraudin, which was combed for three months for political allusions. The ultimate objection was to the phrase "My father, who dealt in *pâtés* from Chartres to Orléans," on the grounds that it was a sly reference to the dukes of the Orléans dynasty. The censor suggested that the line be changed to "from Amiens to Pithiviers." Another time, Adolphe Choler was censored for using the phrase *"foule d'imbéciles!,"* which the censor believed would be heard by the audience as "Fould *imbécile"* and interpreted as a reference to Achille Fould, a Minister of State.[22]

13

One safe political target was the Legitimist newspaper, the *Gazette de France,* edited by Gustave Janicot, although the editorial duel between the Legitimists and the Republicans lacked verve since neither group was in power. At one point, Janicot suggested that all Republicans were the sons of clodhoppers, to which Rochefort responded: "I who, at a time when so many people assume the *de* who are not entitled to it, have discreetly left the *de* which does belong to me under cover; but I take out all my prerogatives today and I sign in an unusual fashion the name I always have the right to sign: Henri de Rochefort de Luçay." [23] One of life's most difficult roles is the uncommon man cast as a democrat; and especially in a century when the aristocracy fretted over its decline and shuddered at the manners of the newly rich, it is small wonder that Rochefort never thoroughly mastered that part.

Even when Rochefort devoted his attention to the nonpolitical matters expected by the editors of *Le Charivari,* he did not escape political imbroglio. After what he called a disastrous cleaning of Raphael's "Saint Michael" at the Louvre, he wrote a strong article about the cleaning procedures used on paintings in that great state museum, adding some tart observations about the authenticity of some recent museum purchases. These charges were especially threatening to Count Nieuwerkerke, the Director-General of Museums and Superintendent of *Beaux-Arts,* because he was already the object of hostility and contempt. Although he was a sculptor, he had done little work and did not enjoy the esteem of the practicing artists or of the men whom he administered. He owed his position, second in rank to the Minister of *Beaux-Arts,* to his being the lover of Princess Mathilde Bonaparte, the Emperor's cousin, a fact that hardly recommended him to the artistic and intellectual circles!

Nieuwerkerke, therefore, did not ignore Rochefort's remarks, but filed charges against him for injury to a state functionary in the exercise of his duties. The staff of *Le Charivari* was horrified, not so much because of a possible jail sentence for Rochefort, but because of possible warnings to the paper. They urged Rochefort to apologize to Nieuwerkerke and back down, but he refused. Before the case went to court, the elderly painter Ingres summoned Rochefort to his studio to tell him that he, too, had been complaining about the treatment given canvases by the "vandals" in the Louvre, but that Nieuwerkerke had not dared to prosecute a painter of Ingres' distinction. Ingres, in short, let it be known that he would appear as a witness for Rochefort in court, and Nieuwerkerke thus was led to drop the charges.[24]

Lawsuits and duels, however, were to become frequent diversions in Rochefort's life. The incident that prompted his first duel, while he was at *Le Charivari,* was typical of the petty causes behind most of Rochefort's challenges. In this case, a private letter from François Ponsard to Rochefort had somehow found its way into the pages of *Le Gaulois,* at that time a mere "cabbage-leaf" read by cafe and theater society. Rochefort immediately sent a challenge to the owner-director of *Le Gaulois,* a pink, rotund young man named Delvaille, who signed himself as Delbrecht or Dell' Bright. The challenged chose a sword, an object Rochefort had never held in his hand. A hurried attempt was made to teach him the salutes, attitudes, and manners required in the duel, but when he arrived on the field of honor, he forgot his lesson and held the sword like a candle. The duel took place in the Chaville woods between Paris and Versailles, with a fine, cold rain falling. In the first pass, the chubby editor gave the skinny representative of the *noblesse d'épée* a cut on the chest. Rochefort's second, Louis Leroy, then intervened to halt the duel, whereupon Rochefort accidentally ran his sword into Leroy's knee.[25]

In 1861, several incidents combined to dim Rochefort's enthusiasm for the theater and to incline him more to political journalism. In the first place, he presented a new three-act comedy at the Vaudeville Theater, *Roueries d'une ingénue* (Tricks of an Unsophisticated Girl), which he admitted was not very good—and apparently the public agreed. Second, Charles Merruau, the Secretary-General at the Hôtel de Ville, having suffered Rochefort's clerical inadequacies for ten years and suspecting Rochefort of opposition to the imperial regime, wrote out an order dismissing him, which he asked Baron Haussmann to countersign. Haussmann balked, probably because he had been a frequent attender of the Vaudeville Theater and was acquainted with Rochefort as a vaudevillist. He also apparently knew of Rochefort's earlier tiff with Nieuwerkerke and concluded that a man of his knowledge of the theater and art was badly miscast in the Hôtel de Ville. Instead of dismissing Rochefort from the municipal service, Haussmann named him Assistant Inspector of *Beaux-Arts* at 2400 francs a year.

This put Rochefort on the political spot: the raise in salary from 300 francs was tremendous and tempting, but to accept such largesse from Haussmann was to accept it from one of the Emperor's most congenial and trusted associates. Either he must resign or admit that he had become a member of the imperial flock. His decision was not made as spontaneously as his later readers may have assumed. Several months went by before, in 1862, he tendered his resignation. He was now left with only about ninety francs a year from *Le Charivari*. But he was free, as he so frequently reminds us in his memoirs, to devote himself to exposing every abuse of power and every violation of the rights of mankind, for he had never been able to harden himself to cruelty, poverty, and all iniquities.[26] The opportunity to indulge in more political writing came in 1863 when Aurelien Scholl revived the *Nain Jaune*, hoping to rival or eclipse *Le Figaro*, the ambition of most new publishers. He joined the staff at a salary of 100 francs a week, a desperately needed augmentation of his tiny income from *Le Charivari*, where he was paid a few cents a line.

The *Nain Jaune* proved not to be successful but not because of its political views. For opposition to the Empire was obviously on the increase by that year. The war of 1859 on behalf of Italian nationalism had pleased few in France and estranged many Catholics from the regime; French business and industrial interests, as eager as their counterparts elsewhere for no governmental interference, were shocked when the Emperor moved toward free trade with Britain in 1860; and the intervention in Mexico made all but the most vociferous expansionists uneasy. This is not to say that the

regime was on the verge of collapse, as the Emperor especially continued to enjoy great popularity throughout the country, but rather
that criticism mounted, above all in Paris. The failure to modify the
press law was increasingly irritating—the modification had been
expected by 1860, and many people of liberal opinion were ungrateful for the liberal steps taken after 1859. The mild Auguste Villemot,
for instance, whose writings were far from subversive, told Rochefort
that even he had been continually red-penciled by the censor, until
he had written the censor a note: "Very well. Henceforth I shall
limit myself to giving market prices. I shall inform my readers that
the coleseeds have fallen, but that the tallows are firm. But still, is
there not in this firmness of tallows something disquieting for the
established order?" [27] (The word tallow—*suif*—also means to blow
someone up.)

University students, traditionally irreverent, grew increasingly
so in the 1860's, shouting at night in the Latin Quarter such phrases
as "What a bum that Louis!" or "That Eugénie, what a slut!" If the
police interfered, they would claim they referred to student ac-
quaintances. The Empress especially was subjected to public abuse,
partly because of her reputation for extreme Catholicism, and because of her reputation for caring for nothing but parties and clothes
(she was popularly called Queen Crinoline). Typical was an incident at the Odéon where she had gone to attend an opening: Suddenly
one group of students burst into song with a line from a popular
song, *"Corbleu, madame,* what are you doing here?" This was
immediately answered by another group of students, "I am dancing
the polka with my little friends." [28] Rochefort shared these sentiments and these tactics, and his students' outlook helps to account
for his coming popularity; his was the taste of the Parisian boulevards and gutters.

Rochefort achieved his first real notoriety in 1864 when he
joined the staff of *Le Figaro* at a salary of 500 francs a month, something more than the combined incomes he had been receiving from
Le Charivari and *Nain Jaune.* Villemessant, the director of *Le
Figaro,* had made the newspaper a highly sophisticated and success-

ful venture; and though not a writer himself, he had a reputation for discovering and using young talent. Staff members of *Le Figaro* were of divided opinion as to the wisdom of hiring Rochefort. Jouvin claimed that Rochefort was "an ignorant and vulgar man of ambition,"[29] but Villemessant announced the new writer in flattering terms: "Each week, beginning today, he will give us a Parisian chronicle; and we are congratulating ourselves with unusual enthusiasm because, while his pen is that of a man of wit, the hand that holds it belongs to a man of honor."[30]

Le Figaro, as a mildly monarchist paper, was regarded as an opposition sheet. Rochefort always presumed that Villemessant's Legitimist politics derived from the fact that he himself was illegitimate and hoped to legitimize himself by assuming both an aristocratic name and the anti-imperial airs of the old aristocrats. The name J.-H.-A. Cartier de Villemessant was, indeed, self-conferred. Yet, Villemessant counted among his friends the Duc de Morny, half-brother of Napoleon III, and it was understood that Morny would protect the paper from legal difficulties as long as it did not become too offensive to the regime. Thus, Rochefort was not hired to riddle the Empire, but to "make fun of everyone, and to make everyone laugh."[31]

By the time he had published four articles for *Le Figaro,* he had managed to involve himself in two duels, to the delight of Villemessant, who thought such activity excellent for public relations. The first was with a favorite of Isabella II, Don Carlos Marfori, Marquis de Loja, who was offended by Rochefort's reflections on the departure of the Queen of Spain from Madrid during an outbreak of cholera. The second was with Prince Achille Murat, cousin of Napoleon III, over remarks concerning a lawsuit involving Murat, the notorious courtesan Coral Pearl, and a horse dealer who wanted payment for a horse delivered to Mlle. Pearl. In the second duel, Prince Murat inflicted a slight wound upon Rochefort's hip.[32] Almost overnight, Paris became aware of Rochefort's singular appearance. Most of the descriptions emphasized the diabolical, "a satanic beard,"[33] for instance, or a "lean Mephistophelean jaw,"[34] which are confirmed by photograph and cartoon. He had a high forehead and high cheekbones, fine hands, a slight body, wildly tufted black hair, a habit of jamming his hands into his trousers' pockets, and a reputation for being nervous, aloof, and easily irritated.

Before Villemessant could realize what had happened, Rochefort selected the key figure in *Le Figaro's* security as his target: the Duc de Morny. It is hard to say which of Morny's attributes galled Rochefort the most. Did he attack Morny as a Republican would attack a member of the imperial family? Did he resent, as an aristocrat, Morny's illegitimate birth and the title necessarily created for him by his imperial half-brother? Or was he especially outraged by the theatricals that Morny produced under the name of M. de Saint-Rémy? Whichever the case, the assault upon Morny came following a new production (1864) of his play *M. Choufleuri restera chez lui.* A very light comedy in collaboration with Ludovic Halévy and Jacques Offenbach, it received the following notice in the *Comédie parisienne* by Albéric Second, known to be friendly to the Empire: "How fortunate it is for us poor writers that the author of this delightful play should be absorbed in higher politics! What would become of us if he could devote his leisure to theatrical matters?" [35]

Rochefort slapped back immediately in *Le Figaro:* "How fortunate is this author whose participation in a fruitful *coup d'état* has saved him from the necessity of living by the pen! If one of us dared bring such an inept production to a theatrical director, he would forthwith have been seized and thrown into the den of the theater's old hag ushers, whose instructions would have been to beat him to death with footstools." [36] At eight o'clock the next morning, Villemessant was on the Morny carpet desperately trying to explain that he had not seen the proofs before publication and promising that future reviews would be more charitable. In the few months that remained for Morny—he died in March of 1865—he persistently tried unsuccessfully to make Rochefort's acquaintance. In later years, Rochefort came to believe that this Morny campaign was a subtle form of police investigation, for Rochefort ultimately believed that he had been the imperial regime's most dangerous enemy. And his

19

memoirs also claim that Morny was a man totally without wit or ability, a shameless cad of the directing classes whose self-indulgence at the expense of the nation had to be unceasingly attacked.[37]

The fact is that Morny was a man of the highest political rank, no matter how illegitimately or illegally he had attained it, and he was without peer in ability and charm among the Bonapartist nobility. He was, furthermore, almost alone among them in favoring the liberalizing of the Empire, and no greater threat could have been envisioned by the Republicans than the Empire deepening its roots through gradual social and political reforms until the dictatorship would have withered away. If that should happen, the Republicans would either have to rally to the Empire or settle back into blind and cranky opposition. No doubt Morny was stung by Rochefort's sarcastic review, but most likely he was also concerned about cultivating Rochefort as an opposition person who needed to be shown the wisdom of rallying to the regime and aiding Morny in his program of liberalization. Alphonse Daudet, then Morny's *attaché de cabinet,* revealed that Morny's first reaction was to take revenge by getting Jouvin, whom he knew to be unfriendly to Rochefort, to review Rochefort's collected works in *Le Figaro*. Then Morny abandoned revenge in favor of seeking a rapprochement, but Rochefort resisted the Morny charms and left him waiting on seven or eight occasions.[38] In theatrical matters, however, Morny was to have the last word. As recently as 1951, his *M. Choufleuri restera chez lui* was produced in Paris, something that cannot be said of any Rochefort plays.

Their clash evidently was less over tunes and cancans than over Rochefort's determination *not* to rally to the Empire as some critical political and literary members of the Republican opposition showed signs of doing. The criticism of the regime in the 1860's, in fact, has too often obscured the internal weakness of the Republican opposition. The Republicans stood together only as envisioning a third Republic as necessarily encompassing all the virtues, all the strengths, and all the beauties. "Cruel, but victorious over the foreigner in '92–'93," wrote Mme. Edmond Adam, "humanitarian and excessively naive in '48, this time the Republic would be the true, the definitive, and, above all, the liberal. . . . France under this Republic can be great, generous, valiant and peaceful, practical and idealistic." [39] But behind this stirring façade of resounding platitudes lay divisions so deep that they could not be healed even by the eventual establishment of that longed-for third Republic.

The "Ancestors," the Republican leaders of 1848, simply claimed to be the party of liberty, exercised little political authority, and to the supposed corruption of the Empire offered their austerity as proof of respectability. They were handicapped by the fact that before 1848 Bonapartism and Republicanism had had much in common, both linking universal suffrage with a strong executive and favoring representative government rather than true parliamentarianism. The Second Empire was such a regime. After 1852, therefore, the Republicans, new to politics, not only rejected graybeard leadership, but came to champion the notion of a weak executive and a strong parliament. In contrast to the aloofness of the "Ancestors," they stood for the *Corps législatif:* five of them were elected in 1857, seventeen in 1863.

This major split within Republican ranks was complicated by inconsistent political behavior by individual Republicans. Before the Duc de Morny died in 1865, he had succeeded in shaking Émile Ollivier's Young-Republican faith, no mean accomplishment considering that Ollivier led the Republicans in the *Corps législatif,* thus preparing the way for his defection in 1870. In fact, Ollivier had never really abandoned the "Ancestral" views; thus, he found himself more congenial to the liberalizing Empire, which retained a strong executive, than to true parliamentarianism. [40] Rochefort, though of the age of the younger Republicans, also inclined to the "Ancestral" posture, but not because he had any distinct views about executive power or parliamentarianism. He simply adopted the virtuous pose of the older generation of Republicans, men like Victor Hugo, Louis Blanc, and Hippolyte Carnot, and accustomed himself to believing that any divergent actions or beliefs were opportunistic.

The Morny-Rochefort clash contained a third facet harder to

pin down than rivalry in vaudeville and politics. It pitted a member
of the old aristocracy against a powerful member of the new, and
the number of lines Rochefort gave to delineating Morny's inabilities
was in suggestive contrast to the generally held view that Morny was
an elegant, skillful nobleman. We would do well to recall the words
of that perceptive social commentator, Marcel Proust:

> Those whose brevet of nobility is more recent have a dif-
> ferent air, a different form of politeness. They have lived
> in closer contact with genuine merit, have been familiar
> with the kind of real superiority which is the source of true
> nobleness—and they have better manners. They were
> bred in a court where they rubbed shoulders with foreign
> ambassadors whom they had to treat with respect, whereas
> the scions of the ancient aristocracy, as a result of their
> noses not being kept to the grindstone, and because they
> have lived in a world entirely given over to pleasure, have
> acquired manners to which only the prestige of race can
> give the name of good, and that only within their own
> narrow circle.[41]

At the beginning of 1866, Rochefort left *Le Figaro* to join the
staff of Polydore Millaud's new journal, *Le Soleil*. He went for a
salary of 1500 francs a month, an unprecedented sum for journalists
in that day, but he soon felt that he had been wrong to leave
Villemessant. *Le Soleil,* presumably a nonpolitical sheet, never
caught on, and eleven months later Rochefort returned to *Le Figaro*.
The articles that he wrote for *Le Soleil* were republished as a volume
in 1867 entitled *La Grande Bohème,* to which he added a preface
intended to infuriate the Bonapartists. The two "great bohemians"
at whom he especially aimed were Persigny and Morny, both self-
styled *comtes* when the Empire was reestablished, both raised to be
ducs by Napoleon III:

> For a long time I worked on the plans for a five-act
> comedy, which I would have called *la Grande Bohème*.
> Ah, it would not have been any ordinary production! Even

though the characters in the play were burdened by a collection of titles and particles, in reality all of them were from unknown parents—though suspected. . . . The public might believe that, thanks to the law against the usurpation of titles, these Guzman d'Alfaraches, who signed public laws with titles that did not belong to them, would be taken into police court. But not at all—and that is precisely where the element of surprise comes in: When we run across them in the third act, these fake counts have become real dukes, quite like Victor Hugo's Jean Valjean who began by taking the silver and to whom the candlesticks were given.[42]

Rochefort's next duel was fought on January 1, 1867, just before he left *Le Soleil*. He had slandered Jeanne d'Arc, calling her a madwoman, and made fun of what he called the Jeanne d'Arc cult. Paul Granier de Cassagnac, the Bonapartist journalist, responded in *Le Pays* and challenged Rochefort. The duel was fought near St. Denis; this time Rochefort was lightly wounded in the side by a bullet.[43]

Villemessant welcomed Rochefort back to *Le Figaro* with a salary of 2000 francs a month. The paper had by then become a daily rather than a weekly, but was still classified as literary and nonpolitical. Rochefort's growing reputation as a polemicist, however, made it impossible to keep up this literary façade, and Villemessant decided to seek authorization to become a political journal with Rochefort as the only political writer on the staff. The few remaining months that Rochefort wrote for *Le Figaro* were full of alarms for the paper's existence. Upon the death of Faustin Soulouque in 1867, for instance, Rochefort wrote an obituary in which the allusions to Napoleon III were so obvious that Villemessant was warned of possible suppression by the Prefect of Police. A brief résumé of Soulouque's career will reveal why it was irresistible to the satirist:

Soulouque, a weak, cruel, incompetent, and superstitious man who aspired to imitate Napoleon I, had become President of Haiti in 1847. After a successful military expedition, he had himself crowned Emperor as Faustin I, then created a new order in imitation of the Legion of Honor called the Order of Saint-Faustin. The aristocrats created to fill the ranks of the order were given ridiculous titles, such as the Duke of Lemonade and the Count of Number Two. Soulouque was finally overthrown and fled the country in 1859, after a career of rapacity and avarice. All Rochefort did was to report the details of Soulouque's life, but his meaning escaped no one.[44]

The final crisis arose from an article Rochefort wrote describing an imperial hunt at Compiègne. According to Rochefort, the hunting authorities had a wise rabbit that knew how to fall over as if struck by a bullet. This talented beast would be placed about eight meters from the Emperor; it would then reappear at five-minute intervals to repeat the scene. The Prefect of Police, Piétri, had another interview with Villemessant, and to save his paper Villemessant had to agree that Rochefort would henceforth be confined to articles on the theater and the arts. This arrangement was satisfactory to neither Villemessant nor Rochefort—the former was now uneasy about such a troublemaker on the staff and not sufficiently a man of political principle to risk all in opposition to the regime; the latter was unwilling to abandon this new and exhilarating indoor sport.

The coincidence of the long-awaited liberal press law early in 1868 suggested a solution: Rochefort would resign from *Le Figaro* to organize his own journal, and Villemessant would raise the money to back the new enterprise. A company was quickly formed after Villemessant himself put up 10,000 francs and an equal amount was supplied by Auguste Dumont, one of the *Figaro* owners. Thus Henri Rochefort was launched as an independent editor of a new paper under an old name: *La Lanterne*.[45]

CHAPTER II

Rochefort the Proud Archer
1868-1870

Rochefort, l'archer fier, le hardi sagittaire
Dont la flèche est au flanc de l'Empire abattu.
VICTOR HUGO

No ONE knows for sure precisely when Napoleon III felt ready to break with the Bonapartist majority to bring forth his Liberal Empire, for many actions and utterances before that break revealed the Emperor to be more liberal than his entourage and his regime. Indeed, even after the Decree of January 19, 1867, His Majesty's public announcement that liberal reforms were being prepared, the more autocratic Bonapartists fought a rear-guard action designed to preserve the dictatorship, so that nearly three years were required to prepare and execute the constitutional changes proposed in 1867. Small wonder that the Opposition doubted that any such thing as a Liberal Empire could be constituted, just as it hoped that the transformation would be impossible. An intransigent Empire could be more easily overthrown, paving the way for the intrenchment of Republican virtues and beauties.

Among the proposals of January 19 was the promise of freedom of the press—in other words, a new press law. That law was not promulgated until May 11, 1868. The government abandoned the system of licensing journals, and individual officials lost the right to warn, suspend, and suppress papers, a reform that infuriated the conservative Bonapartists. But the law did not provide for jury trials for press offenses, a fact that made the reform unacceptable to most of the Left Wing.[1] The appearance of many new papers in the wake of the reform suggested considerable confidence in the law despite almost universal criticism of it.

The first issue of *La Lanterne* appeared on Saturday, May 31, 1868. It was really a pamphlet rather than a newspaper as the format was a tiny 32mo, about the size of a large pack of cigarettes. Its price had been settled at a dinner honoring the vaudeville star Hortense Schneider, who was leaving on a provincial tour. A number of theatrical and newspaper celebrities were present, and each one had an opinion about the ideal price and probable circulation of Rochefort's pamphlet. The compromise price was for forty centimes, about double that of an ordinary newspaper, a price Rochefort considered outrageously high. A flame-colored cover not only attracted readers' attention at the newsstands, but rubbed off on the readers' hands; and a small lantern and a rope adorned the cover to remind the reader that *"La Lanterne* can at once serve to enlighten men and to hang malefactors."[2] Rochefort had had between four and five thousand readers at *Le Figaro,* and expected a similar sale for *La Lanterne;* but the printer, confident of a larger sale, prepared 15,000 copies of the first issue—to Rochefort's consternation.

The estimates proved to be wildly conservative: the first issue sold over 100,000 copies, and 125,000 were put out on the second Saturday. Rarely had investors done so well. Villemessant and Dumont got their initial investment back out of the sales of the first issue! The first sentence of the first issue caught the public instantly.

Not only did Rochefort never equal it again, but it has been called one of the profoundest witticisms on the psychology of the French: [3] "France has thirty-six million subjects, not counting the subjects of discontent."

For nearly three months *La Lanterne* came out each Saturday like a firecracker. The present-day reader may wonder at its success, for many of the allusions have grown dim, and the indifference to facts is striking. No positive political philosophy was even pretended, in fact, no pretense to be just was made. Rochefort brought the exaggerated burlesque of vaudeville into print, a technique likened by one historian to "the daring naughty boys who write on walls." [4] A recent critic's judgment also seems warranted: "As for his style, he hadn't any; but style was not what was asked of him. He was funny—that sufficed." [5]

Let us sample some of the fare that convulsed Paris a hundred years ago:

> I, who speak to you, when at the Ministry of the Interior to inquire about the probable outcome of my request for authorization of the *Lanterne,* was accused by the high functionary who received me of being an outspoken enemy of the present state of things and a supporter of those famous former parties. This insinuation was quite unfounded, as . . . I am profoundly Bonapartist. You will allow me, however, to select my own hero from the dynasty. Among the Legitimists, some prefer Louis XVIII, others Louis XVI, and still others, finally, are all for Charles X. As a Bonapartist, I prefer Napoleon II; it is my right. I shall even add that he represents, to my mind, the ideal sovereign. No one will deny that he occupied the throne, since his successor calls himself Napoleon III. What a reign, my friends, what a reign! Not one tax, no useless wars with their ensuing levies; none of these distant expeditions through which we expend six hundred million in order to reclaim fifteen francs [a reference to the Mexican expedition especially], no consuming civil list, no pluralistic ministers at one hundred thousand

27

francs apiece for five or six functions. There, indeed, is a monarch such as I can understand. Ah! yes, Napoleon II, I like you and I admire you without reservation. Who, therefore, will dare to insist that I am not a Bonapartist? [6]

The French intervention in Mexico, a complicated and unpleasant adventure as little understood then as now, was one of the Opposition's favorite targets. It particularly suited Rochefort, because the Duc de Morny had been one of the financiers involved: "M. de Morny has already given *M. Choufleury* [sic] there [Bouffes-Parisiens], and they are saying in the corridors that M. Rouher wants to present a counterpart to this witty comedy under the title: *M. Juarez restera chez lui.* The Minister of State, indeed, knows better than anyone else why the President of Mexico is at home and how he returned us to ours." [7] Hardly a Saturday went by without some reference to Mexico: "From another letter from Belgium, was find that the madness of Princess Charlotte, widow of Maximilien, has taken quite a peculiar turn. During her seizures, she cries out from minute to minute: 'God, how dirty everything is! Come! Let us wash immediately!' I am not an alienist, but if she finds that everything is filthy and the need of a cleaning makes itself felt to her, it seems to me that we have not a more lucid princess in all Europe." [8]

Good taste was no more a requirement than good style: "*Theaters:* Today, unfortunately, as fresh news, I cannot offer you much, save that it is said in well-informed circles that Mlle. Roze has not yet recovered her dog. In this whole business her big mistake, in my opinion, is her failure to state what she will give as a reward to him who brings back the dog to her." [9] And one can still hear the backroom snickering over the following drama of which only the first act is described here:

THE WARS OF THE SECOND EMPIRE

(Military play in three funds and six loans)

(In the fourth loan, the *Dance of the Dollars,* Ballet-pantomime which will end with a loan from Bengal.)

ACT ONE: The Crimean War.—The scene is the main room in one of the Parisian city halls, where the crowd is subscribing to a necessary loan so that the war may begin. A bride enters with her spouse. The mayor's assistant is so preoccupied that instead of asking her if she consents to take Robinard, maker of buffalo combs, as her husband, he says to her:

"Do you consent to take some of the loan *en cours d'émission?*"

"Yes," responds the bride—blushing.

Immediately, then, an employee begs her to be willing to make her first payment. The bride protests, her fiancé is outraged, the mother-in-law swoons. Tumult. End of the first loan.[10]

Not everyone, of course, was amused. Gustave Flaubert wrote to George Sand that "I do not even read or rather have not read the *Lanterne!* Rochefort bores me, just between us. One must have real audacity to dare say even timidly that he is perhaps not the first writer of the century."[11] Flaubert asked the novelist Octave Feuillet whether he had found some talent in Rochefort. Before answering, Feuillet looked to the right and left, then said: "I find him very mediocre, but I should be unhappy to be overheard saying so; I should be thought to be jealous of him!"[12]

No doubt of it though, Rochefort could evoke laughter, especially when he tackled topics that had universal appeal and were not solely directed against the Second Empire and its creatures: "There is a fortune to be made by opening a public institution which advertises: *Baccalauréat ès Croix d'Honneur* or the Art of Getting Yourself Decorated in Twenty-Five Lessons. Using the Robertson method, the instructions would include the measures to be taken, the platitudes to be perpetrated, and the affronts to be endured. The pupils should be shown how one begins to develop incontestable titles to the public gratitude. They should be given the names and addresses of the Excellencies at whose doors it is necessary to wait. They must be shown the cafes where one may profitably speak well of the government. . . ."[13]

In a similar vein: "One of the most amusing of the sinecures among so many inscribed on the budget is the one of the Inspector General of Regional Contests. One person, whose name escapes me, receives twenty thousand francs a year to eat *pâtés de foie gras* continually and to see fireworks set off. He is obliged, one must admit, to swallow so many insupportable speeches and so many sickening toasts with his *foie gras* that, all considered, I ask that the stipend be raised from twenty thousand francs to twenty-five thousand francs with the right to put cotton in his ears." [14]

Because so much in *La Lanterne* was designed to heap ridicule on the imperial family and its regime, it is surprising that many members of the Opposition were irritated by Rochefort's popular success. Some were merely anxious about their own newspapers in competition with *La Lanterne*. Even Villemessant, with a financial interest in the pamphlet, began to fear that subscriptions to his *Figaro* would flag. [15] Others feared that Rochefort was abusing the new press privileges, which might, in consequence, be withdrawn. Many of the Republican leaders, furthermore, were offended by the vulgarity of much of what they found in *La Lanterne,* just as they were jealous of the sudden notoriety of a self-styled Republican who had never run for office or demonstrated much solicitude for party discipline. Had Rochefort merely appealed to the lowest ranks of society, more orthodox Republicans would not have feared for the limelight. But the evidence is that his readers were the bourgeois and the well-to-do, the vast majority of whom, in fact, probably supported the imperial regime when they went to the polls. [16]

Even the Emperor's dog suffered the political attack later to plague Fala, though posthumously: "Nero is dead! . . . I do not need to point out to our fatherland, already so tried, the enormous loss that has just transpired, even though, according to the Constitution, Nero was not responsible. . . . I am told that he has been buried in the private garden at the Tuileries. I should have preferred to think of him interred at Saint-Denis between Turenne and Philip-Augustus. One must never do things halfway. . . . There is talk of opening a new avenue planted with trees. It will bear the name Nero Boulevard." [17] Then, the following week, a new bulletin on the subject: "I understand that Nero has left some *Memoirs,* though for easily understood considerations, they will be published only in sixty years." [18]

In the aftermath of military defeat and political collapse in 1870, it was easy to regard the witticisms in *La Lanterne* as the darts that undermined the prestige of the regime and amounted to a call to revolution. In truth, those who indulged themselves in guffaws at the expense of the regime were the same ones who had delighted in Offenbach's *La Grande Duchesse de Gérolstein* the previous year —they sought nothing but entertainment and, like most citizens the world over, were irresponsibly amused by the discomfiture of the powerful who govern. Revolutionaries are rarely recruited from their ranks.

Rochefort never shrank from the question of legitimacy, both that of the regime and of members of the imperial family, a topic that one might presume should not have concerned a man of such advanced egalitarian views. In the first place, the Bonapartes were not counted among the legitimate dynasties of Europe, as they had been born of revolution. Then, within the family, leading members were dependent upon their bastardy in the competition for position. No secret was made of the fact that Morny was the illegitimate half-brother of the Emperor, nor that Comte Alexandre Walewski was the natural son of Napoleon I. Indeed, when the Emperor appointed Morny to be the presiding officer of the *Corps législatif* in 1854, *Punch* signaled the event with a cartoon showing Morny in the presidential chair, saying: "My mother is Queen Hortense; my father is Count de Flahaut; Emperor Napoleon III is my brother; Princess Louise Poniatowski is my daughter; all that is natural." [19]

As *Punch* obliquely suggested, the legitimacy of Napoleon III was actually in serious doubt, and it was a much investigated matter by his political opponents and by other members of the family who were jealous of his precedence. Rochefort wrote:

A subscriber has asked for an explanation about the following situation: Why is it that the birth certificate for a legitimate child costs two francs and for an illegitimate

31

child seven francs fifty? Each time that a liberal writer allows himself to write in favor of illegitimate children, he is called a socialist, an enemy of the family, a renegade, and even a swindler. But these epithets are certainly no excuse for this figure of seven francs fifty compared to two francs. . . . As for me, I am all the more surprised by this discrimination, as France has never seen so many illegitimate children occupying magnificent offices. True, that it is here a question of recognized children, and that most of them are not so recognized.[20]

The above lines are the more interesting in that when they were written Rochefort had three illegitimate children of his own: Noémie, born April 2, 1856; Henri-Maximilien, born March 2, 1859; and Octave, born July 14, 1860.[21] What is more, the most recent research on the birth of Napoleon III, while no absolute proof exists either way, implies legitimacy. Just as the Emperor and Morny, sons of Queen Hortense of Holland, resembled each other, so did the Emperor resemble King Louis of Holland physically and in temperament. Also, King Louis had an illegitimate son, later known as the Comte de Castelvecchio, who was clearly the brother of Napoleon III.[22]

Readers of *La Lanterne* soon began to speculate about how long the government, despite the liberal press law, would tolerate the insulting Rochefort whose words could be easily construed as subversive to the dignity of the imperial family and the nation it personified. On June 25, after only four issues of the pamphlet had appeared, the *Indépendance belge* published a report to the effect that the French government, having examined both the sales of *La Lanterne* and its contents, had concluded that it was a straw fire. The betting was that the wit was already on the wane and that the paper should be allowed to die a quick and natural death, an estimate that was correct and a decision to which the government would have been wise to adhere. Stung by the report in the Belgian paper, Rochefort replied that "The true editor of *La Lanterne* is not I but the government itself. It commits the errors and I limit myself to transcribing them chronologically in my paper. . . . I shall add that the French Empire's paper being a daily, it is quite a handsome concession on my part to appear only on Saturdays." [23]

He had, meanwhile, published a comment that provoked one of the earliest editorial responses of real insight into Rochefort's temperament: He wrote, "We are told that the early heat from which we are suffering may be attributed to the presence of a comet not yet perfectly visible. It is common knowledge that in all epochs, the appearance of a comet has preceded a great event. I am only waiting for one particular great event in the world, but I have so little luck! You will see that it will not happen this year." [24] Edmond About, in *Le Gaulois,* responded to these lines: Granting that Rochefort's convictions were sincere, he added that Rochefort was condemned by temperament to perpetual opposition and raised the question of what would happen to Rochefort on that day when his political dream should suddenly be realized. [25]

What was at hand, actually, was a time of troubles for Rochefort, growing especially from the eighth issue, in which he was guilty of inciting the assassination of the Emperor:

Monday, July 20, 1868: Anniversary of the Battle of Pharsalus which determined the destruction of the Roman Republic and inaugurated the reign of that special kind of despotism which arrests thought and imprisons men to the tune of "Long Live Liberty!" Caesar, about whom, an author, more known for his political *coups d'état* than for his literary works, has lately written a history (I believe that the Commissioner of Tracts has granted him the trademark),* Caesar, as I was saying, on seeing Cassius, exclaimed "That young man disturbs me: He is quite thin for a Senator," and perished, assassinated in fact in open session by Senator Cassius and several others who carried the limbs of the dead tyrant out under their robes. Today, Senators are old and very fat. When one of them carries something under his toga, it is a melon. [26]

* Napoleon III completed his two-volume *Life of Julius Caesar* in 1866.

Whether the government would have cracked down immediately on Rochefort for this audacity remains a question, for, in the same issue, he left himself open to legal assault on a technicality that the government was not slow to exploit. The wrangle arose over the case of a lawyer named Sandon, who had been held in an insane asylum, presumably at the whim of one of the Emperor's ministers. Rochefort noted:

> When M. Guéroult, in the Chamber, cited the fact that M. Sandon had been put in Charenton without motive and released eighteen months later without explanation, M. Rouher could find only the following sentence to answer the honorable chief editor of *L'Opinion Nationale:* "Don't speak of that!" I hope that the public will be satisfied with such a frank explanation from the Minister of State. Here is a man who does not fear embarrassing questions. . . . In M. Guéroult's place, I would have obeyed M. Rouher's invitation while continuing my speech: "I tell you gentlemen that at the last ball given by the Comtesse de la Gourgandinière, the guests were truly the most select: a councilor of state, three pharmacists, and six butter dealers." Interrupted at once by the shouts of the majority, the Deputy from the Seine would then have made this declaration: "When I beg the government to justify having held for eighteen months at Charenton a citizen who, before, during, and after his incarceration has been in complete possession of his good sense, M. the Minister of State finds the topic so little worthy of his immense talent that he invites me to speak of other things. I speak thus of other things and I ask him why he did not go to the Comtesse de la Gourgandinière's ball, where he would have been so happily received?" [27]

The law specifically prohibited the publication of false information, and the government, holding that Rochefort had misrepresented the Sandon case, sent him a long "clarification" which he was ordered to publish in his next, the ninth, issue. Receiving this "clarification" on Thursday when his Saturday issue was already going into print, Rochefort merely noted that he had received a communication from the government on the Sandon case, but failed to publish the "clarification" as required by law.[28] The communication, incidentally, seems to have been largely a reproduction of a Senate committee's inquiry into the case, which had already been published the previous February in the *Moniteur,* the official journal. It would have required more than three quarters of Rochefort's ninth issue to publish this report, which concluded that Sandon had been an irresponsible and ambitious blackguard.

While avoiding the matter for the moment, Rochefort evidently was unsure of his ground, for on the very day that his ninth issue appeared, he sought out Émile Ollivier, leader of the parliamentary Republicans, for "advice about the colossal communiqué that had just been sent to him." [29] Ollivier advised compliance with the law, but this good advice came too late—the law was already broken and the government was already preparing to fine Rochefort fifty francs for the infraction. What is more, the government was no doubt encouraged to take more drastic steps by Rochefort's apparent intransigence, an appearance that was heightened when the tenth issue was published. Not only did he publish the required communiqué in such tiny print as to discourage the most devoted readers, but he reviewed the incident in a manner to charge the government with deliberate provocation so that a prosecution might be undertaken against him.[30]

Through the Ministry of the Interior, far more serious charges were being prepared to silence him permanently. The eleventh issue was seized, but fortunately for Rochefort he was not in his office or at home when the police made their move. Warned by Villemessant and Ernest Blum of a probable jail sentence, he had fled to Brussels, expecting his children to follow the next day. Villemessant gave him 10,000 francs in the emergency, which Rochefort came to believe was an expression of Villemessant's eagerness to see the demise of *La Lanterne.*[31] The government found Rochefort guilty on two counts: insulting the person of the monarch, punishable under articles 1 and 9 of the Law of May 17, 1819; and arousing hatred and distrust of the government, punishable under article 4 of the Decree of April 11, 1848. For these offenses, Rochefort was condemned to one year in prison and fined 10,000 francs.[32]

One might well wonder why the government did not stick to its earlier decision to ignore Rochefort and allow *La Lanterne* to peter out. As Flaubert wrote to Princess Mathilde Bonaparte, "If I were the government, I should make fun of many things with which it is preoccupied, and I should busy myself with a great number which it neglects. . . . And I believe that had the *Lanterne* continued to appear, within a month at the very most the mob would have itself beaten the author to death." [33] Rochefort himself, of course, by breaking the law, goaded the government into action by making himself a tempting target, but it is quite probable that Napoleon III had little confidence in those who advised ignoring Rochefort. " 'Sire,' said someone to the emperor, talking of this *Lanterne,* 'the paper is read, but most of those who read it despise it.' 'I know,' replied he,' but there are women whom one despises and whom nevertheless one does not disdain to court.' " [34]

For a few days in Brussels, Rochefort stayed at the Hôtel de Flandre, joined there by his two elder children, the youngest remaining with his mother in Paris. Victor Hugo, then living in Brussels with his two sons, Charles and François-Victor, insisted that the Rocheforts join the Hugo family; and François-Victor gave up his room to the additional exiles.

Rochefort had no idea of abandoning *La Lanterne,* especially since the governmental action had been directed only against his person and the publication itself had neither been suppressed nor suspended.[35] However, the thirteenth issue, the first to be written at the Hugos', was the last straw for the French government. The offensive words were as follows: "The Archbishop of Paris, on the occasion of the Chief of State's *fête,* which is also that of the Assumption, received the cross of the Legion of Honor from the Emperor at the proposition of the Holy Virgin. The Archbishop of Paris being the representative of Christ on earth, I have come to wonder if our Divine Master was really crucified as tradition affirms, and if Pontius Pilate did not simply say to the Jews: 'Ah, you want a cross for this virtuous man. Well, I give him the Grand Officer's.' " [36]

The government chose to regard these tasteless remarks as an attack upon a legally recognized religion and thereupon seized the thirteenth issue and forbade further importation of *La Lanterne* from Belgium. Another ten thousand francs and thirteen months in jail were added as garnish to the original sentence. Shortly after, Villemessant came to Brussels to liquidate the association in the paper, paying Rochefort 30,000 francs. Even so, Rochefort resolved to continue the paper on his own, determined to smuggle it into France.[37]

Not wanting to be compromised, the Belgium government asked Rochefort to date his issues from a Dutch or German town. Thus, while he lived in Brussels and there produced his Saturday offerings, he rented a room in Aix-la-Chapelle from which to date the forbidden journal. It now appeared in two formats, the original one for sale in Belgium, and an even smaller one designed to be sent through the mail in envelopes. Whole packages of these envelopes were carried across the frontier to French post offices to save postage, but the police grew increasingly efficient at interception. Some were carried to Paris by travelers and distributed to subscribers in person, but this arrangement was too risky and small scale to be practical. For several months Rochefort had the aid of a wealthy Belgian cigar smuggler who had "bought" an official in the French Embassy in Brussels and could send his cigars duty-free into France under diplomatic immunity. He lent Rochefort one of his trunks, and all went well until a trunk of cigars arrived by mistake at the Quai d'Orsay.

Charles Hugo and Rochefort then fell upon the idea of filling busts of Napoleon III with copies of *La Lanterne*. They got fifteen plaster busts of "the mustached person" and passed them through customs with the story that, as the Emperor had aged, new portrait busts were being provided for all French mayors. Since France then had about 36,000 towns, this traffic inside His Majesty seemed splendid. Early in the game, unfortunately, one of the busts was jolted in customs, burst open, and gushed forth red brochures.

The most successful ruse, which worked for over a year, had the disadvantage of transporting only about fifteen copies of the paper. Rochefort stuffed copies of the paper into the frieze of a picture frame that he blackened to make it look like a Renaissance antique. The frame was sent by an art dealer in Malines to the mother of Rochefort's children, who posted the copies in Paris and returned the frame to the dealer.[38]

One who reads those issues of *La Lanterne* from Brussels will be struck by the decline of wittiness. The style and format remained the same, and occasionally a quip had the old verve, but a new bitterness provided the tone: *"La Périchole,* the new operetta by Offenbach, would probably have succeeded only two years ago. Given this week at the Variétés, it nearly fell flat. Not that Offenbach's music is evidently below his usual, but the public, witness for sometime to events of such seriousness, has come to have a distaste for farces and jokers. This explains why the French Government has become equally insupportable for the public."[39]

The following reference to Louis-Napoleon's attempt to land at Boulogne in 1840 better illustrates the new tone: "My great consolation in the midst of these persecutions . . . is to tell myself that political rights return when governments go away. I remember a man who was similarly deprived of them after having—on the Boulogne beach—smashed the jaw of a poor soldier who was accompanying his officer. One has to believe that political rights were restored to this well-known conspirator, as he has since been able to put a crown on his head."[40]

Yet, amusement, if rarer, was still present: "The decision has been made to put in the new Louvre a *bas-relief* representing Napoleon III on horseback and in the costume of a Roman Emperor. It remains to be seen to which Roman Emperor Napoleon pretends to be compared. If it is Caracalla, they cannot put up too many *bas-reliefs* in my opinion. If it is Marcus Aurelius, allow me to hold on to the trees to keep from collapsing from the hilarity which is choking me." [41] Then a few issues later, he added, "The equestrian statue which represent Napoleon III as Caesar . . . is the work of M. Barye. Everyone knows that M. Barye is the most famous of our sculptors of animals." [42]

Having announced in one issue that "M. Walewski, former Minister of State, former President of the *Corps législatif,* former member of the Privy Council, former whatever you want, has just died of apoplexy in Strasbourg," [43] Rochefort followed his statement up with remarks about his widow: "The great beggarwoman of the Empire . . . has just received a pension of twenty thousand francs for life from the coffers of the French people. Xenophon had a retirement of only ten thousand, but Louis-Bonaparte inaugurates for his servants a retirement of twenty thousand. It is his own way of surpassing the heroes of antiquity." [44] And, finally, one last remark: "There is a suggestion of giving a Parisian street the name Rue Walewski. This public avenue will be unbaptised in such a short time that I can see no harm in entitling it as such. I shall even add that if all the Empire's servants are willing to promise to disappear two weeks from now, I shall be the first to propose that the Rue Vide-Gousset be henceforth called Rouher Blind Alley." [45]

Recognizing the declining position of *La Lanterne,* the Hugo set in Brussels organized a newspaper in 1869, *Le Rappel.* Hugo's two sons, Charles and Françoise-Victor, Paul Meurice, and Auguste Vacquerie comprised the initial editorial team, encouraged by Désiré Bancel, a French Republican teaching in Brussels. Rochefort and Edouard Lockroy were soon added to the staff. Lockroy, who was a son-in-law of Hugo, has been called among other things a scatterbrain. [46] In the first issue, which appeared on May 8, 1869, they took dead aim at the upcoming spring elections in France with the hope of getting Rochefort elected to the *Corps législatif.* [47] Most of the more orthodox Republicans were as unenthusiastic about this prospect as they had been earlier, for the party stalwarts were being eclipsed by a renegade upstart. "Rochefort and Bancel are the lions of the moment," wrote George Sand, "and Barbès is fondly remembered. Of Ledru-Rollin and his crowd, it is merely a question of whether they ever existed." [48]

Napoleon III, meanwhile, was also moving toward the elections of 1869, but his backers were seriously divided. Rouher, leader of the conservative Bonapartists, was not only determined to defeat Republican candidates, but to defeat Émile Ollivier, the rejected Republican leader running as an Independent and obviously the "Emperor's man" in the liberalizing of the Empire. Ollivier stood for election in two districts, the Third of Paris and in the Department of Var. As the Third was strongly Republican, Rouher's efforts were superfluous; but in Var, the Emperor intervened by refusing to allow an official candidate to be designated. The balloting began on May 24, and Ollivier was overwhelmed two to one in the Third by Désiré Bancel, Rochefort's friend in Brussels. In Var, however, Ollivier won a solid victory—to Rouher's dismay.

In his later years, Rochefort would insist that he had been drafted against his will to run in May of 1869, for that election left durable scars in Republican ranks.[49] In fact, Rochefort had publicly made himself available six months before the election: "I received from several inhabitants of one of the most populous of the Parisian quarters letters which tell me that the democrats of this district, now represented by a deputy who is inclined to be lukewarm, have decided to oppose my candidacy to his in the next elections. . . . If the voters who question me accept my opposition plans, I deliver my destiny to them. We shall thus have the opportunity to witness together how the government which has violated everything means to respect a deputy whom the law renders inviolable." [50]

Thus it was that Rochefort pitted himself in the Seventh District of Paris against the distinguished parliamentary Republican, Jules Favre, against an obscure Socialist named Cantagrel, plus a long-forgotten official candidate. In the first balloting, Favre received 12,000 votes, Rochefort 10,500 votes, Cantagrel 7,000 votes, and the official candidate trailed with 4,000. A runoff was therefore necessary between the two leaders, Cantagrel urging his voters to support Rochefort, the official support going to Favre. Though apparently the underdog, Favre won the runoff by several thousand votes.

The election produced forty Opposition deputies, of whom thirty were Republican, giving the Opposition only eight more seats than it had had in 1863. On the other hand, the Opposition was less scattered than before and could be more effective through Republican discipline. Moreover, Opposition candidates had received many more votes than in 1863, so that even though the government had won solidly, there was room for anxiety. Ollivier profited from the situation by rallying 116 deputies—none of them Republican— who petitioned the Emperor favoring responsible government.

On July 12, the Emperor responded by granting the *Corps législatif* the power to choose its own officers and by increasing its power to initiate and amend legislation, with the right to vote the budget by sections. These were all major liberal concessions, though he stopped short of decreeing ministerial responsibility.[51] Recognizing defeat for his position, Rouher resigned from the ministry, and the Emperor named him to the presidency of the Senate as a consolation. It was Ollivier's victory, but it was common to attribute Rouher's fall and His Majesty's liberal concessions to the darts coming from the radicals on the Left. As Ludovic Halévy put it, "Rochefort has obviously been the pill which has led the Emperor to evacuate Rouher."[52]

Rochefort's defeat in May turned out to be temporary. Léon Gambetta, in his first attempt at gaining office, had won two seats, the First District of Paris and one district in Marseille. He decided to opt for Marseille, vacating the seat more likely to be won by a Republican. The First District of Paris included Belleville, La Vallette, La Chapelle, and Montmartre, already famous for radicalism. Three other Parisian seats were vacated in like manner, all to be filled in the supplementary elections of November 21–22, 1869. As a public meeting was to be held to hear the candidates for the First District on the evening of November 5 in the Grand Salon in La Chapelle, Rochefort decided to risk reentry into France to secure the nomination. Crossing the frontier at Feignies the morning of the fifth, he was immediately detained by the local authorities while they telegraphed the Prefect of Nord for instructions. This official at once telegraphed the Minister of the Interior, who rushed the question to the Emperor; and His Majesty commanded that Rochefort be allowed to proceed to the political meeting.[53]

This imperial charity is somewhat hard to understand unless we remember that, besides the fact that Napoleon III was not tyrannical by temperament, Rochefort's chances for election seemed doubtful. Banking on his rejection was a good gamble, especially since the Emperor expected to reduce the radical opposition further with immediate constitutional reforms. Moreover, the hostility of leading Republicans to Rochefort was well known. Literary figures also by and large distrusted Rochefort, though they had little political influence. At the time of the Rochefort-Marfori duel, Flaubert had written to Ernest Feydeau, "Yes, I envy Marfori; only he is clumsy. What a loss for literature should he have smashed Rochefort's foul mouth!" [54] Now he wrote to his niece, Caroline, on November 15 that the Opposition was losing public favor and that Rochefort probably would not be elected.[55] The same week, George Sand wrote to Edmond Plauchut in Le Mans: "In politics, I do not like Rochefort's role. I do not like this adulation of the people, this surrender of his will, this absence of principles. . . . A man who respects himself does not say: 'I shall take the oath or I shall not take it, depending on your wish.' If he knows no more than his constituents, if he waits for their every caprice before acting, then the first idiot to turn up might as well be elected as he. All that ultra-democratic air is froth." [56]

At the public meeting of November 5, which Rochefort did not arrive in time to attend, numerous radical hopefuls vied for popular favor. Cantagrel, earlier beaten in the Seventh District, was available; Hippolyte Carnot, earlier beaten by Gambetta in the First District, wanted to try again; the radical journalist Jules Vallès and a workman named Stanson believed themselves qualified; and Gambetta had asked his secretary, Clément Laurier, to stand for the seat he had vacated. Laurier must have been confounded by Rochefort's decision to enter the contest. Evidently a man of principle, he had written Rochefort in midsummer about the supplementary elections, asserting that he felt Rochefort to have a prior claim to the nomination because of his condemnation by the Empire. Thus, he would not contest the nomination if Rochefort wanted it.

Rochefort responded to Laurier:

> I would enter the Chamber only to make one or two uproars. The Empire now lies dead for a man determined, as I am, on a call to arms at a favorable moment; it is not the government that one must keep the eye on, but those who want to replace it at the expense of the Republic. Bonaparte gone, all the laws of general security and others fall with him. . . . Thus I want to keep a freedom of action that the position of deputy would not give me; I plan to return to Paris, to spend the four months in prison which remain for me, and to put myself at the head of a socialist journal which will prepare the way while awaiting the fall [of the regime]. Under these circumstances, my dear Laurier, I determine not to run and I pledge to support your candidacy energetically.[57]

How did Rochefort secure the seat against Gambetta's favorite and a well-known Republican like Carnot? A crowd of about 3000 in the Grand Salon received the news of Rochefort's detention at the frontier, realized he would not be present at the meeting, and immediately erupted into a protest demonstration of many minutes. It gave Rochefort the psychological advantage over his rivals as *the* opponent of the Empire. Then came the news of the Emperor's decision to release Rochefort, and Clément Laurier withdrew his candidacy in favor of Rochefort.[58] Later, Vallès, Cantagrel, and Stanson also withdrew, leaving only Carnot and the official candidate, Frédéric Terme, as opponents. Beyond that, Rochefort was nearly the perfect candidate to excite the enthusiasm of a lower-class constituency. An anonymous police agent has left us a perceptive estimate of Rochefort's appeal. He described him as "noisy rather than violent, vain rather than prideful, good by instinct but cruel by temperament," capable of the most delicate sentiments as well as anger and vulgarity to a point *"à l'ordure."* He classified Rochefort as a perfect example of the legendary *gamin* of Paris whose ability was the product of "Parisian civilization: a bit of mud and a bit of gold." [59] Thus could the idol of the mob prevail over the opinion of most Republican leaders.

One sample of a Rochefort speech as reported in *Le Figaro* should illustrate the Rochefort campaign technique.* "In the Middle Ages, the monks had two desks in their churches, one occupied by the advocate of the Good Lord, the other by the advocate of the bad devil. They debated. After a half-hour, it was agreed that the devil had to give way to the Good Lord and allow it to be said that the Holy Virgin was immaculate and that St. Joseph was the happiest of husbands." [60] His campaign program was equally aimed at a special constituency: (1) individual freedom; (2) laws to protect every citizen from arbitrary arrest after displeasing a minister; (3) all lawbreakers to be held responsible, even if they are governmental officials; (4) free schooling, elimination of scandalously low salaries, freedom to associate publicly and to express opinions in a newspaper. He signed this program as the Socialist Revolutionary candidate for the First District.[61] On the first day of balloting, Rochefort received 18,051 votes, to 13,000 for Carnot and 2,000 for poor Frédéric Terme.[62]

His election was, of course, regarded by the government as an insult to the Emperor by the people of Paris. But Émile Ollivier, not yet a member of the government but increasingly close to the Emperor, preferred Rochefort to those "who think as he does but do not have his boldness." In private interview with the Emperor, Ollivier found the Emperor "smiling, gay, seemingly better than ever," and able to talk about Rochefort's election without anger. His Majesty's real annoyance was directed against those members of the Opposition, mostly Monarchists, who simply sought power. He said to

* *Le Figaro* did not support Rochefort in the campaign.

Ollivier, "I want as ministers men who love the people and who desire to alleviate their poverty." To which Ollivier added, "In the aftermath of the insult which the people of Paris have just given him, that reveals a lofty soul." [63] Perhaps Napoleon III did not really take Rochefort seriously—as many of the radicals did not. Jean-Baptiste Millière, who had presided over the November 5 evening at the Grand Salon, reputedly told Rochefort after his election, "In electing you, we knew quite well that you were not a legislator, but an enemy of the Empire." [64]

When Rochefort entered the Chamber for the first time, he avoided respectability as much as possible by going at once to sit by François Raspail, the aged radical who was treated as a pariah by the rest of the Opposition. Next, Rochefort avoided the ceremony in the Louvre where it was the custom to present newly elected deputies to the Emperor. After the master of ceremonies had called out Rochefort's name three times in vain, the Emperor laughed, leading the others present to respond with laughter and applause. [65] Finally, Rochefort founded a new journal, *La Marseillaise,* to publicize his ideas, taking as collaborators a bevy of extremists: J.-B. Millière, Raoul Rigault, Paschal Grousset, Arthur Arnould, and Gustave Flourens.

The first act of the new deputies, Rochefort and Raspail, was a joint proposal to reform the army, that is to say, to scrap the Law of 1868 in favor of a three-year universal military service law. The nature of the military establishment had been a political issue ever since the end of the Napoleonic era. Republicans and Bonapartists favored the mass citizen army of that era, while those of more conservative bent, in power after 1815, preferred the small, professional army to a people-in-arms. The military chiefs themselves usually preferred professionalism, and it was one of the ironies of the Second Empire that a Bonaparte could not prevail over his generals in his desire to have a trained militia. Nor was Napoleon III backed by the Bonapartist majority in the *Corps législatif* on the issue, as his party regarded compulsory military service as unpopular and inexpedient.

After the Prussian victory over Austria in 1866, which was also a victory for the universal military service principle, Napoleon III received the support of two prominent newspapermen in his drive for a new military law, August Nefftzer in *Le Temps* and Eugène Forçade in the *Revue des Deux-Mondes*. As the Ministry of War still resisted the Emperor's view, Napoleon moved against the military by removing Marshal Randon as minister early in 1867, appointing Marshal Niel who was more congenial to the Emperor's hopes. Niel, however, had no taste for parliamentary maneuvers and soon lost patience with those who sought to block new legislation with lengthy committee inquiries; and he could get no help from the parliamentary Republicans. Whereas Niel and the Emperor wanted a standing army backed by militia, the Republicans wanted to destroy permanent military establishments in favor of universal military training. In the end, Niel accepted a halfway measure, the Law of 1868, which permitted the conscripting of 100,000 men a year (which actually produced 75,000 a year, thanks to various exemptions). The conscripts were able to buy replacements, a gesture especially to the well-to-do urban dwellers.[66]

The Rochefort-Raspail army bill in 1869 would have abolished this conscription and replacement system, along with the regular army, and substituted three years of compulsory military service for all Frenchmen. Jean Forçade-Laroquette, the Minister of the Interior, denounced the proposal as ridiculous and childish, whereupon Rochefort answered that evidently the government sought to do no more than ridicule the words and acts of the Left, adding that the Emperor himself had set the pattern by laughing when Rochefort's name had been called "the other day." "This," he continued, "was a gross insult on the Emperor's part to universal suffrage, on which he pretends to support himself. And in any case, if I am ridiculous, I shall never be to the degree of the individual who paraded on the Boulogne beach with an eagle on his shoulder and a piece of bacon in his hat."[67] This reference to a well-known and apocryphal story about the Emperor's past forced the presiding officer to call Rochefort to order, and Gambetta, sitting near him, suggested he sit down.* The rest of the Left did not support the Rochefort-Raspail bill, failing to appreciate their leadership, though in many cases agreeing with them in principle.

Thus, by 1870, France was still defended by a professional army, and the limited number of reserves training after the Law of 1868 were still inadequate to make a significant contribution in the opening campaigns against the Prussians. Certainly this inadequacy was one of the chief reasons Napoleon III resisted so strongly those pushing him toward war that year. After the shocking defeat, when fault-finding became a national sport, the Republicans laid the mess at the door of the imperial military system. That system had its short-comings, but in an increasingly technical age, the opposition to military professionalism amounted to a summons to return to slings and arrows; while the Republican opposition to Marshal Niel's program helped to impede implementing the best answer to the military dilemma.

On November 29, 1869, one week after Rochefort's election to the *Corps législatif,* Napoleon III went before that body to open a special session called to consider liberal amendments to the Constitution, notably the establishment of responsible government. In response to His Majesty's appeal for parliamentary support, a new petition was drawn up requesting responsible government, this time signed by 136 deputies, the additional votes coming from Republicans. This enabled the Emperor to dismiss his conservative cabinet in December and to ask Émile Ollivier to nominate a liberal cabinet, leading to the Government of January 2, 1870.

As Napoleon III continued to preside at cabinet meetings, the post of Prime Minister did not exist. The leading minister, Ollivier, took the title of *Garde des Sceaux* (Keeper of the Seals) and was Vice-Premier. The responsible government established was imper-

---

* In 1840, Louis-Napoleon and a small party sailed from Britain to Boulogne in an attempt upon the July Monarchy. Someone devoted to symbolism had tied an eagle to the mainmast, giving rise to the story that Louis-Napoleon had worn bacon in his hat to keep an eagle happy on his shoulder, a version much more satisfactory to the wits on the boulevards.

fect, a transitional form actually, reflecting the understandable difficulty in moving from dictatorship to limited monarchy within one reign. Moreover, the Senate decree of the previous September, authorizing liberal reforms, had stated that the ministers would be "dependent" on the Emperor, but "responsible" to the *Corps législatif* and "impeachable" by the Senate. The ambiguity therein probably derived from the intention to express the Ministry's simultaneous responsibility to Parliament and loyalty to the Crown, an ambiguity that only could have been worked out in time. The Republicans, though they had signed the petition favoring responsible government, remained in opposition to the reformed regime, because it was not yet republican in form; but many of them despaired for the future of their party now that the Empire was liberalizing its institutions.

Suddenly, on January 10, the new regime received a rude jolt: Prince Pierre Bonaparte shot an employee of Rochefort's *La Marseillaise,* and the prospects of a political funeral restored Republican hopes. Inciting revolution in the wake of a corpse was the oldest trick in the revolutionary handbook. Writing to Vienna, the pro-French Austrian Ambassador, Richard von Metternich, said: "The Rochefortists had to have a corpse! What a stroke of bad luck that it has to be a Bonaparte who provides it. The unrest is extreme, and one must expect most anything in a country where one can anticipate no more than a week in advance. At the moment, the public at large and the outcome seem to be on the side of the Emperor." [68]

Prince Pierre was *persona non grata* at the Tuileries. His difficulty in part lay in his descent from Lucien, for Lucien and his line had been excluded from the imperial family by Napoleon I. (Lucien had defied Napoleon by taking a commoner as his second wife.) Napoleon III confirmed that exclusion when he reformed the official imperial family in 1852. Three years later he created the civil family to provide for relatives not included in the imperial family. Members of the civil family, including Prince Pierre, were entitled to be called Highness and Prince, but could not use the title Imperial, and they drew a pension from the Civil List.

Prince Pierre, the third son of Lucien, was fifty-four at the time of the murder in 1870. His previous record seemed to justify his continued exclusion from state employment. He had a reputation for violence, having fought for Bolivar in South America, against the Pope in 1830 in Romagna, and having shot a Papal agent sent to arrest him. In 1848, he was elected to the Constituent Assembly of the French Republic and sat with the extreme Left where he became most famous for his insulting language. His cousin, when President, sent him to a post in Algeria with the Foreign Legion, from which he returned to France without leave and was then cashiered.[69] Denied official employment under the Second Empire, he finally announced his intention to run for the *Corps législatif* in the elections of 1863, hoping to represent the First District of Corsica. Napoleon III asked him to withdraw from the contest, and when the Prince refused, the Emperor wrote that while he could not legally prevent him from running, he could, as head of the family, legally prevent Pierre from taking a seat in the Chamber. In fact, the government actively supported an official candidate, Charles Abbatucci, for the seat, who was victorious.[70]

The man shot by Prince Pierre on January 10, 1870, was known as Victor Noir, though his real name was Yvan Salmon. He was from a Jewish family that had been converted to Catholicism, and he had taken his mother's maiden name, Noir. He was not, however, a practicing Catholic, and the evidence is that he was nearly illiterate. Of extraordinary size and strength, he had been hired at the age of twenty-one as a doorman for *La Marseillaise,* Rochefort's new journal. Occasionally his name was signed to unusually violent articles, which meant a bit of extra pay for him. As for the political incident that caused his death, he was very nearly an innocent bystander, and in the complexities of that incident, which have never been completely unraveled, it is easy to lose sight of him.

The initial polemic involved two Corsican newspapers—*La Revanche,* a radical sheet devoted to the overthrow of the Empire, and *l'Avenir de la Corse,* organized specifically to combat *La Revanche* and actually published in Paris by an employee of the Ministry of the Interior, Della Rocca. Rochefort's *La Marseillaise* and *La*

Revanche had more than hostility to the Empire in common: since Paschal Grousset was on the editorial staff of *La Marseillaise* and also served as the Paris correspondent for *La Revanche,* it is difficult for us to calculate to what degree the papers were independent of each other.

In December of 1869, the two Corsican journals exchanged insults relative to the merits of Napoleon I. On December 30 Prince Pierre wrote a letter to *l'Avenir* in support of its views and called the gentlemen of *La Revanche* wretches, cowards, and Judases.[71] Louis Tomasi answered back in *La Revanche,* on January 8, 1870, that he who had been a Republican in 1848 was in no position to reproach them as "traitors" considering his later support of the Empire. After reading Tomasi's article, Prince Pierre decided that the issue had to be solved by a duel, and he took steps to select two witnesses.[72] Grousset, meanwhile, also favored a duel, and he appointed as his witnesses Victor Noir and Ulric de Fonvielle, the latter another member of *La Marseillaise* staff.

Before either party could make a move to arrange a duel, an article appeared in *La Marseillaise* taking the side of Grousset and *La Revanche:* "There are in the Bonaparte family some strange individuals, whose wild ambitions cannot be satisfied, and who, seeing themselves regularly cast in the shadow, burn with spite at being nothing and to have reached no power. They are like those old girls who have never found a husband and weep over the lovers that they have not had either. Let us rank Prince Pierre-Napoleon Bonaparte in this category of lame unfortunates; he makes war on radical democracy, but achieves more of a Waterloo than an Austerlitz. . . . Scratch a Bonaparte, find a ferocious animal." [73]

This offering was signed by Ernest Lavigne, whom Rochefort always claimed was the author; [74] but the style was Rochefort's and Prince Pierre knew it. Thus, on January 9, he wrote to Rochefort saying, "After having abused each member of my family, you now insult me with one of your penned contrivances. My turn must come. Only I have an advantage over the others of my name; I am a private citizen as well as a Bonaparte. I can thus ask you if your chest backs

up your pen. . . . I live, not in a palace, but at 59, rue d'Auteuil.
I promise that if you present yourself, you will not be told that I have
gone out." [75] Rochefort then appointed two seconds of his own, J.-B.
Millière and Arthur Arnould of *La Marseillaise* staff.[76]

On the day of the murder, January 10, Prince Pierre apparently
had the flu, for he was visited by his physician that morning. About
two o'clock in the afternoon Victor Noir and Ulric de Fonvielle
knocked at Prince Pierre's door, leaving outside in their carriage
Paschal Grousset and Georges Sauton. Correct procedure required
that Grousset's seconds make the necessary arrangements for the
duel with Prince Pierre's seconds, not with the Prince himself, and
Grousset and Sauton should have remained at home. The most serious violation of correct procedure, however, was that Noir and de
Fonvielle entered the house armed.

Prince Pierre was not only surprised to have to meet the seconds
himself, but he was annoyed to find they were Grousset's seconds—
he was much more eager to tangle with Rochefort. As both the seconds did, in fact, come from *La Marseillaise,* the Prince instantly
concluded that he was the victim of a Rochefort trick and demanded
to know whether Grousset and Rochefort were conniving against
him. Victor Noir's response was to advance a step and slap the
Prince, who fell back and drew out his own pistol. He fired at Noir,
who staggered and fled from the house. Fonvielle tried to fire back
but could not get his pistol loaded; he too fled when fired at.

Shortly after, the physician stopped in and found Pierre with a
puffed-up cheek from the blow, which proved to be valuable evidence in Pierre's defense.[77] The Prince made no attempt to flee, but
wrote a note to the Emperor telling of the shooting and turned himself in as a prisoner. Ollivier, getting the news, ordered the arrest of
Prince Pierre and then went to the Tuileries to tell the Emperor what
he, Ollivier, had done. He found Napoleon III nearly in a state of
collapse.[78]

Rochefort, meanwhile, had been at the Chamber; when he got
the news, he went to the newspaper office to compose a call to arms.
It appeared in *La Marseillaise* the following morning: "I have been

so weak as to believe that a Bonaparte could be other than an assassin! I dared suppose that a straightforward duel was possible in this family where murder and snares are tradition and custom. Our collaborator, Paschal Grousset, shared my error, and today we weep for our poor and dear friend, Victor Noir, assassinated by the bandit Pierre-Napoleon Bonaparte. For eighteen years now France has been held in the bloodied hands of these cut-throats, who, not content to shoot down Republicans in the streets, draw them into dirty traps in order to slit their throats in private. Frenchmen, have you not had quite enough of it?" [79]

The Government of January 2 was understandably annoyed that this scandal had arisen so early in its term of office, and it took swift action. Having arrested Prince Pierre on the tenth, Ollivier seized *La Marseillaise* on the eleventh, with the Emperor's approval, for its call to revolution. Rochefort tried to continue the attack in the Chamber that day. Obtaining the floor to question Ollivier, he proceeded on the assumption that Prince Pierre had waited at his home for his victims—"a trap" he called it in his memoirs.[80] And, assuming that the government would try to whitewash Prince Pierre, Rochefort demanded an ordinary jury trial. That is, he claimed that one who had murdered "a child of the people" must be tried by the people themselves, as the judiciary was devoted to the imperial family. Eugène Schneider, then the presiding officer of the *Corps législatif,* called Rochefort to order for condemning judges whom he did not yet know. Rochefort responded that in the light of the justice meted out during the Second Empire, he wondered whether they were living under the Bonapartes or the Borgias. He sat down only after appealing to all citizens to arm themselves and to take justice into their own hands.[81]

Ollivier then explained the government's view of the situation, speaking directly to Rochefort: "You question the government while insulting it; the government will answer you and not insult you." Deploring the incident, Ollivier gave assurances that the rank of the defendant would not excuse him, and that all the necessary steps to bring him into court had already been taken. Unfortunately, under a

Senate decree of June 4, 1858, special criminal jurisdiction was provided for members of the Bonaparte family; the jury was to be recruited from among the General Councilors, members of the Departmental Councils. Ollivier told the Chamber that the cabinet did not favor such a trial, but that for the moment the Senate decree would have to be obeyed, with the hope that it would be abrogated in the future. He finished with a powerful warning: "A murder has been committed by a highly placed person: we shall prosecute him. . . . As for these exhortations designed to inflame popular sentiment, we are unmoved and unfearful. We are the law, we are *le droit,* we are moderation, we are liberty, and, if you stand in our way, we shall be force." [82] Rochefort later described these words as "threatening." [83]

Victor Noir, who had died a few minutes after fleeing Prince Pierre's house, was to be buried on January 12. The casket was at the Noir home in Neuilly where a large crowd gathered; estimates of its size ranged from 80,000 to over 200,000 people. How much of it was a mob raised by Rochefort, and not the merely curious, is, of course, unknown. Rochefort entered the Noir home for the funeral, not as the firebrand who had threatened the government in print and speech the previous day, but as one depressed with the knowledge that Émile Ollivier was ready with troops in case of insurrection. Customarily, when trouble was anticipated the government readied its troops without display, keeping them under wraps to avoid unnecessary provocation; but Ollivier wanted it made unmistakably clear that the government meant to stand firm, and the Emperor gave orders that the troops should be openly deployed.[84]

The radical leaders argued about the burial of the corpse. Gustave Flourens and Auguste Vermorel insisted that the procession go to Père-Lachaise in Paris, even though the government had denied permission; while Rochefort and Delescluze were for giving way and going to the Neuilly cemetery where they would be unmolested by troops. The Noir family favored the latter course, too, since they were more concerned for the deceased than for revolution. The procession seems to have started in some confusion with the leaders still bickering. When it reached the avenue de Neuilly, a right turn would have led to the Neuilly cemetery, a left turn into Paris where troops were massed. At that point, Flourens and several friends tried to seize the horses pulling the hearse and turn them toward Paris, but Louis Noir succeeded in turning the cortege to the right.[85]

Rochefort not only lost control of the situation but of himself. He offered as an excuse extreme hunger, saying that he had not eaten for three days because of the crisis. Thus, in the crush, he had extreme stomach pains and lost consciousness. Whatever the cause, it was known that he had fainted and had disappeared during the critical moments of the procession; and some of the radical leaders never again trusted him.[86] Later in the afternoon, when Rochefort had recovered, he did appear at the Porte Maillot with a group of demonstrators. As there was no violence, the police allowed the group to proceed, and it was blocked by troops only at the Palais de l'Industrie. Rochefort, insisting on his parliamentary immunity, was allowed to pass through, presumably on his way to the Chamber; but the demonstrators were restrained.

By evening the city was calm and the threat of revolution was over. The Noir affair marked the apogee of Rochefort's career as a polemicist, for though he would still write violently about numerous important causes, he never again enjoyed the popularity and the faith that he did on January 11, 1870. But there is one curious aspect of the Noir affair that adds to its significance. Although Rochefort failed to overthrow the Empire in his call to arms, those who marched behind Noir's coffin, Delescluze, Flourens, Vermorel, Millière, and Raoul Rigault, among others, were those who rose again on March 18, 1871. In other words, the men of the Commune were mustered for revolutionary action fourteen months before they would seize control of Paris.[87]

Flourens objected so strenuously to Rochefort's softness during the Noir funeral that he felt obliged to resign from *La Marseillaise;* but Vermorel, even more sharply critical of Rochefort's behavior, began a personal campaign against Rochefort among the extreme Left. In response, Rochefort got up in the *Corps législatif* to denounce Vermorel as an agent of the police. Vermorel at once demanded the formation of a *jury d'honneur* "in the interest of justice and democracy," selected nine citizens all known for democratic views, and wrote to Rochefort asking him to select a like number to complete the jury so that the charges could be judged. When Rochefort ignored the summons, a member of Vermorel's team, Roselli-Mollet, appealed to Rochefort again.[88] It was publicly announced on February 6 that the jury had been selected. The hearing was to take place on February 20, and the jury urged anyone with relevant facts to appear and testify.[89] Without much question Rochefort was in difficulty with the Left, but before the hearing could take place, the government moved against him. The government thus prevented the meeting of the *jury d'honneur* and helped to restore Rochefort's reputation. Vermorel did not achieve vindication until after his death in the last days of the Commune, when Rochefort publicly retracted his charge.[90]

The most consistent of Rochefort's qualities was a simple faith that he was somehow exempt from the consequences of his rashest words and acts. He attended the parliamentary session of January 17, when the question of prosecuting him was on the agenda, expecting that the entire Left would support him in the debate; and he was indignant when, except for Raspail, the leading Republicans backed the "cynical Ollivier."[91] It is true that as a deputy he had parliamentary immunity. But his call to arms had not been made as a deputy in the *Corps législatif*, but as an editor on a newspaper. A committee had been charged by the *Corps législatif* to examine the problem of immunity, and it had returned its report on January 13. Taking as a precedent the parliamentary session of July 3, 1849, the committee unanimously decided that for parliamentary immunity to confer private privilege upon members of the Chamber would be an intolerable inequality. Rather, they found that the intent of the principle is to give both the individual member and the Assembly as a whole a guarantee of political independence and dignity. Thus, in deciding whether or not prosecution is justified, it must be determined whether that prosecution is really directed against the man or the deputy. In Rochefort's case, the committee found that prosecution was justifiable.[92]

Ollivier had much the better of the debate on the seventeenth.

He said: "We do not fear revolution, because the people do not want one. . . . We would repress one reluctantly, for repression would mean shedding blood; . . . but the government is resolved to prevent there being any *days*." The Chamber voted overwhelmingly to accept the committee's report, and a police court hearing was set for January 22. Rochefort failed to appear, claiming that his parliamentary immunity gave a police court no jurisdiction over him. Therefore, he had to be sentenced *in absentia:* six months in prison and a fine of 3000 francs for inciting revolt and for contempt for the Emperor.[93] Ollivier, who for political expedience hoped that Prince Pierre would be sentenced to at least several years in prison, had recommended a light sentence for Rochefort for the same reason.[94]

The failure of the parliamentary Left to support Rochefort in January took on a new significance in February. This was the month that the Ollivier government undertook the study of important liberal reforms, reforms that would disarm all but the extreme Left. With the party of "order" becoming the party of liberty, these irreconcilables felt seriously threatened; and the leaders of the Internationale resolved to reach an understanding with Rochefort when he should be free and to build a stronger party organization in the industrial cities of France.[95]

Rochefort, meanwhile, had not accepted Ollivier's invitation to turn himself in at the Sainte-Pélagie prison, hoping to embarrass the government by making it use force. Late in the afternoon of February 7, the *Corps législatif* voted that Rochefort must be arrested to serve the sentence already levied by the Sixth Police Court. Rochefort slipped out of the Chamber, surrounded by friends, and evaded the police who were waiting for him. He had scheduled a political meeting for that evening at a hall in the rue de Flandre, and the police picked him up when he arrived there at eight thirty. When news of the arrest reached those in the hall, Gustave Flourens, who could always be counted on for a muddle-headed performance, rose to proclaim the revolution, saying, "I begin by arresting the police officer." Pulling a pistol from his pocket and grabbing a sword from someone, he ordered the audience to follow him. Off they went in the direction of radical Belleville. Later in the evening, the police were reinforced by mounted Paris Guards, and the mob was dispersed.[96]

The government then turned to its other annoyance, Prince Pierre. Since a common-law jury trial was forbidden, he was brought before the High Court on March 21, 1870. The court convened at Tours to take the case away from the heated opinions of Paris. Charged with the murder of Yvan Salmon and the attempted murder of Ulric de Fonvielle, Prince Pierre took the line that he was victim of a trap, that he almost always carried a weapon and did not have it just for that encounter. The testimony to the effect that Noir had struck Pierre was clearly established, while Noir's autopsy had revealed no other injury than the pistol wound. On the third day of the trial, Rochefort was brought into court from prison, but he shed no light on the case—though he had ample abuse for the court and the defendant.

The Attorney-General summed up the evidence on March 26: Victor Noir had evidently struck Prince Pierre, and Fonvielle had not drawn his pistol until after Pierre had fired at Noir. He found it significant, though, that Grousset had waited until January 10 to challenge Prince Pierre for a letter published on December 30, and he questioned whether Grousset was really seeking a duel when he took a friend along with his two witnesses to Auteuil. That was hardly the usual procedure. Indeed, Grousset knew that Rochefort's two seconds were expected momentarily to call on the Prince. In other words, six men from *La Marseillaise* were in or around the house at the time of the murder. And when the Attorney-General quoted a remark made by Fonvielle shortly before the incident, "When it is a matter of the Bonapartes and of Bonapartists, the lie is a weapon to be used," he completed his recital of doubt about the real motives of the gentlemen from *La Marseillaise*.

An acquittal from the criminal charges was given the following day. A civil process then began, and Prince Pierre was sentenced to pay the Salmon family 25,000 francs in damages for the loss of their son.[97] No matter what the evidence, an acquittal was bound to appear to be a whitewash, and the government would have preferred a prison sentence. Yet, justice was apparently done, and it is useful to note that Rochefort's memoirs, while full of accusations of partiality on the part of the court, give no satisfactory account of the trial.[98]

As for Rochefort in prison, he was hardly an ideal guest for his hosts. Both he and his friends of *La Marseillaise* continually made protests on his behalf. At the end of his first week in jail, for example, he wrote to Piétri, the Prefect of Police: "My situation, quite special as a deputy and as a chief editor of a political journal, forces me to ask . . . if these dispositions [the examination of his mail] do not constitute a real violation of the law. . . . As arbitrary censorship has been abolished in press matters . . . and as I have not been deprived of my civil rights, I have kept the right to write in newspapers. . . ." He went on to threaten that if the opening of his mail did not cease he would be obliged to abandon his duties as a deputy and as a collaborator on his paper.[99]

La Marseillaise harped on its contention that Rochefort was denied visitors in prison, claiming that he was not even allowed to see his children,[100] a charge specifically denied by Rochefort in his memoirs where he tells us that his youngest child, Octave, came almost every afternoon.[101] But even though Rochefort was presumably denied humane treatment, *La Marseillaise* wanted it clear that Rochefort was constantly concerned with the welfare of others, an impression inspired directly from the prison cell. He wrote the following to an assistant editor, Barberet, for publication: "I read in the *Cloche* that an old woman, the widow Marie Foit, has collapsed from starvation in Belleville where she lives. . . . I should like to send her help directly; but all my letters being seized by M. Piétri, I am not naive enough to send money by this route. Will you be good enough, therefore, to take the required sum from the journal and have it sent to the unfortunate woman." But, alas, noted Barberet, the money arrived too late—the widow was dead.[102]

The Government of January 2 soon had problems more serious than Prince Pierre and Henri Rochefort to face. On July 2, 1870, the crisis of the Hohenzollern candidacy for the Spanish throne began. This served as Bismarck's trap for the French, into which they fell with astonishing lack of finesse. The Spanish throne having been vacant since 1868, Bismarck had arranged secretly for a Hohenzollern prince to be chosen by the Spanish, for he believed that the French would strongly resist the threat of dynastic encirclement. For a brief moment, it appeared that the liberal majority in the cabinet, backing the Emperor, would avoid a showdown with Prussia. But the great majority of Bonapartists hoped that by forcing the Emperor to take a strong stand in the face of the Prussian challenge, authoritarian government could be restored. Public opinion rallied to the extremists, as it will in times of crisis, and Napoleon III and Ollivier were swept into war against their will. If the majority was confident of victory, His Majesty was not. He had not obtained the military reforms he had deemed essential, and, unlike the French military chiefs, he had taken seriously reports on the excellence of the Prussian Army sent by Stoffel, his military attaché in Berlin. But in the face of the assurances given by Marshal Lebœuf, the Minister of War, about the readiness of the French Army, the Emperor's opinion was taken lightly.

Hostilities opened on July 14, and the initial reverses were so shocking that by the end of the first week of August the Emperor telegraphed the government in Paris to prepare the city for siege. The conservative Bonapartists used the bad news to unseat the liberal cabinet on August 9, while the Leftist Opposition indulged itself in plans for the overthrow of the dynasty. Not all the Republicans, let it be said, rejoiced in the French defeats. "As to what is *the obligation*," wrote George Sand, "it is to beat back the enemy above all else; I find intolerable the insults, the cock-and-bull, the puns, the tasteless humor in certain journals. Perhaps these braggarts, who laugh midst the blood of nations, will hide in their caves if the Prussians enter Paris." [103]

La Marseillaise had ceased publication toward the end of July, as the outbreak of war had put the editorial staff in a difficult position. They did not want to support the Emperor, nor did they wish to appear unpatriotic by opposing the commander-in-chief. What is more, Rochefort's term in jail would come to an end on August 7, and it seemed the better part of wisdom to avoid annoying the regime to insure his release.[104] Their discretion was in vain, as the government had determined to use its emergency powers to detain Rochefort past the term of his sentence, considering it foolhardy to release an avowed revolutionary in a time of military crisis. The pretext was a complaint signed by a printer, Rochette, and four months were added to Rochefort's sentence. His editorial staff published a protest in another journal,[105] but he sat in jail until Napoleon III's personal surrender at Sedan brought an end to the Second Empire, on September 4, 1870.

CHAPTER III

The Critical Months of Rochefort the Equivocal

September, 1870-May, 1871

Part 1

THE GOVERNMENT OF NATIONAL DEFENSE

Political genius lies in consistent negation. Opposition to brilliantly successful policy is forgotten in the delirium of victory; a vote against that which fails proves one's formidable insight and is remembered through the ages.

ROGER DE MORAINE

ON May 8, 1870, the government had gone to the country to ask approval of the limited monarchy called the Liberal Empire, and the plebiscite gave back 7,336,000 affirmative votes to 1,560,000 against. Of those voting *no*, some were authoritarian, some were Royalists who would not cooperate with a Bonapartist regime in any form, and some were Republican irreconcilables. On the surface, at least, the Empire seemed powerfully reconstituted, with the Opposition small and badly divided. Gambetta's despairing remark, "Never

61

has the Emperor been stronger," [1] affected the Left deeply. What the total vote did not show, however, was that a majority of Parisians had voted *against* the regime. This fact suggests at once a deep division between the capital and the provinces and that the Opposition, if small, was strongly and strategically concentrated.[2] Thus, three days after the Battle of Sedan, and two days after Napoleon III's personal surrender, while the Bonapartists and Royalists hesitated, the Parisian Republicans proclaimed the fall of the Empire and the establishment of a Republic, certain that they would at least be supported in the capital:

> *September 4, 1870*. Citizens of Paris, the Republic is proclaimed. The government has been named by acclamation. It is composed of citizens: Emmanual Arago, Crémieux, Jules Favre, Jules Ferry, Gambetta, Garnier-Pagès, Glais-Bizoin, Pelletan, Picard, Rochefort, Jules Simon. General Trochu is charged with full military powers for the national defense. He is called to the presidency of the government. The government asks the citizens to be calm. The people must not forget that they are in the presence of the enemy. The government is, above all, a Government of National Defense.[3]

Of this initial list of government members (the executive power), all were moderate Republicans except Rochefort. Why, then, did the others include him? For one thing, it would have been pointedly inconsistent to exclude him, since, like the other men on the list, Rochefort had been elected to the *Corps législatif* as a Parisian deputy in 1869. (Gambetta had been elected from Paris, but had chosen to represent Marseille.) As no other Parisian Republican deputy was to be excluded from the government, it might have been dangerous to exclude the one deputy who was popular with the extremist elements and the workers of the city. True, some of the radicals had not forgiven Rochefort for his collapse at the Noir funeral nor for his vicious attack upon Vermorel in its aftermath, but the months in prison had done much to refurbish his reputation among the multitude that joyfully released him from Sainte-Pélagie on September 4. Moreover, as Jules Favre, a former electoral rival of Rochefort in 1869, had taken the lead in forming the revolutionary government, to have excluded Rochefort would have likely encouraged his open opposition to the shaky regime. Favre had no taste for Rochefort, but firmly believed that it was better to have him inside the government than outside.[4] The decision to limit the government to deputies previously elected in Paris was a deliberate attempt to keep the government free of any other men dear to the Parisian radicals.[5]

For a brief moment, the framers of the government hoped that Adolphe Thiers, though an Orleanist, would take the presidency of the government. Not only had Thiers had great administrative and parliamentary experience, but he had been one of the few vociferous opponents of war with Prussia and had grown in prestige with each bulletin of the military disaster he had predicted. But Thiers remained consistent in his views by refusing to participate in a government dedicated to pursuing the war against Prussia; he preferred to leave the mess in Republican hands. Hence it was necessary to turn to General Trochu, the military governor of Paris.[6] Trochu may not have had Thiers' prestige, but he had been something of a military reformer and, as such, a critic of the now-discredited imperial military system. And he enjoyed a sudden popularity in Paris which the moderate Republicans hoped would offset that of Rochefort.[7] Apparently Trochu accepted the presidency of the government without knowing that Rochefort would be included and regarded his inclusion as "a breach of good faith." [8] Glais-Bizoin, who first showed the list to Trochu, was able to convince him that it was expedient to have Rochefort in the government, and Trochu later admitted that the government's survival during its first three critical days owed much to the reluctance of the radicals to attack a regime of which Rochefort was a member. Yet, the two men could never have been congenial colleagues, the one an outspoken anticlerical and enemy of religion, the other a devout Catholic.

Once it was decided that Rochefort would be included, orders were sent to release him from Sainte-Pélagie, but he had already been set free by the mob.[9] Masses of people were on the boulevards to celebrate the fall of the Empire, seemingly indifferent to the proximity of the Prussians, and Edmond de Goncourt saw Rochefort "with his rebellious mop of hair, his nervous countenance, acclaimed as the future savior of France."[10] Surrounded by close friends, notably his former associates at *La Marseillaise,* Paschal Grousset and Ulric de Fonvielle, Rochefort pressed toward the Hôtel de Ville where he had been told the Parisian deputies were deliberating. Some of the Parisian radicals, realizing that they were to be omitted from the new government, spoke of seizing the municipal government of Paris and establishing a rival regime with Rochefort as mayor; but Rochefort entered the Hôtel de Ville and offered his support to the man already appointed mayor by the Government of National Defense, Étienne Arago, a long-time Republican.[11]

The self-acclaimed government of September 4 still had not settled on cabinet posts when Rochefort arrived. By eleven o'clock that evening the portfolios were distributed, five of them going to men already members of the revolutionary regime, four going to men sympathetic to the regime. Jules Favre was to be Minister of Foreign Affairs, Gambetta was made Minister of the Interior, Picard was to head Finance, Crémieux was to head Justice, while Jules Simon took Public Instruction, to which Cults and Fine Arts were added. As for the four new men, General Le Flô took over the War Office, Admiral Fourichon the Navy, Frédéric Dorian the Ministry of Public Works, with Joseph Magnin to preside over Agriculture and Commerce.[12] General Trochu presided over meetings of the government, and Jules Favre took over in case of his absence.

Rochefort's first assignment was to a committee to examine those papers in the Tuileries that Empress Eugénie had not destroyed before she hastily fled Paris. Juliette Adam, that arbitress of Republican notions of virtue, called these papers "a pile of ordure"[13]—a description that probably refers to the fact that many of the documents written by the Emperor or the Empress revealed the imperial couple to be bad spellers and grammarians (hardly surprising considering he was German-educated and she Spanish), and that many of the papers concerned matters of patronage.[14] Rochefort was also asked to inspect the art works in the chateaux of St. Cloud and Meudon—they were likely to be occupied by the Prussians in the anticipated attack upon Paris—and to supervise the removal of any treasures.[15]

The overall situation facing the Government of National Defense after September 4 would have tried the skill and patience of the most experienced statesmen. First, they had assumed power in the midst of military disaster, expecting that they could best assure the defense of the national interest by making the war seem merely to have been Napoleon III's war and thus quickly negotiate a soft peace with Prussia. This assumption suggests that it was not merely the imperial government that had fallen into Bismarck's trap the previous July! Second, the Government of National Defense had to mobilize the remaining resources of France to prepare Paris for siege and to retrieve the military situation generally, both to strengthen the hand of the negotiators and to convince the masses of Paris, whose patriotism had been deeply aroused, that a Republican government had the determination to roll the Prussians back as in 1792. In the third place, the government, as a revolutionary regime, was weakly based, fearing both further revolutionary action by radicals in Paris and the conservatism of the hostile provincials. Only national elections could give the government real authority both at home and abroad; yet, such an election might destroy the Republic and leave the country without a government.[16] Finally, the government felt threatened from the start by the creation of a radical Central Committee which acted as a bullying lobby for radical legislation and hovered in the wings as a successor government should the moderate Republicans falter.

And who were the men to meet this immense challenge? They were mostly lawyers, some with brief parliamentary experience, who had lived their political lives in the house of opposition. Not one of them was a professional diplomat. It has been often observed that prolonged opposition is rarely a school for leadership, for negation

breeds pessimism, not courageous policies. As we think of government as both the maker and the enforcer of law, we naturally associate lawyers and government, and no doubt lawyers have often been
effective politicians. A lawyer's training, however, inclines him to
win cases, whereas in politics and diplomacy, successful solutions to
disputes amount to compromises that accommodate the interests of
more than one party. The rather dismal record of the Government of
National Defense has sometimes been attributed to its members
being men of mediocre talent. Would it not be fairer to say that,
whatever their motives for assuming power on September 4, they
faced an appalling situation and that their professional talents and
instincts were not the best suited to the job at hand? Not to speak of
the fact that they were inexperienced in public administration!

   After September 4, Bismarck continued to recognize the legitimacy of the imperial government, because it was to his advantage to
deal with a defeated regime and because, in fact, the Government of
National Defense had yet to demonstrate that it could command the
support of the French nation. Since the members of that government
were assuming that the war could be made to appear to be Napoleon
III's war and that a peace that would not cost France in territory
could be made by a Republican regime, they realized that they had
to establish the legitimacy of the Government of National Defense
and get down to the business of negotiating with Bismarck. This
raised the question of national elections. On September 8, Favre and
Picard proposed immediate national elections to the other ten members of the government and won the support of Trochu, Ferry, and
Garnier-Pagès. They argued that there was no alternative to national
elections, Garnier-Pagès especially insisting that the quicker the government demonstrated its confidence in national opinion, the more
favorable the vote would be for the government. Gambetta led the
opposition to the proposal and was backed by Rochefort, Crémieux,
Arago, Simon, and Glais-Bizoin (Pelletan was absent at the voting),
thus defeating it six to five. The majority believed that an election
would only serve reactionary parties, and that certain Republican
defeat would paralyze the government's military preparations. Elec-

tions should not be held, it was then voted, before October 16. Certainly the question was an agonizing one, but its solution left Favre in an impossible negotiating position and implied that the government, if it could not seek the immediate support of the nation, must rely on that of Paris.[17]

Evidently the members of the government were unanimous on one subject: that Paris, once invested, could not be defended for long. That fear focused the government's dilemma, for Paris was seen as the source of political strength and of military weakness. The decision to keep the government in Paris, was, thus, dictated by political necessity, but it offered no end of military and administrative problems after the investment began on September 19. On the morning after rejecting immediate national elections, the government decided to attempt to meet both its political and military dilemmas by sending some of its members into the provinces as "delegates." On September 11, Crémieux, the Minister of Justice, was selected to establish himself at Tours. This choice was dictated by the fact that he was the oldest of the governmental members and the least able to endure the rigors of a siege.[18] Four days later, with alarming reports of local resistance to Parisian authority reaching Paris, the government decided to send Glais-Bizoin and Admiral Fourichon to Tours to support Crémieux.[19]

If the government had to rely on Parisian support and shrank from national elections, why not hold municipal elections in Paris alone as a gesture to the Parisians? Rochefort, advancing himself as the interpreter of popular wishes, repeatedly urged this solution upon the majority.[20] But as his suggestion represented the views of the most radical elements in Paris, the majority was understandably suspicious of its wisdom and meant to avoid an open dependence on the radicals which they were certain would antagonize the provinces. Rochefort was the only member of the government to enjoy the confidence of the Parisian extreme Left, which had established a Central Committee comprising delegates from the arrondissements of Paris. Men like Blanqui and Delescluze did not want for the moment to attack the government because of the war; neither did they want national elections or a national assembly, preferring France to be governed by the Paris Commune.[21] As Blanqui put it on September 28, "If elections take place, the reactionaries will certainly win. Representative Assemblies are outmoded, condemned, bad, not only in times of crisis, in time of war, but always."[22]

Jules Favre, meanwhile, without the support of immediate national elections, sought help from a different quarter. On September 9, he asked Adolphe Thiers to represent the government in London as a move to bring neutral pressure on Prussia to negotiate with the Government of National Defense. Thiers, though reluctant to serve in that government, undertook out of patriotism not only to visit London, but to go to Russia, Austria, and Italy as well.[23] In their hope to build up a league of neutrals interested in a soft peace for France, Favre and Thiers had to hope that the great powers would find it in their interest to maintain the balance of power on the continent and not to allow a sharp increase in German strength. To their gradual dismay, they found the great neutrals absorbed in other interests, the same interests, on the whole, that had prevented the imperial government from finding an ally during its last years and months of power. Russia and Austria, for instance, had a common cause with Prussia in Poland, while Russia and Italy each had major objectives to be achieved in the event of a French defeat: the remilitarization of the Black Sea in the case of Russia, the occupation of Rome as the national capital in the case of Italy. No significant help came to France from the great neutrals.

Whatever he later wrote about favoring all-out war against Prussia, Rochefort approved this early attempt to seek a settlement. On the sixth of September, he spotted Auguste Villemot of *Le Figaro* in the rue Jacob. "I was just on my way to your house," he told Villemot. "Soft pedal your articles; avoid saying to [Emperor] William that he has a pug nose, that Bismarck is a jackass, and that Moltke is a cuckold. We are going to try to come to terms with these gentlemen, and we must humor them, at least for a time."[24] Even Trochu, who of all the members of the government was least happy about Rochefort's presence in the regime, testified that Rochefort was moderate and cooperative during September and October.[25] Not that they had always agreed, but Rochefort was evidently not obstructing the primary policies of the government.

Weeks before the failure of Thiers' mission became evident, the Government of National Defense had to modify its September 8 stand on national elections, largely because the Foreign Minister could not obtain an interview with Bismarck. Having just strengthened its shadow government in Tours on September 15, the government, the following day, advanced the national elections from October 16 to October 2 as a sign that it was determined to establish its legitimacy.[26] Two days later, Jules Favre gained access to Bismarck at the Royal Headquarters at Ferrières. The government also felt obliged to concede municipal elections for Paris to coincide with the national elections.

Favre was not in Bismarck's presence long before all his optimism vanished. He learned to his dismay what the agents of Napoleon III had earlier learned, and which, to their credit, they had not accepted as a means of retaining power, that Bismarck meant to secure the German frontier by detaching two French provinces in addition to charging the French a large war indemnity. Favre's lack of diplomatic experience proved fatal for his government and his cause. Losing all aplomb, he failed to take the only sensible line left to him, negotiating as he was from a position of military weakness. Indeed, as his government had been assuming all along that this was Napoleon's war, it would have been consistent to insist that the Republic would be friendly to Prussia and the German world; then to offer to guarantee the German frontier against further aggression, thus eliminating the Prussian claim to the two frontier provinces; and finally to arrive at an indemnity as a further measure of the Prussian victory. After all, Bismarck already had the victory necessary to complete his dream of German unification, and he had, in 1866, shown himself ready to make peace before an enemy had been totally crushed. Moreover, he could not know what the fortunes of war would be if the Prussians would be drawn deeper and deeper into France. But Favre failed to exploit what opportunity he had, and in response to Bismarck's proposed terms, replied that France would cede "neither an inch of her territory nor a stone of her fortresses." [27]

Because he made no counterproposal, Favre left Bismarck no alternative but to pursue military operations to a point where the French would have little negotiating position and toward a settlement that would establish a military barrier, Alsace and Lorraine, between the two countries. This barrier would be an inferior solution because it would breed irredentism.[28] No one can say for sure what Bismarck actually would have done had Favre made the logical counterproposal. But Bismarck was an astute politician with respect for the recuperative powers of the French, and the very fact that he had received Favre at all would suggest that he was not indifferent to a negotiated settlement before the possibility of neutral intervention, which he knew Thiers was seeking.

The Government of National Defense, upon hearing Favre's report, found itself obliged to be enthusiastic for a struggle to the bitter end, a conflict that it had had no confidence could be won. Not merely Favre, but no one suspected that Bismarck might have been bluffing, so that the determination to carry on the war was general, especially among the radical elements of Paris. And since national elections had been decreed only as a source of strength for negotiations with Bismarck—and negotiation was now ruled out—the government voted unanimously to postpone elections indefinitely in order to give full attention to the national defense.[29] Paris by then was fully invested, but though the siege began on September 19, the government maintained cable communications with Tours until the twenty-seventh.

The last dispatch sent from Paris to Tours by the submerged cable contained the phrase "the Rochefort barricades are underway." [30] As part of the effort to put Paris in a state of defense, Rochefort had been named president of the Barricades Commission by the government and was charged with building blockhouses capable of halting the Prussians should they penetrate the outer fortresses of Paris. This gave Rochefort a position of military command, and he set up offices in the Ministry of Public Works. "Hardly a day passed," he later wrote, "without seven or eight Archimedes coming in to propose some infallible means of destroying the besieging army at one blow." [31] Indeed, such was the enthusiasm of the Parisians to assist in the war effort that most of the governmental members were besieged with inventions and proposals whose chief characteristic was rarely realism—the proposal to turn the lions in the Jardin des Plantes on the Prussian lines was a favorite—and a reading of which can be both amusing and sobering. [32] For on the whole, they not only embarrassed a sorely tried government, but helped to instill that popular feeling of invincibility which later gave way, in defeat, to popular suspicion of betrayal by generals and ministers.

Some contemporary observers believed that Rochefort was given the Barricades position on the assumption that he would prove to be incompetent and ridiculous. [33] In fact, he was the governmental member closest to the popular leaders in Paris, whose cooperation was especially needed in raising the blockhouses. True enough, Rochefort's frailty and nervousness hardly commended him for military command. Edmond de Goncourt described going to the Bois de Boulogne to watch the guns firing at the besiegers. He saw Jules Ferry, Pelletan, and Rochefort, "who talked and laughed feverishly." [34]

Presumably the radicals in Paris were pleased that national elections had been postponed indefinitely, especially as the municipal elections in Paris still were promised for October. Yet, relations between the radical Central Committee and the official agencies of government remained uneasy. The Government of National Defense, aware that the provinces were anti-Republican, never reached a satisfactory understanding with the advanced Republicans of the city. Among the first acts of Étienne Arago and Charles Floquet, mayor and deputy mayor of Paris, had been the selection of mayors for the twenty arrondissements of Paris. This they did on September 5, making the appointments public on the sixth. It is unclear whether Gambetta, as Minister of the Interior, approved all the appointments, though apparently he was consulted. Because some of the nominees

—Bonvallet, Greppo, and Ranc notably—were considered to have radical friends, several of the more conservative members of the government proposed canceling the appointments in favor of popular election. This suggestion implied their confidence that radical candidates would not win an election. At the moment, however, as electoral policy was undetermined, the appointments were allowed to stand.[35]

Even so, the radicals had gone right on with what amounted to the formation of a rival government. These radicals made no attempt to pretend that they were founding a literary discussion club. At the first meeting of the Central Committee, on September 11, the agenda included the defense and feeding of Paris and the problem of organizing national defense in the provinces. The chief radical leaders, Blanqui, Delescluze, Pyat, and Flourens, also organized demonstrations to press their program on the government. The first of these came on September 20 to reproach the government for military inactivity and to demand sorties en masse against the Prussians.[36] Rochefort had already raised that issue in the government, suggesting a *levée en masse* during his first week in office. General Trochu had replied that the fire-power then available to the Prussians made such an operation impossible.[37] Trochu, let it be added, was a true professional with a commendable knowledge of military science. As such he had little faith in masses of men against superior technical resources and little liking for civilian suggestions about how to run a war.

A second demonstration took place on September 22 and added to the earlier demand the insistence that a municipal council be elected at once. From that time on, *"Vive la commune"* would always be a rallying cry for those dissatisfied. The government watched this organized discontent with misgivings and was finally forced to take action on September 28 after some of the radicals in the Twentieth Arrondissement passed decrees deposing their mayor and confiscating the property of Godillot, a footwear manufacturer. Rochefort thought that the incident ought to be ignored considering the insignificance of the perpetrators, but the majority in the government voted their prosecution.[38]

The events of the next few days led Rochefort to oppose the majority in the government again. October 7 was a critical day; Gambetta had left Paris by balloon that day for Tours to try to invigorate the aged delegation already there, a departure that captured popular imagination. But the radicals were more interested in a simultaneous governmental decision to postpone municipal elections until the end of the siege.[39] Delescluze had already pronounced that "the people of Paris must proceed alone in elections, and these elections should take place . . . whether the government likes it or not;"[40] and the Central Committee had no intention of allowing the decision to go unchallenged. On October 8, Gustave Flourens appeared at the Hôtel de Ville at the head of six battalions of the National Guard, where he was confronted by the entire government. Again the demand was for mass assaults upon the Prussians and for municipal elections; and again Trochu refused, adding that the presence of the battalions was a serious breach of military discipline. The demonstration was poorly organized, became confused, and lost coherence. [41]

Two days later, Kératry, the Prefect of Police, informed the government that at a radical meeting presided over by Flourens and Blanqui twelve battalion commanders had signed a resolution calling for the overthrow of the Government of National Defense and for the establishment of the Commune. The resolution had been defeated 48 to 19, but Kératry thought it was high time to forbid these meetings. The government refused to do this but did decide to order the arrest of Flourens and Blanqui. Only Rochefort voted against the decision to arrest Flourens, though he was joined by Emmanuel Arago in the case of Blanqui.[42] Dissatisfied with the halfway measure, Kératry resigned as Prefect of Police and was replaced by Edmond Adam.

Knowing that Rochefort was regarded as the most radical member of the Government of National Defense, and seeing him apparently defend radical activity on both September 22 and October 8, one would assume that he was simply voting where his sympathies lay. His motives, however, seem to have been more complex and less honorable. In the first place, Rochefort had been swept out of prison and into power before he had had time to consider the consequences. His inclusion in the government had been an expedient, and while all the other members of the government were perfectly civil to him, he knew their varying degrees of animosity toward him. Jules Simon was the only one who showed him any warmth or friendship.[43] Rochefort further set himself apart from the others by refusing a salary as a member of the government,[44] an action that not all the members could afford to take. (Trochu accepted only his military pay.) Though he never specifically said so in his memoirs, one gathers that Rochefort's position in the government was uncomfortable for him.

Why did he not then resign when he found the government uncongenial and throw himself into the ranks of the radicals who had, after all, been his comrades at the Noir funeral? For one thing, he was a patriot and, like most Parisians, was opposed to capitulation; and whatever he would later say and write about his dislike and mistrust of Trochu from the outset,[45] his faith in Trochu's military skill was actually unshaken in early October. Juliette Adam, wife of the new Prefect of Police and close friend of Rochefort, was as dismayed by her husband's assumption of office as she was by Rochefort's loyalty to Trochu. "If only M. Trochu had some guts!" she wrote on September 28.[46] Several weeks later she noted: "October 14: Trochu is not for capitulation and opposes Ernest Picard on that score. *That* is the only reason Rochefort supports Trochu resolutely."[47] Finally, having entertained Rochefort and his son Octave at dinner, but having been unable to sway him from Trochu, she complained that Rochefort's "one naïveté is to believe, seeing General Trochu in military dress, that he is a soldier."[48]

Granting his patriotism and confidence in Trochu, the fact remains that Rochefort was disturbed by the government's growing unpopularity; and while he suggested measures to reverse public opinion, such as seeking closer relations with the Parisian journalists,[49] he confided to Edmond Adam his desire to leave office.[50] There is no conclusive evidence about Rochefort's loyalties during that troubled month before he did actually resign office. But on the basis of what does exist, and considering his lifelong tendency not to be a dependable party man, it is reasonable to assume that he was drifting into the neutrality of ambiguity as the going got rough and uncertainties mounted. Thus, he could "resolutely" support General Trochu *and* vote against the arrest of revolutionaries who sought Trochu's overthrow. Moreover, believing himself to be a man of virtue and invariably correct in his behavior, he expected that this ambiguity would be understood by all sides as a measure of his goodwill and integrity. In this way, he prepared himself and his neighbors for a high-principled defection from the Government of National Defense, which took place in the wake of the next radical assault upon the government.

Let us return for a moment to Adolphe Thiers' European pilgrimage. He had arrived in St. Petersburg on September 27 to find the Russians friendly to him personally—as a well-known Monarchist—but fearful that a Republican France would be a source of trouble for the conservative monarchies of Europe. Thiers tried to warn the Czar that the impending unification of Germany would upset the balance of power, endangering Russian security, but Alexander II preferred to emphasize the community of Russo-Prussian interests in Poland and in containing the Hapsburg Empire. At the same time, he promised Thiers not to be hostile to France. Perhaps the combination of Thiers' warm personal reception by the Czar, Chancellor Gorchakov, and Russian society led him to be more hopeful of Russian help than the situation really promised, for Russia promised him nothing more than that she would back a just peace. Whatever the reason, on October 1 Thiers sent an optimistic telegram to the members of the Tours delegation, since Paris was then cut off:

> Prussia and Russia have made engagements which greatly hamper the action of the Russian government. Nevertheless, the Emperor has told me that he would do everything that he can to produce an acceptable peace settlement—short of war; and as he is a perfectly honest man, one can count on his word. . . . I am promised that

when the conditions of the peace are debated, the assistance in our favor will be great. Opinion on this settlement will be spoken, and if it not be equitable, they will openly declare that it will receive neither the approbation nor the satisfaction of Russia, and that it will be an act of force deprived of any European guarantee. They would prefer that by some set of circumstances this peace would be debated by the Powers, and then it could be turned in our favor. They would also prefer a military success on our part in order to answer Prussia who complains that the fruit of her victory is being disputed.[51]

Naturally this news raised the hopes in Tours and, when Gambetta arrived, justified a supreme effort to organize provincial resistance to obtain a military success against Prussia. The Tours delegation also ordered the regular French ambassador in St. Petersburg to get the Russian government to commit itself more specifically; but he telegraphed the unpleasant news, on October 14, that France ought not to expect anything from the great powers—in other words, that the Thiers mission had failed. Thiers reached Tours on the twenty-first, the same day that the British government officially proposed that both belligerents agree to an armistice so that the French could conduct national eletions. As Russia, Austria, and Italy backed this British proposal the following day, the Tours delegation felt obliged to resume negotiations with Bismarck for such an armistice. Thiers accordingly departed for the Prussian headquarters at Versailles on October 29.[52]

In Paris, meanwhile, matters were also coming to a head. Communication between Paris and Tours by pigeon had been sporadic, and all military thrusts from Paris to achieve communication with the South had been quickly checked. On October 26, the Government of National Defense was informed by pigeon from Tours that Marshal Bazaine was *suspected* of negotiating for the surrender of Metz where he was undergoing siege. Rochefort at once concluded that the rumor was not only true, but that Bazaine was undoubtedly involved in a plot to restore Napoleon III, to be supported by Prussia in exchange for signing the disastrous peace terms. Leaving the Hôtel de Ville, Rochefort met Gustave Flourens on the steps and spilled the news. Flourens, instinctively believing the worst, took himself at once to Félix Pyat's radical paper, *Le Combat,* which printed an inflammatory article the following morning without bothering to check the facts.[53] Flourens, of course, ostensibly had been arrested several weeks before by order of the government, but the Prefect of Police felt that he did not have sufficient manpower to attempt the arrest of two popular and well-guarded radical leaders.[54] Now, through Flourens as intermediary, *Combat,* under the heading "Surrender of Metz," announced that the government had news of Bazaine's capitulation but was hiding the truth from the Parisians in its usual way.

Having imprudently tipped off the radicals before the government knew anything for certain about Metz, Rochefort joined other members of the government in denying that they had any such news. Their denial carried sufficient weight to draw an angry crowd to the offices of *Combat,* where Félix Pyat was threatened with mistreatment. Moreover, the following day, October 28, the government was able to announce a military success. A sortie in limited strength to the north had captured Le Bourget, a position the government dearly wished to hold for both military and political reasons. But sudden cold weather had frozen the earth, making satisfactory entrenchments impossible, and the troops were exposed to bitter cold and to murderous fire on three sides from an enemy greatly superior in numbers. The inevitable retirement was ordered on the thirtieth.[55]

Thiers, who had obtained a safe-conduct pass from the Prussians in Versailles, entered Paris the same day to discuss armistice terms with the Government of National Defense. He brought with him undeniable proof that Metz had indeed fallen, and, horrifying coincidence, that Bazaine had actually capitulated the very day *Le Combat* had rushed the rumor into print as fact! Having already been accused by that journal of withholding the truth from the public, the government had no option but to admit the loss of both Metz and Le Bourget. Besides announcing military disaster,

77

the government officially published that it had authorized Thiers to negotiate for an armistice so that a national assembly could be elected, but only if the Prussians agreed to allow the revictualing of Paris during the armistice and if the election, even in the occupied territories, were freely conducted.[56] Thus did Paris get its bad news compounded, and there were now grounds for suspicion that the government had not been strictly honest with the citizenry. Rarely has fate dealt so cruelly with well-intentioned men doing their patriotic best against fearful odds.*

With the precedent of radical insurrection already established and with the radical elements of the population only too ready to believe themselves betrayed by the moderate Republican government, an uprising was to be expected. Mayor Étienne Arago urged vigorous police measures to nip any uprising before it gained momentum. Edmond Adam either misunderstood the seriousness of the situation or, as an advanced Republican himself, felt too sympathetic to the radicals to take adequate defensive measures.[57] Thus, on the morning of October 31, a crowd gathered at the Hôtel de Ville unobstructed, shouting for the Commune, for a war to the bitter end, a *levée en masse,* and denouncing an armistice. Trochu summoned the governmental members remaining in Paris, and all, except Rochefort, arrived shortly after one in the afternoon. Delegations of demonstrators were received, but the government had no success in explaining its policies; and in the meantime a dangerous mob was seeping into the rooms and corridors.[58]

Virtually unprotected and uncertain whether units of the National Guard would come to their rescue, the government yielded and announced that municipal elections would be held, though they gave no specific date. When the Mayor of Paris sent the announce-

---

* Various French defeats in the Franco-Prussian War, such as the surrender of Metz, have so often been attributed to treason or to halfheartedness on the part of commanders not in sympathy with the republicanism of the Government of National Defense that it is important to note that no such indictment appears in the best recent study of the war, that by Michael Howard. Instead, we get a portrait of incompetent military administration before the war, ineffectively combated by Napoleon III; of regular army troops who fought magnificently but whose bravery could not overcome incompetent generals, notably Bazaine.

ment to the arrondissement mayors, however, he added a date, say-ing, "I have the honor to advise you that in consequence of the deliberations in which you have taken part, the municipal elections will take place tomorrow, Tuesday, at noon." [59] In the midst of this confusion, Rochefort arrived to join the government. Pale and speaking with difficulty, he stood on a table and tried to get the mob to retire, reminding them that the government had already granted municipal elections; but he had absolutely no influence. Evidently his arm was grabbed by someone who said he was taking him to see Flourens, and Rochefort disappeared from the Hôtel de Ville, not to be seen by the rest of the government until the following day.[60]

The chief reason that the government's concession had no effect is that the radical leaders, encouraged by their success in intimi-dating the government, had lost interest in municipal elections and were concentrating on overthrowing the Government of National Defense, which was evidently at their mercy. In the late afternoon of October 31, several revolutionary committees had been drawn up and the names on them read to the mob in the courtyard of the Hôtel de Ville. The mob applauded some names, hooted at others, including Rochefort's, and shouted out names not then included, notably that of Frédéric Dorian, the popular Minister of Public Works.[61] The final lists, one for a Committee of Public Safety and one for a provisional municipal council, were brought into the Hôtel de Ville by Flourens. At that point there was some uncertainty as to whether Rochefort was to be included. As the Government of National Defense refused to give way to Flourens, he decreed their resignations and named Dorian to be temporary president until the Commune could be established.[62]

Several members of the government meanwhile had managed to escape in the confusion and were bringing military help for the cornered government. Picard, the first to leave, telegraphed General Ducrot, who brought two brigades from the front lines into the city. Trochu managed to meet him at the Louvre, where they decided to send soldiers into the Hôtel de Ville through a tunnel that led from a nearby barracks. General Le Flô, the Minister of War, having come into the Hôtel de Ville in mufti, left unnoticed to rally National Guard battalions not commanded by radicals. During the evening of that chaotic day, the few thousand insurgents found themselves caught between troops in the building and troops moving in from the avenues. Before daylight the insurrection was over and the mob dispersed, but the five members of the Committee of Public Safety, Flourens, Blanqui, Delescluze, Millière, and Ranvier, had escaped custody.[63]

Even though the Government of National Defense, backed by the great majority in Paris, had survived the insurrection, it suffered an irreparable wound to its prestige, and the loyalty of some members was called into question. Had some members of the government reached an understanding with the radical leaders for the establishment of the Commune on October 31? Why had Étienne Arago, for instance, gone beyond the governmental decision to allow municipal elections by setting the date? Why was Dorian's name prominent on the list of the would-be government? Where had Rochefort been when the government convened—and where did he go when pulled down from the table? Trochu later defended all his colleagues, insisting that there had not been a single instance of complicity with the radical leaders,[64] while Dorian reminded his questioners that concessions made to radicalism on October 31 had been made under threat of force.[65]

Conservative opinion was never entirely satisfied with these explanations, probably because, given his known antagonism to Rochefort, Trochu's excuses were too sweeping. On the other hand, whatever Flourens assumed on that day of insurrection may or may not have derived from actual agreement with anyone else, radical or otherwise; for Gustave Flourens was not so much a politician as a character out of Edgar Allan Poe. A man of vast, inherited wealth, he spent his days wandering from one end of Paris to the other, rarely with twenty cents in his pocket, seemingly indifferent to food and rest, really a humane visionary without practical experience in politics, indeed, without experience of any kind.[66] Moments of delicate political crisis are Edens for the abnormal, and as their zealotry derives from emotional extremism rather than political conviction, their entry into the arena confounds the analysis of political alliances and events.

As for Rochefort's position during those last days of October 1870, his own description inspires little confidence when set against other evidence. He tells us, for instance, that he wrote out his resignation from the Government of National Defense on the evening of October 29; that is, after the official denial of Pyat's story of Bazaine's capitulation, but before Thiers confirmed it on the thirtieth. The letter of resignation did not list his motives, as he assumed that the other members understood them. By this he meant that he could not morally associate himself with a government that had broken its pledge to hold municipal elections earlier that month. He then entrusted the delivery of the resignation to his friend Ernest Blum, expecting to see it published in the official journal. Not finding it published, he went to the Hôtel de Ville on the thirty-first to demand its publication and thereby came upon the mob gathering "to demand the real news about Metz and municipal elections."[67] And finally, though he had no responsibility under the circumstances, he tried to intervene on behalf of his ex-colleagues.

Had Rochefort really resigned on October 29, surely the fact would have been recorded by Juliette Adam with whom he dined the next day,[68] not merely because she was a confidante of his, but because the issue of resignation was much on her mind (she wanted her husband to abandon the Prefecture of Police). And surely, had Rochefort resigned on the twenty-ninth he would not have attended a meeting of the government on November 1, which he did according to all other accounts.

At that session, the two principal topics were the promised municipal elections and what to do about the insurrectionary leaders. These issues were actually inseparable, since after the radicals had forced the government to concede on the matter of municipal elections, Dorian, apparently without the approval of other governmental members, but temporarily a prisoner of Delescluze and Millière, reassured the two that the elections would be held and that as a measure of good faith no reprisals against the insurgents would be taken.[69] Thus, on November 1, several members of the government, backed by the Prefect of Police, Edmond Adam, preferred indulgence for the insurgents to the risk of breaking an agreement. Rochefort, however, insisted that the radical attack upon the Hôtel de Ville had been so serious that it ought to be punished with the utmost rigor. The rioters, he argued, had abandoned their posts in the face of the enemy in order to overthrow violently the government charged with the national defense. Failure to take immediate action against those guilty would be to invite further attack. He also urged the government to abandon Paris at once for a more secure city and to leave Paris under the military governor.[70] He took these positions in the knowledge that the majority was against retaliation, and for the moment nothing was done.

On the issue of municipal elections, the majority was inclined to cancel them on the grounds that they had been promised under duress. Rochefort now reversed himself in essence by arguing that the agreement must be kept; but the majority canceled the elections called for that day and postponed them until November 6. In protest, both Rochefort and Edmond Adam sent in their resignations on November 2, though it is peculiar that when Rochefort left the session of November 1, he gave no hint that he was walking out for the last time.[71] Edmond Adam seems to have believed that an attempt to arrest the radical leaders was imminent, and the issue of the elections provided an escape from an action he would have had to supervise.[72]

Rochefort's erratic behavior is not merely to be seen in the ambiguity of his November 1 positions, when, on the two issues relating to the insurrection, he cast what amounted to votes for and against a strong line of governmental action, in each instance for the losing position. For more than a month before his resignation, Rochefort's votes on critical decisions had lacked consistency, as earlier noted, so that there was nothing novel about his votes on November 1. What may escape us when first confounded by his equivocation is the consistent way he voted for the minority view.

In some respects, Rochefort was both in the government and against it, but he was not conclusively loyal or disloyal either to his colleagues or to those who sought to establish the Commune. Therein lay the real ambiguity.

Many months before, Edmond About had publicly recognized the essential negation of Rochefort's politics, claiming that Rochefort was condemned by temperament to perpetual opposition and wondering what would happen on that day when Rochefort would find himself in the positive position of power.[73] What About implied came to pass in 1870: Rochefort still managed negation. When he did resign on November 2, after advocating the arrest of the radical leaders, he associated his resignation with that of Edmond Adam, who opposed their arrest. Who could know where Rochefort really stood!

Ernest Cresson, Adam's successor at the Prefecture of Police, respected Adam as a man of integrity, but could not understand his feeling bound by an agreement with revolutionaries forced upon the government in the face of the enemy.[74] Indeed, the crisis of October 31 exposed an unresolved conflict between party politics and personal honor, with chaos just around the corner. No one seemed to know how to crack down on the home front in order to face the enemy more efficiently without compromising personal honor and jeopardizing the democratic nature of the Republic—which was, in fact, a minority regime ruling without consent of the governed. One looks in vain for the ingredients of political success, and the wonder is that the Government of National Defense survived as long as it did. Probably for the majority of Parisians, militantly patriotic though they were, the prospect of being led against the Prussians by Blanqui and Flourens, men of the sticks-and-stones school, was a bit too much to risk.

When on November 3 Cresson told the government that the radicals were again plotting an assault upon the Hôtel de Ville, he secured from the government an order for the arrest of twenty-four men. Many went into hiding, and of those brought to trial, only Jules Vallès received·a mild sentence of six months.[75] Municipal elections were still scheduled for the sixth; but on the first, when they had been arranged, the government decided to hold a prior plebiscite on November 3 to ask the Parisians whether, in the light of the insurrection of the previous day, the government still had their confidence. The plebiscite of November 3 gave a rousing vote of confidence, 557,000 to 62,000, which gave the government both a legal basis for the first time and the courage to proceed with municipal elections.[76] Those elections were duly held, but as they were limited to providing new mayors and deputy-mayors for each arrondissement, no real Commune was established to provide a centralized government as a rival of the Government of National Defense.[77]

Meanwhile, the news got worse. Thiers' negotiations with Bismarck for an armistice broke down on November 7 over Bismarck's stubborn refusal to allow Paris to be revictualed during an armistice. And while for a moment the French hoped that this would induce the other great powers to intervene, the Russian denunciation of the Black Sea clauses in the Treaty of Paris (1856) on November 11 dashed any hope for sympathy from that quarter.[78] The siege would have to continue, and the food supplies were becoming seriously depleted. Morale in Paris seemed to collapse, when suddenly a pigeon arrived from Gambetta on the fifteenth with the astounding news that provincial recruits had driven the Prussians from Orléans. And Orléans of all places, for was it not at Orléans that Joan of Arc had won the victory which proved to be the turning point against the English! Victory seemed now assured, and the Parisians, not content to be liberated by others, once again clamored for sorties in strength that would presumably link up with provincial armies converging on Paris. But Trochu dared not launch these sorties without far more information about the exact progress of the provincial forces. In fact, the plight of Paris was forcing the use of the provincial troops before they were adequately trained and supplied, and what successes they did enjoy only increased the disillusionment when final surrender came.

For the moment, however, the Parisians settled down to the grim task of maintaining culinary appearances as the ultimate proof that Paris still lived. A variety of creatures hitherto deemed inedible appeared in markets and on menus, and epicurean instructions became available in newspapers. Rat was not really bad; according to one gourmet it had a taste somewhere between pork and young partridge. As for dogs, another wrote: "Killed properly, well skinned, suitably seasoned, cooked rare and garnished with a sauce, dog is an excellent food; the meat is delicate, pink, and not tough." [79] Dog brains were even more esteemed. A central rat market opened on the square before the Hôtel de Ville. The rats were sold alive, but killed for their purchasers by bulldogs, the only canines not generally used for food. Cats, horses, crows, and sparrows were also eaten; indeed, it was estimated that Paris had 25,000 fewer cats after the siege than before. The animals in the Jardin des Plantes met a similar fate, though they were usually sold to restaurants and became the fare for the more well-to-do. Or, as in the case of Castor and Pollux, the two elephants who fell victim on December 30 and whose trunks brought eighty francs the kilo, a butcher might obtain the whole carcass to be sold to his better-heeled customers.

But if the foods were novel, the menus kept their traditional form and offered diners a choice of meats:

> Horse Consommé with millet
> Dog liver brochettes à la Maître d'Hôtel
> Thin slices of cat back in mayonnaise sauce
> Filet of dog shoulder in tomato sauce
> Civet of cat with mushrooms
> Dog Cutlets with small peas
> Rat Ragout à la Robert
> Leg of Dog with tiny rats
> > Endive Salad
> > Begonia au jus
> Plum Pudding au jus and à la horse marrow
> > Dessert and wines [80]

Few such luxuries were available to the poor, of course, and their lot became desperate before the end of the siege. Edmond de Goncourt wrote than on January 21, 1871, he was followed in the rue Saint-

Nicolas by a girl who said to him, "Monsieur, do you want to come home with me—for a piece of bread?" [81]

Just as the news of the capture of Orléans on November 15 spared the Government of National Defense renewing the armistice talks with Bismarck, ruptured the week before, so the admission that the city had been lost forced the government to reconsider an armistice after December 5. (The defeat also forced the Tours delegation to move to Bordeaux.) Several members of the government, led by Favre, were understandably anxious about the constant danger of insurrection and wanted an armistice so that an elected National Assembly could assume the burdens then borne by the Government of National Defense. General Trochu, who had been popularly criticized for inaction for so long and who had been ready for an armistice earlier, now argued that Paris must hold out as long as provincial forces were fighting to come to their rescue and must prepare to cooperate with them. If the Army of the Loire had suffered a setback at Orléans, it was still in the field, and the majority of members agreed with Trochu that it was hardly the moment to seek an armistice. [82]

Thus, during December, the Government of National Defense waited for the favorable provincial news that would justify a major offensive from Paris, while suffering Paris grew increasingly irked by the government's inertia. Rochefort, once enthusiastic about Trochu as a military leader, was quoted by the journalist Nefftzer as saying that Trochu had little military talent: that he was merely a politician and an orator. [83] On the last day of the month, Trochu presided over a Council of War at which it was concluded that there could be no armistice without one major attempt to break through the Prussian lines; this decision was necessary not merely because of military honor and the pressure of public opinion, but because cooperation with the provincial armies required it. Despite Trochu's distrust of the unprofessional National Guard battalions, it was agreed that they would be employed along with the Regulars, but no firm date was then set for the offensive.

On January 8, the government received a military report by

pigeon which, by briefly reporting limited successes by the armies of Bourbaki, Chanzy, and Faidherbe, created the impression that the Prussians were on the verge of Napoleon's predicament in 1812.[84] Trochu, doubting that such an optimistic reading was warranted and far from confident that his Parisian garrison could rout the Prussian besiegers, saw no alternative to planning the last-ditch offensive, which, on January 15, was set for the nineteenth. Versailles was the target, three separate columns to attack in the area of St. Cloud and to converge near Garches. Whatever the military odds, the operation was hampered from the start by unusually bad weather, fog and rain, which prevented the impact of simultaneous assault upon the surprised Prussians. Despite the fantastic confusion, the French took several key strong points, including the redout of Montretout, which had been a major objective and the capture of which sent a ripple of excitement through the streets of Paris. But another key point, the Buzenval ridge, held fast, and as the French were unable to match the Prussian build-up in artillery, Trochu had no choice but to order a general retreat. Parisian elation gave way to despair and fury, and the ground had been laid for another insurrection.[85]

Before that broke out, however, the members of the Government of National Defense had a crisis of their own in General Trochu's refusal to direct any more large scale sorties on the grounds that it would be a military crime to do so. He thus became too great a political liability for the harassed government, which on January 20 replaced him as supreme commander with General Vinoy, but retained him as president of the council.[86]

With the insurrection of January 22, 1871, Rochefort moved back into public eye, though not as one of the insurgents. This time, unlike on October 31, the government was prepared for trouble. It began in the Nineteenth Arrondissement, where Delescluze had been elected mayor and where a number of proscribed radical leaders had been hiding. The insurgents approached the well-guarded Hôtel de Ville and opened fire; the defenders immediately responded, and reinforcements were summoned. Fighting lasted barely fifteen minutes, and the insurgents were unquestionably routed, but they had forced the government into the unpardonable situation of shooting down the patriotic citizenry. Cresson, the Prefect of Police, forced the government to outlaw the radical clubs on the twenty-third and to order the arrest of Delescluze and Félix Pyat of *Le Combat;* Delescluze was imprisoned the following day.[87]

Delescluze's arrest produced a bogus legal controversy as to whether the government had had a right to perform the arrest, and the general commanding the First Military District was persuaded to sign an order for Delescluze's release. When Cresson refused, he was condemned as an outlaw by Rochefort in *Le Combat.*[88] But the government and General Vinoy continued to back Cresson, and Delescluze was not released until after his election to the National Assembly. Rochefort would later argue that he had abstained from agitation and criticism of his former colleagues until after the surrender of Paris, for fear of complicating the national defense in the presence of the enemy.[89] The record does not bear him out.

In the meantime, Jules Favre had gone to Versailles on the day following the insurrection, for the military, internal, and food situations required capitulation. On January 28, 1871, Bismarck granted a three-week armistice for the purpose of national elections, which would provide a government able to negotiate a peace settlement. The armistice also applied to the armies of Generals Chanzy and Faidherbe, and allowed Paris to revictual during the three weeks.[90] It was bad enough that the beaten and discredited Government of National Defense had had to admit defeat, but Jules Favre committed one more diplomatic blunder that led to further military debacle. The final paragraph of Article One of the armistice stipulated: "Military operations in the Departments of Doubs, Jura, and the Côte-d'Or, as well as the siege of Belfort, shall continue independently of the armistice, until such time as an agreement can be reached on the demarcation line the drawing of which across the three mentioned departments has been postponed until a later understanding."[91]

Once the armistice was signed, Bismarck gave Favre permission to send the following telegram to the Bordeaux delegation, which implied that the armistice applied to the entire country, including the forces in the east under Bourbaki: "We are signing today a treaty with M. de Bismarck. An armistice of 21 days is agreed upon; an Assembly is to be convoked at Bordeaux for February 12. Make this news known to all France. Have the armistice put into effect. Convoke the voters for February 8. A member of the Government will leave for Bordeaux." [92] The telegram was signed by Favre and countersigned by Bismarck. It happened that the French forces in the east were in the best position to give the Prussians serious trouble. Omitting them from the armistice to confront an augmented enemy was, in the first place, risking destruction of one's best bargaining cards before negotiations for the peace treaty could begin. Second, thanks to the misleading words in Favre's telegram, those forces in the east lost momentum before their omission from the armistice was discovered, a loss that proved to be fatal to what hopes they had. Naturally, Gambetta at Bordeaux, who had been unshakable in his faith that the provincial forces could ultimately win out, was furious at Favre; and in sending Jules Simon off to Bordeaux to prepare for the election of a National Assembly, the government feared it might not have Gambetta's cooperation and that it might even face civil war with regions under Gambetta's control.[93]

Arriving in Bordeaux on February 1, Jules Simon soon discovered considerable opposition to his mission, and two days later he telegraphed Paris for assistance. Pelletan, Arago, and Garnier-Pagès were then dispatched to Bordeaux to aid Simon. Here is one example of electoral reports reaching Bordeaux that week: "Yesterday, [radical] congress at Béziers, stormy session. Assembly, by 77 no against 17 yes, decided that it is not necessary to have elections. However eventually arrived at following list of candidates: Floquet, Ledru-Rollin, Baille, Ballue, Louis Blanc, Victor Hugo, Rochefort, Delescluze. Two delegates, Guesde and Tresfond, departed for Bordeaux, to ask Gambetta annulment of the electoral decree; actually they represent tiny minority." [94] Perhaps they were a tiny minority, but the names had an ominous ring for men who had faced serious insurrections by the determined few in Paris. Civil war, indeed, was to come, but not until after the elections for a National Assembly; and it was not centered in rural regions but in Paris, where revolution had twice failed, October 31 and January 22.

Part 2

THE COMMUNE

How now, Thersites! what, lost in the labyrinth of thy fury?

Troilus and Cressida
Act IV, Scene 3

EVEN though Gambetta may have felt frustrated upon receiving the news of the armistice, and though he may have been inclined to continue the war despite the loss of Paris, he did, in fact, begin preparations for national elections as instructed by telegram. In the hope of returning a Republican majority in those elections, the Bordeaux delegation decreed that partisans, officials, and official candidates of the fallen imperial regime were ineligible for election. But when Jules Simon arrived from Paris, he had to point out that the armistice terms provided for free elections and that the decree must be withdrawn. No doubt Bismarck had been convinced that free elections would favor the more conservative provinces as against radical Paris and, thus, amount to a defeat for the radical bitterenders; and as he was apparently arguing for impartiality, the Government of National Defense could not but agree. The radicals, for their part, inevitably saw those free elections as a conspiracy by the Government of National Defense against the Republic. Gambetta struggled against Simon over the issue for several days before Simon, supported by the arrival of three more government members, won the withdrawal of the decree.[1]

Rochefort wasted no time in founding a newspaper so as to influence the coming elections. *Le Mot d'Ordre* was established on February 1, 1871, the day Jules Simon reached Bordeaux, and the first issue was published on February 3. Rochefort was the editor-in-chief, with Eugène Mourot as his secretary, and Henry Maret, Georges Richard, and Martin Bernard were hired as collaborators.[2] Presumably the name of the new journal was suggested by Louis Blanc,[3] but in Rochefort's notebook, there appears the following curious sentence: "I called my journal *Le Mot d'Ordre* because at a moment when the Republic was attacked, the shout must be 'Vive la République,' but I hestitated a long time as to whether I should not call it *Le Régicide*."[4]

The Department of the Seine was entitled to forty-three deputies in the coming National Assembly, and Rochefort published a list of the forty-three he was backing, which included himself. The list comprised a rainbow of radical views: some 1848 socialists like Louis Blanc; orthodox Republicans like Gambetta and Edmond Adam; radical Republicans like Floquet and Clemenceau; Blanquists like Edouard Vaillant; members of the Internationale like Assi and Johannard; the recent insurgents Félix Pyat and Delescluze; those heros of literature and life, Victor Hugo and Garibaldi; and one former member of the Government of National Defense, the already-compromised Dorian.[5] Noting that the elections were required to be free, Rochefort asserted that the political prisoners of October 31 and January 22 were entitled to election and repeated his earlier demand for Delescluze's release: "Those who have arrested Delescluze and are keeping him in prison are putting themselves above the law."[6]

The Paris elections were held on February 5 and resulted in victory for nearly three-fourths of Rochefort's candidates. Rochefort himself did well, coming in sixth with 163,000 votes.[7] The five ahead of him were Louis Blanc (216,000), Victor Hugo (214,000), Garibaldi (200,065), Edgar Quinet (199,000), and Gambetta (191,000). Jules Favre was the only member of the former government to win in Paris, with 81,000 votes, while Thiers succeeded with 102,000. Nearly all the Parisian forty-three, however, were counted as Republican or radical. Three days later, when elections were held in the provinces, the returns were different. Some Republicans were elected from the larger cities, but the overwhelming number of deputies were Royalist or Imperialist. The issue in the election, however, was not so much form of government as whether to have war or peace. The Republicans, especially Gambetta, were known to favor fighting to the end; thus, votes for non-Republican candidates were votes for peace.

Yet the country had simultaneously voted against the Republic, for of the 675 deputies who took their seats in Bordeaux, at least 400 were regarded as espousing some form of monarchy. Gambetta, true enough, had been elected in ten departments, but Thiers was the champion, with victories in twenty-six departments. He was a former minister of King Louis-Philippe and had an enduring reputation for having approved the squelching of the Parisian radicals in 1848; moreover, his speech in 1866 warning about the dangers of German unity and his recognition of French isolation in 1870 gave him immense prestige. Thus, Thiers was almost an inevitable choice to lead an Assembly bent on peace and monarchy.[8]

The Assembly had been scheduled to open on February 12, 1871, but the slow arrival of deputies forced postponement until the thirteenth. The entry of the Parisian deputies, who had sallied forth from their citadel of sophistication as knights errant to save the country from the reactionary yokelry, was applauded by a partisan crowd, for Bordeaux was quite Gambettist. And one Republican journalist, Gaston Crémieux, was moved to shout "Hicks!" at the rural conservative deputies as they filed in.[9] Rochefort wrote to his collaborators that the Assembly was obviously going to be dominated by Orleanists and old fogies. Though a permanent presiding officer for the Assembly had not yet been selected, he noted, the temporary chairman was M. Benoît-d'Azy, "who is twelve hundred years old but looks only about 525; he looks like Mme. Adélaîde [sister of Louis-Philippe]." [10] This inauspicious opening tone was immediately reversed when Jules Favre opened the session by delegating the powers of the Government of National Defense to the new National Assembly, after which he and his colleagues gave their resignations from the ministry. Whatever their sentiments about the armistice, the deputies knew that Favre had sacrificed any claim to popularity by signing it, and they did him the honor of having a dignified ceremony.

The Assembly then moved to organize the new government, especially selecting a presiding officer for the Assembly and a head for the executive department. Since it was virtually certain that Thiers would head the executive power, he took the lead to insure that a known Republican would be elected president of the Assembly, thereby hoping to reconcile the Republican minority to his own office. His choice was Jules Grévy, a moderate from Jura known to favor peace—unlike the Gambettists—and thus a Republican more acceptable to the Monarchists. This compromise succeded in getting Grévy elected, but the extreme Left abstained from voting. [11] Then came the matter of a title for Thiers. The Orleanist Dufaure proposed "Chief of the Executive Power of the French Republic," a title that recognized that the form of the government was Republican but that avoided the title "President," obnoxious to the Monarchists.

At the time the Monarchists were divided between Legitimists and Orleanists, with a handful of Bonapartists, so that the establishment of a republic in name was a temporary convenience for them. But they wanted to avoid the republican forms as much as possible so as to hint at the provisional nature of the regime. Hence, while Thiers was objecting to his probable title (*Chef*) as too suggestive of cuisine, the Monarchists wanted to strike out mention of the French Republic. At the session of February 17, 1871, Dufaure's proposal was accepted, but with the qualification that the title for the executive would be provisional "until a final government for France can be formulated." [12] Thiers accepted this compromise and quickly

chose his cabinet, submitting it for Assembly approval on the nineteenth. It contained some surprises, considering the Monarchist majority in the Assembly: of the nine posts, three went to men formerly
in the Government of National Defense: Favre (Foreign Affairs),
Picard (Interior), and Simon (Public Instruction and Cults); and
two mildly Republican officers took over the War and Navy departments, General Le Flô and Admiral Pothuau. The remaining four
ministries went to Monarchists: to the Orleanists Dufaure (Justice)
and Lambrecht (Agriculture and Commerce), the Legitimist Baron
de Larcy (Public Works), and a Bonapartist, Pouyer-Quertier
(Finance).[13]

The cabinet may have had a Republican majority, but it did not
represent the greater number of the Republican deputies in the
Assembly. For them, the cabinet was made up of *capitulards,* whatever their party designation; and, given the election returns, they had
gone off to Bordeaux in full expectation that the new government
would be *capitulard.* Thus, Rochefort had left Paris expecting to be
gone for only a few days, having no intention of remaining in an
Assembly that would vote for peace.[14] Like other members of the
extreme Left, he had no real understanding of the meaning of loyal
opposition nor of conforming to the rule of the majority. Several
days before the government was formed, he wrote: "The Parisian
delegates meeting in Bordeaux will have to decide whether they are
there to save the country or to disarm it." [15]

Acceptance of defeat, revealed by the assemblage of deputies
at Bordeaux and by Thiers' departure to arrange final terms with
Bismarck, went far beyond the mechanics of politics and diplomacy.
No doubt there were millions for whom peace meant a formalized
return to the daily essentials—the plowing, sowing, and reaping; the
buying, shelving, and selling—for whom defeat was a momentary
perplexity studded with agonizing casualties, after which life simply
had to resume its plodding regularities. They did not search for
explanations. That further agony was reserved for those few who
were conscious, and the conscience, of the whole nation.

Soul-searching, the crown of disaster, began in the autumn of

1870 as the magnitude of the catastrophe dawned. Making the fallen Napoleon III the scapegoat perhaps sufficed for those with only superficial interest, but those of greater sensibilities began to look deeper for explanations. Some, like Gustave Flaubert, asserted that money had become king in the nineteenth century, raising the vulgar to power and making frivolity and sloth the outward signs of arrival. Others, like Louis Veuillot and Amédée de Margerie, noted the loss of Christian faith and the consequent decay of public morality. Ernest Renan blamed social ideals based on a faith in indefinite progress, and Hippolyte Taine claimed that any political system based on the assumption of the goodness of human nature was bound to fail.[16]

Rochefort arrived at his verdict rather too quickly and published it immediately in a form that was as impolitic as it was untimely. He saw the military expeditions of the Second Empire as alienating all the world, which could but rejoice at the French disaster, and inevitably bringing a just retribution. If this were true, then his insistence on fighting the Prussians to the last ditch might be seen as a foolhardy flight in the face of Divine Will. He opened his article by calling attention to the large number of generals elected to the National Assembly, saying that he was glad to see them there as

> they will explain to us no doubt what special methods they used to get themselves so continually beaten. . . . It will not get back Alsace and Lorraine for us, but at least we will know how we lost them. . . . While going to Bordeaux to settle our accounts with Prussia, perhaps there would be some merit in settling some of our own. However unpleasant this thought may be, its truth must be recognized: namely, never did a country, especially the French nation, so much merit what happened to it. The time has perhaps come to examine our consciences, the only things we have not delivered to the enemy, and ask ourselves if it is possible to have been so punished without having been profoundly guilty. . . . Our conquerors are not crueler toward us than we have been toward our vanquished. . . . So long

as we smoke out Africans and rob Chinese objects, we can do nothing but bow our heads when the Saxons come to take down our family souvenirs from the walls. The political wailers have much complained that the great powers remained indifferent during our disasters. This coldness, in my opinion, is even more than we could have hoped for. They were perfectly within their right to jump for joy when writing to each other about each one of our defeats: "If ever we are pillaged, it will not always be by them!" We have made wars in savage style and we get savagery in return. It belongs to us to overthrow the ancient system and to replace militarism with patriotism. Thus, I can congratulate the people for having sent so many generals to the Chamber only on one condition, that it henceforth send out citizens in the armies.[17]

For others, the problem assumed a variety of guises; moreover their soul-searching was personal, not merely national, and the guilt they found was both internal and external. One looks in vain through Rochefort's words for evidence of self-doubt.

At the parliamentary session in which Thiers' title was confirmed (February 17, 1871), a deputy from Haut-Rhin, Émile Keller, made an emotional appeal on behalf of the deputies from Alsace and Lorraine against the probable cession of the provinces. He was vociferously applauded by Rochefort and the Left. Thiers answered that the Assembly must have confidence in the wisdom and patriotism of the negotiators.[18] Given the attitude of the Left, which implied that the Right was indifferent to the territorial losses about to be suffered, not to speak of what Rochefort had just written in *Le Mot d'Ordre,* it is hardly surprising that when Rochefort rose to speak on the eighteenth, he was greeted by a mumbling from the Right. He rose to complain about the heavy army guard around the Assembly hall, claiming first that only a monarchical conspiracy against the Republic could justify such precautions. When the Right responded with laughter, he shouted, "We are here in sufficient numbers to defend [the Republic], and we swear that we shall not let her be whisked away."[19] The session quickly degenerated into tumult. The president rang his bell vainly, bringing the session to a close after the cry of "Hicks!" was again directed against the Right.

Thiers and Favre, having established themselves at the Ministry of Foreign Affairs in Paris on February 20, went to see Bismarck at Versailles the following day. There they heard his conditions for peace: cession of Alsace and part of Lorraine, an indemnity of six billion francs, and a German occupation of Paris until the treaty ratifications were delivered. The French negotiators had long known Bismarck's harsh intentions, but the magnitude of the indemnity staggered them when added to the territorial losses. Bargaining continued for several days until Bismarck scaled down his demands, reducing the indemnity to five billion francs and agreeing to let the French keep the fortress of Belfort in Alsace, which had not been captured. In order to keep that symbol of honor, Thiers agreed to the entry of German troops into Paris, a concession that became a further grievance against him in the capital city. A preliminary convention was signed on the afternoon of February 26, and Thiers, who had retained his poise throughout the painful negotiations, wept all the way back to Paris.[20]

Yet, he lost no time, but set out almost at once for Bordeaux, where he presented the treaty terms to the Assembly for ratification on the evening of February 28. As Émile Zola put it—he was covering the Assembly for *La Cloche*—"the Left was for principles, M. Thiers for the facts."[21] The great majority in the Assembly believed that what M. Thiers had negotiated was the best that could be done, while the Left contemptuously saw him as the "King of the Capitulators." "We have," Rochefort wrote, "a parliament like that of Cromwell. It was then called the Rump Parliament. Ours, one must say, is beneath the Rump."[22] In the debate on the terms, the Right sat silently, ready to support the unpalatable terms; while members from the Left took turns at the tribune, Louis Blanc being the only one who made any effective sense. When it came to a vote on March 1, 1871, the treaty was ratified 546 votes to 107 with 23 abstentions. Jules Grosjean made one final and moving protest on behalf of the deputies from Alsace and Lorraine. Pledging unending filial ties with France, those deputies then tendering their resignations from the Assembly. Gambetta joined them in resignation.[23]

The scene that followed revealed that not only the Left felt a sense of betrayal:

> COMTE DE TRÉVENEUC: Why should not the representatives of Alsace continue to sit among us?
>
> ROCHEFORT: You should have kept Alsace; then you would have kept their representatives too; it is you who have surrendered them.
>
> COMTE DE TRÉVENEUC: What! It is we who have surrendered them! We fought for them while you were organizing riots at home! [24]

A few more resignations from the National Assembly followed. Félix Pyat and Ledru-Rollin wrote letters of resignation, while Rochefort, Tridon, Ranc, and the Marxist Malon signed the following: "The voters who have given us our mandate have named us representatives of Republican France, one and indivisible. By its vote of March 1, the Assembly has given up two of our provinces; it has dismembered France; it no longer represents the will of the country. Four generals, in voting against peace, have given the lie to M. Thiers when he maintains that the struggle has become impossible. Consequently, our conscience forbids us to sit any longer in the Assembly, and we ask you [Grévy] to present our resignation to it." [25] Most of the generals present, including the old opponent of Napoleon III, Changarnier, had voted for the treaty, presumably "giving the lie" to M. Rochefort.

During the crisis of the Victor Noir funeral, Rochefort had collapsed. At Bordeaux he did not collapse until he had given his resignation. Unable to stand the return trip to Paris, he went to the Atlantic resort of Arcachon where he suffered from a fever so high that he thought he was dying. Indeed, his old associate Paschal Grousset published that he had died and foresaw a magnificent funeral and the adoption of Rochefort's children by the state. "Behind his coffin there will be 200,000 patriots, those who, last year, accompanied the coffin of Victor Noir to Neuilly."[26] While we may doubt that the "hicks" would have insisted on state support for Rochefort's illegitimate children, the issue did not arise. Mourot, Rochefort's secretary at *Mot d'Ordre,* went to Arcachon and brought him back to Paris when he was able to travel. The illness was critical only in that it kept Rochefort out of circulation during the days when the Parisian radicals were organizing the Commune.[27]

Now that it had made peace, The National Assembly prepared to assume normal governance of the country; but the two extremes, Left and Right, were so occupied by schemes to pillory scapegoats for the recent unpleasantnesses that saner spirits feared for the success of the Assembly in binding the national wounds in order to promote the national recovery. Louis Blanc, backed by a flock of radical signatures, spoke on March 6 for the arraignment of the members of the Government of National Defense. When the Right questioned how this would affect Gambetta—who had been a member but had voted against the peace terms—Louis Blanc left the tribune without answering. The Right was demanding the death penalty for Flourens, Blanqui, and others who took part in the October 31 insurrection.[28] Even the question of where to move the Assembly was divisive: Louis Blanc and the Left insisted on Paris, center of radical sentiment; the rural and conservative majority, fearful of the municipal hostility, preferred the country for at least the time being. Some wanted Orléans, others Bourges or even Fontainebleau. On March 9, however, Thiers spoke out for Versailles, wanting to associate the government with Paris as much as possible, if not inside the walls. The decision to move to Versailles, another affront to the Parisians, was made on March 10 and the Assembly adjourned the following day to reconvene on the twentieth.[29]

Immediately before adjournment, the Assembly voted some critical decrees that also smacked of vindictiveness and partisan interest, decrees that proved to be worse than unwise. Most of them were financial, and though they were to be generally applied, they worked a special hardship in Paris where, because of the siege, normal financial operations and obligations had been suspended. On March 6, the Minister of Justice, Dufaure, proposed that the moratorium on debts be ended, and the Law of Maturities (March 10) fixed the time limits for settling these obligations. Similarly, rents, generally not paid during the siege, were to be collected within a given time. Psychologically this was even more dangerous, since in effect it was those who had stayed in Paris who were now required to pay people who had fled the city during the siege.[30] Indignity was thus added to inconvenience, and the Parisians had further evidence that there was no rural gratitude for their "indomitable spirit" and their resistance to Prussian shells. Thiers saw the danger of civil strife and shortly before adjournment made a speech asking the deputies to put aside party issues in the interest of national recovery. The warmth of their response was construed as a pledge of political neutrality, the so-called Pact of Bordeaux between the Assembly and the Chief of the Executive Power.[31] They were soon to discover that suspicions of betrayal cannot be erased with a round of applause.

At the time the Assembly voted the Law of Maturities, General Vinoy in Paris contemplated another step which proved to be equally impolitic. On the grounds that no government was possible as long as certain sheets daily preached sedition and civil disobedience, Vinoy ordered six radical newspapers shut down on March 11, 1871. Rochefort's *Le Mot d'Ordre* was the first on the list of the banned.[32] This untimely decree ended by forbidding the publication of any new journal dealing with political or social matters "until the raising of the state of siege by the National Assembly." [33] Another item had been added to the long list of Parisian grievances.

With the National Assembly scheduled to reconvene in Versailles on March 20, Thiers moved his cabinet into Paris on the fifteenth to begin the business of government. He found the city in an ugly temper and soon concluded that it would be wise to disarm the National Guard, many of whose units were commanded by Parisian radical leaders. The first step was to seize 227 cannon in the Montmartre and Belleville districts; these guns had been bought by public subscription during the siege. The operation was designed to be carried out on the night of March 17–18 by 12,000 Regulars under General Vinoy, but by daylight it still had not been completed, and the Parisians began to obstruct the removal of the guns. Some of the troops deserted, and two of Vinoy's generals, Lecomte and Thomas, were shot by the mob, though not by order of either National Guard officers or the Central Committee, that body which had so plagued the Government of National Defense. Thiers did not mean to become subject to the mob, and he packed himself and his ministers off to Versailles on the afternoon following this fiasco. The Central Committee, therefore, found itself in control of Paris, but by default rather than insurrectionary action.[34]

The Central Committee then did the expected by announcing municipal elections for March 26, an extralegal action bound to be regarded as revolutionary by the Rightists in Versailles. Picard, the Minister of the Interior, countered with a proposal that the Department of Seine-et-Oise be declared in a state of siege, while Clemenccau argued that this was the way of madness—that the Assembly itself should arrange for municipal elections in Paris. On the twenty-second, Thiers entered the debate on the side of punitive action. He claimed that the Left in the Assembly would not be able to impose its will upon those radicals now at the Hôtel de Ville, who had no intention of bowing to any decree voted by the Assembly, and that the Left at Versailles could not hope to recapture leadership of the Parisian mob. Referring to the incident of the Montmartre guns, Thiers concluded, "Paris has given us the right to prefer France to her." [35]

Was Thiers' opinion simply a realistic view of the situation or did he welcome the opportunity for a showdown with the Parisian radicals, even if it meant civil war? Indeed, did the Rightist majority in the Assembly crassly hope that a showdown with Paris would compromise the Republic beyond repair, just as some of the Parisian radicals saw the situation as the opportunity to defy the *capitulards*? Opinions on these matters have always been intensely partisan. But one thing is certain: Fear and lack of good faith on both sides prevented any compromise, though there were gestures from both sides.

The Assembly, for example, did vote to prorogue the Law of Maturities for one month, recognizing that the law had heated Parisian tempers; and the mayors of the Paris arrondissements came to Versailles and asked to be heard. Members of the Right objected, but Grévy overruled them and on March 23 admitted about fifteen mayors into the hall. All wore tricolor sashes, hardly in the spirit of conciliation, setting off a wild Leftist demonstration for the Republic which forced Grévy to adjourn the session.[36]

On the following day, one mayor spoke for the group and asked the Assembly to invest the mayors with full power to assure order in Paris. Though haste was essential, as the Central Committee expected to hold municipal elections in two days, the Assembly failed to reach an electoral understanding with the mayors. Émile Zola listened to the debate with deepening horror, sick at the thought of civil strife and fearful that the Republic would succumb. His sympathies were for Thiers, whom he saw trapped between the intransigent extremes yet standing for moderation and reconciliation. "If M. Thiers," he wrote, "does not reduce the enthusiasm of these gentlemen [the Royalists] to reasonable and patriotic limits, we shall have within a week the white terror instead of the red terror." [37]

The Central Committee, meanwhile, not only declared invalid the Law of Maturities on March 24, but went ahead with municipal elections as scheduled. About 47 per cent of the registered electorate voted to fill the ninety seats of the municipal government on the twenty-sixth, and the results gave no radical faction a ruling majority. Only sixteen moderate Republicans gained victory, notably Méline, Tirard, and Marmottan. Sixteen members of the Internationale were elected, including Varlin and Theisz; and six Blanquists, notably, Raoul Rigault, besides Blanqui himself who had already been arrested by the Versailles authorities. Then a flock of revolutionary veterans and Leftist journalists were elected, representing a variety of socialist and Jacobin views, among them Jules Vallès, Paschal Grousset, Gustave Flourens, Auguste Vermorel, Charles Delescluze, Arthur Ranc, Arthur Arnould, and Félix Pyat. One notices at once the absence of Rochefort, whose illness had taken him out of circulation. Yet, many of the elected were former associates, and one is justified in suspecting that he, too, would have been elected had he been available.

The new municipal government, called the Commune, assumed office on March 28, 1871, apparently replacing the Central Committee, thirteen of whose forty-two members had won election to the Commune. In fact, the Central Committee continued its activities, constituting a rival regime as it had to the Government of National Defense, and the Committee's pronouncements were generally more radical than the intentions of the majority in the Commune. The consequent confusion was twofold: The Commune government never succeeded in developing a clear-cut program of social or economic reform, while those beyond Paris too often concluded that the most extreme socialists and communists had control of the Commune and meant to pursue a social revolution.

Recent studies have shown quite conclusively that the Commune was pathetically disorganized and inefficient, held together by patriotic anger and humiliation, and sadly lacking in military leadership when it came to defending itself against an attack from Versailles.[38] Supplementary elections had to be held on April 16 to fill thirty-one seats vacant through resignations or through multiple election in the first round. Only twenty-one of the vacancies were actually filled, and public disaffection was evident in the 12½ per cent of the electorate that turned out. The newly elected were more Jacobin than socialist.[39]

Yet the Commune was in a state of rebellion, and its first acts were designed to give Paris both autonomy and security. It brought to an end the old conscription laws, limited the defense of Paris to the National Guard, and made every able-bodied man a member of that Guard. It voted for the separation of Church and State and ordered the continued postponement of rent and debt payments.[40] Finally, it suppressed three newspapers classified as reactionary.[41] This last act brought Rochefort into the public eye once again, for he had returned from Arcachon to resume charge of *Le Mot d'Ordre*. When General Vinoy had evacuated Paris on March 18, his suppressive decrees had gone with him. Now the Commune regime was the suppressor, and Rochefort published a warning: "We advise the Commune to take care. It can choose freedom or terror, but it cannot harbor both at the same time." [42]

Neither the Central Committee after March 18 nor the Commune after its election planned a military offensive against Versailles; they left the initiative with Thiers. Thus the Parisians failed to take advantage of the few days in which they enjoyed a military superiority. Thiers rushed provincial troops toward the capital, determined to make an end of the rebellion before the Prussians found some pretext for further interference in French affairs. On April 2, his guns opened fire on Communard positions around Courbevoie, directly west of Paris, forcing the Communards to retire. Five Communard prisoners were taken and shot by the Versailles troops, avenging the death of the two generals on March 18, but also insuring that savage reprisals would increase the horror of the civil war. [43]

Rochefort, having already chided the Commune about censorship, now turned his fury on the National Assembly. Convinced of a friendly understanding between Versailles and Berlin, he wrote: "We know of newspapers so reactionary that they want to put Napoleon III, the Count of Paris, and the Count of Chambord on the throne, all at once. These papers . . . have just published, with a remarkable coincidence, the following note: 'M. de Bismarck has told M. Thiers that he would give him every consideration in the payment of the war indemnity in order to further the suppression of the uprising which has broken out in Paris.'" Rochefort told his readers that "every consideration" meant supporting the French Army with Krupp batteries and regiments of the Prussian Guard. [44] No question now but that he must support the Commune, convinced as he was that the choice between the Commune and Versailles was a choice between Republic and Monarchy. "The duty of those deputies elected to represent Paris," he wrote, "from the opening shot against the city which had elected them, was to come in person to her defense against the infamous yokels who were trying to destroy her." [45]

For some Republican deputies in the National Assembly, how-

ever, the issues were hardly that clear-cut, and they were aghast at
the opening of hostilities. For them the fighting not merely pitted
Frenchmen against Frenchmen, but Republicans against Republicans. Louis Blanc, for instance, believed that the Parisians did have
a legitimate right to elect their own municipal government; but he
also suspected that there were men in the Central Committee who
intended to extend the governance of the Commune to all of France,
and that was illegitimate. Beyond that, Blanc thought it obvious
that the Prussians would reoccupy Paris if the Commune should successfully defy Thiers, a factor that made this rebellion in the presence
of the enemy criminal.[46]

Georges Clemenceau, another Republican deputy, had been
mayor of the Eighteenth Arrondissement (Montmartre) until the
municipal elections of March 26. Like Louis Blanc, Clemenceau
respected the right of Paris to local self-government, but he had been
rejected by his constituency. His response was a frantic search for
compromise, despite Thiers' evident belief that force was the only
practical measure under the circumstances. If compromise failed,
Clemenceau thought that the future of the Republic lay in rallying
provincial Republican sentiments so that the victorious Assembly
would hesitate to reestablish monarchy. Hence, to abandon the
Assembly for the Commune would be to abandon the Republic.[47]
Clemenceau's efforts were warmly backed by Floquet, Allain-Targé,
Lockroy, and other Republicans in the Assembly, thus denying the
Communard's claim that they alone stood fast in the Republic's defense. Granted that the Republicans in the Assembly were the minority, they did deserve recognition; but Rochefort lumped all the
deputies together as those "wretched puppets piled up at Versailles"
for the purpose of outlawing the Republic.[48]

In the meantime, the Communard military decided to respond
to the Versaillese attack on Courbevoie with an offensive against
Versailles the following day, April 3. Ten days before, sending out
an armed mob against the tiny forces available to Thiers would have
stood some chance of success, as Thiers himself admitted, but by
April 3 Thiers' strength was greatly augmented. Commanded by

Duval, Bergeret, and Flourens, the casually organized citizens set out for Versailles as if on a delightful holiday. At last they were to be allowed that sortie repeatedly denied them by General Trochu! This picnic was abruptly halted when they came up against regular troops on the Chatillon plateau and near Mount-Valérien. Both Duval and Flourens were captured and executed, as were any regular army deserters found fighting for the Commune. The survivors scampered back to Paris, a city now besieged for a second time. One immediate result of this affair was the Hostages Law, sponsored by Delescluze, which provided for the arrest and trial of anyone thought to be pro-Versailles. Those convicted were to be held as hostages, three to be shot for every Communard prisoner shot by the Versaillese.[49]

Rochefort believed at the time, as well as later, that the Hostages Law was justifiable. Reprisals were legitimate since it sufficed for the Versaillese to refrain from shooting "our prisoners" in order to save the lives of those whom "we" have taken.[50] Yet he was also concerned about the injustice of the arbitrary choice of hostages to be shot. Were not some prisoners, he later wrote in *Le Mot d'Ordre,* more deserving of death than others, so that the choices ought not to be made out of a hat? [51] Crime, in other words, has its degrees. Other writers, both then and since, were more concerned about pinning down the guilt for starting the horror of prisoner-execution. Some blamed the Versaillese for the incident after Courbevoie; others pointed to the mob that assassinated the two generals on March 18.

It is less useful to assign blame for the pitch of savagery reached in the murder of prisoners than to observe that civil strife has historically spawned a frenzy and a savagery that go beyond that normal in war. For civil war is the final calamity after a prelude of communal or national crises, which, going unresolved or precipitating humiliation, finally flare into furious violence. Old scores are settled, private feuds are worked out, debtors assault creditors, and each side easily imputes treason or betrayal to the other side, justifying the wildest vengeances.

Walking through his arrondissement on that fatal March 18,

the conciliatory Clemenceau, physician, journalist, and politician, saw barbarism and did not mistake it for heroism:

> Suddenly a terrific noise broke out, and the mob which filled the courtyard burst into the street in the grip of some kind of frenzy. Amongst them were chasseurs, soldiers of the line, National Guards, women and children. All were shrieking like wild beasts without realizing what they were doing. I observed then that pathological phenomenon which might be called blood-lust. A breath of madness seemed to have passed over this mob: from a wall children brandished indescribable trophies; women, dishevelled and emaciated, flung their arms about while uttering raucous cries, having apparently taken leave of their senses. I saw some of them weeping while they shrieked louder than others. Men were dancing about and jostling each other in a kind of savage fury. It was one of those extraordinary nervous outbursts, so frequent in the Middle Ages, which still occur amongst masses of human beings under the stress of some primeval emotion.[52]

There seems to be little doubt that Rochefort supported the Commune in its early days. Aside from his gentle warning about censorship, his articles clearly showed him to be an enemy of the National Assembly from which he had recently resigned. Yet he would soon fall out with the Commune, too, much as he had eventually separated from the Government of National Defense the previous year. During those critical weeks in April, Rochefort met a lawyer, Jean Destrem, who as an administrator of Rochefort's legal affairs became devoted to his cause. Destrem would ultimately argue that Rochefort had known from the start that this insurrection in a blockaded city was hopeless and, given the presence of the Prussians in France, even criminal. On the other hand, according to Destrem, Rochefort felt sympathetic to many of the insurgents, and his anger increased with the casualties among the Parisian defenders. Destrem's point, published in a pamphlet in 1871, was that Rochefort wanted to be an enemy of Versailles without being a friend of the

Commune.[53] This appraisal reflected Rochefort's attitude toward the end of the Commune but obscured his earlier support for the insurgents. We must account for the change in attitude.

Shortly after the establishment of the Commune, Rochefort turned his attention to the failure of the Central Committee to disband, saying that the continued existence of the Committee could only constitute a threat to the established regime.[54] "The first obligation of the Committee," he wrote, "having declared that it was relinquishing its powers, is really to relinquish them." [55] He also published as fact a current rumor that the Assembly was about to name the Duc d'Aumale of the House of Orleans as Lieutenant-General of the Kingdom, thus justifying the Commune as the only hope for Republicans. And once the bombardment began, he judged that "M. Thiers' gendarmes have made holy the men who deliberate at the Hôtel de Ville." [56] In short, Rochefort clearly published where his sentiments lay.

At the same time, he did not refrain from criticizing those who governed in Paris for their military incompetence, forgetting—if he ever knew—that revolutionaries are rarely enthusiastic about criticism. Rochefort had never had any illusions about Flourens' ability to command troops, and after Flourens' death in such capacity, Rochefort wrote, "Our national guardsmen, victim of leaders as full of courage as inexperience, have been dislodged from nearly all their positions and have seen all their attacks beaten back. . . . All these disasters have as their origin the incredible casualness which has presided over military operations." [57]

Perhaps he thought to soften this criticism by presenting another article offensive to Versailles in the same issue. His thesis was that the defenders of order in Versailles, callously killing women and children and blowing up houses not belonging to them, might have second thoughts if their own property was at stake. His words deserve quotation, because they were later cited in his court-martial: "M. Thiers owns a wonderful house on the Place Saint-Georges full of all sorts of art works. M. Picard has on the streets of this Paris, which he has deserted, three houses bringing an enormous income;

and M. Jules Favre occupies in the rue d'Amsterdam a luxurious house which belongs to him. What would these property-owning statesmen say if the people of Paris responded . . . with pickaxes? If, for each house in Courbevoie hit by a shell, they knocked down a section of the wall at the palace on the Place Saint-Georges or at the house in the rue d'Amsterdam?" But Rochefort concluded his article in a different vein: "Inasmuch as the Assembly sitting at Versailles, if it should learn that the people's justice had demolished M. Thier's house, which had cost two million, would immediately vote him another house costing three million; and as [the taxpayers] would pay the bill, we see ourselves obliged to advise against this form of expiation." [58] Before the end of the Commune, a mob did ransack Thiers' home. Rochefort would argue that he had opposed such an act.

His real difficulties began, however, in the revival of his quarrel with Félix Pyat. This quarrel grew out of Pyat's publication of the news of Bazaine's surrender of Metz back in October of 1870, rumor of which Rochefort had foolishly communicated to Gustave Flourens who had carried it as fact to Pyat. Pyat, now a member of the Commune, had always believed that Rochefort knew that Metz had surrendered but that he had tried to conceal the news along with the other members of the Government of National Defense. Rochefort attributed Pyat's continuing hostility both to the fact that he was a man embittered by long exile and to their rivalry as journalists for subscriptions.[59] Flourens' death provided Pyat opportunity to remind the readers of his journal, *Le Vengeur*, of Rochefort's conversation with Flourens about Bazaine's "treason." Rochefort replied in print that it was hardly the time, considering Flourens' glorious death, to resurrect the issue, which cast doubt on both Flourens and Rochefort. Indeed, he noted, impartiality and circumspection should be the primary qualities of a man in Pyat's high governmental position.[60]

Impartiality and circumspection were no more Pyat's primary qualities than they were Rochefort's, and Rochefort's next move goaded Pyat even more. Rochefort had seen his name in several

109

newspapers listed as a candidate for one of the vacancies on the Commune, and on April 9, he wrote: "Needless to say, I should be extremely honored to be a part of the Commune of Paris. But there are serious reasons why I could not fulfill the great duties which that position would impose." He went on to explain that he was still a convalescent and simply did not yet have the strength to undertake public life.[61] (Years later Rochefort would assert that he had declined to run to avoid associating himself with the chaos in the Hôtel de Ville,[62] a revelation that somewhat obscures his real motive.) In the same issue of Le Mot d'Ordre, however, Rochefort sought to destroy the bad effect of his refusal by criticizing the postponement of the supplementary elections from the tenth to the sixteenth. Thus he proved his enthusiasm for the Commune, while leaving us to ponder his equivocation.[63]

Pyat had no doubt about what Rochefort meant, and he published a manifesto on April 10, ostensibly adopted by the citizens of the Ninth Arrondissement, declaring that those who had refused to be candidates for the "perilous supplementary elections" should henceforth not be named on any "sincerely Republican list" for election to the Commune.[64] Rochefort did not let the matter drop. Rightly suspecting that the citizens of the Ninth Arrondissement had neither seen nor signed Pyat's manifesto, he published this notice: "The following resolution has been passed in the Twenty-Second Arrondissement:* 'M. Félix Pyat, having been convicted of receiving 100,000 francs from Prussia, thanks to which he established a maternity home in Batignoles, rue des Dames, the people decree that M. Félix Pyat may not be included on any sincerely Republican list in the next elections.' " As for danger to be risked, Rochefort pointed out that being a member of the Commune was hardly more perilous than being the publisher of either Le Mot d'Ordre or Le Vengeur, considering that both journals had been suppressed by Vinoy the rifleman.[65]

The more one reads Rochefort in this troubled period, the more one senses his genius for equivocation. After commenting that the

* Paris has only twenty arrondissements.

destruction of Thiers' house would be an act of justice, he advised against it as impractical; after recognizing the legitimacy of the Hostages Law, he wrote an article condemning capital punishment.[66] One of the first and most notable of the Parisians to be arrested under that law was Darboy, Archbishop of Paris. On several occasions Rochefort made it clear that *Le Mot d'Ordre* had not favored the arrest of the archbishop or of any other priest;[67] yet he would add that he thought all religion was useless, and had he the decision to make, he would probably "allow Monseigneur of Paris to digest in peace the 400,000 franc annual salary that he received for nearly ten years under the Empire."[68] Did he mean to provoke without openly advocating, or was the equivocation instinctive? If he really wanted Monseigneur Darboy left in peace to enjoy his ill-gotten gains, why did he repeatedly advocate the confiscation of ecclesiastical property and wealth for the purpose of paying off the Prussian indemnity? "We should infinitely prefer to see the Commune make its requisitions in the churches than in the homes of the negotiators."[69]

On April 16, the promised supplementary elections to the Commune were held, and Rochefort, fearing widespread abstention, appealed to the voters to go to the polls no matter how they intended to vote. If as a result of the elections the Commune should run afoul of an Opposition, so much the better; for then the Commune would have to defend its plans and principles with greater energy. Furthermore, the Parisians must show Thiers their solidarity.[70] When only an eighth of the voters turned out, Rochefort declared that the results were meaningless, for one could not be sure whether this measured opposition or apathy. A common complaint was that the Commune was dictatorial. "You no longer have the right to complain if they exercise [dictatorial power], since you have given it to them" through abstention.[71] Had he left it at that, members of the Commune might have had reason to be pleased with Rochefort; but he canceled this credit by calling for new elections, saying that otherwise the Commune would have neither prestige nor authority.

An aura of suspicion, bad enough during the siege of 1870,

grew worse under the Commune; for a besieged city, if nothing else, becomes a closed corporation for the suspicious and those with axes to grind. In the humiliation of defeat, hunting scapegoats had been a national pastime, and betrayal was ascribed to them as the only possible explanation for the catastrophe. Now, a real doubt about the ultimate form of the French government extended tensions; and if the deputies in the National Assembly were divided on that topic, the members of the Commune were even more factious and mutually suspicious. Honest dissent was easily seen as a subtle plot to seize power, and as the military position of the Commune became increasingly impossible, the charges, countercharges, and hatreds rose to a frenzied crescendo. When Rochefort hinted that men elected to the Commune by a tiny minority lacked authority, he became in their eyes a traitor to the cause. He had, of course, refused to stand for election to the Commune, so that there was room for reasonable —as well as hysterical—doubt about his enthusiasm.

Rochefort's call for new elections, therefore, aroused a second round of attack upon him. But this time it came from an opponent far more dangerous than Félix Pyat, the grotesquely misshapen Pierre Vésinier, publisher of *Paris-Libre,* on which two other members of the Commune collaborated. Vésinier was also editor of the *Journal Officiel,* but he published his attack upon Rochefort in his private paper. The essence of the attack was that *Le Mot d'Ordre* was not truly Republican and sounded each day more and more like *Le Figaro,* the journal from which Rochefort ought never to have resigned.[72] Rochefort's response to the hunchbacked Vésinier recalled the taste and wisdom of *La Lanterne:* "The two-horned creature called Vésinier, whose appearance and style make one want to vomit more than debate," represents a regime that suppresses sheets that criticize it, yet allows three of its members openly to attack Republicans who have no means, "even illegal," to suppress papers that vilify them.[73] This was also an oblique reference to one of the editors of *Le Siècle* who had recently been arrested by the Commune, a Proudhonist named Chaundey.[74]

Rochefort kept up the attack, not against Vésinier by name, but against "eccentrics" in general: "Let us be suspicious of reactionaries, but let us also be suspicious of eccentrics." [75] And hearing of a proposal to arrest his old enemy, Félix Pyat, Rochefort took the line that it was not his mission to defend Pyat, but to recall that Pyat had fought for thirty years for the principles underlying the new order now established in Paris.[76] Through it all, Rochefort was careful to use abusive language about Thiers and the National Assembly in Versailles: "This bloody Tom Thumb . . . the old snake in glasses . . . the pontiff who officiates at Versailles . . . *la poltronnerie française émigré à Versailles.*" "Napoleon III is really too modest," he wrote, "to set himself up in London. We are convinced that if he should land in Seine-et-Oise, those who govern there would receive him with open arms and at once put him in charge of organizing the massacre in the streets of Paris." [77]

By May of 1871, the climate inside Paris was precisely what Flaubert called it: "totally epileptic." [78] With the Versaillese pressing hard, the Communal leadership dissolved into the gelatine of mutual mistrust. Even Rochefort, so long the opponent of dictatorship, believed that the only remedy was a "temporary" dictator to lead the troops, a man who would have the power to remove those whom he suspected and those who were suspicious of him.[79] A dictatorship was, in fact, established on May 1 and 2, the executive power going to a five-man Committee of Public Safety, augmented by a Revolutionary Tribunal with Raoul Rigault as the public prosecutor. The military commander-in-chief, General Gustave Cluseret, was removed and arrested, to be replaced by the highly patriotic Colonel Louis Rossel, a move Rochefort publicly supported.[80] Yet, on May 5, Rochefort published his opposition to the establishment of the Committee of Public Safety, claiming that the best way to solidify resistance to Versailles would be to hold new municipal elections, not to set out on a hunt for traitors.[81]

That very day, the outer defensive forts began falling to the Versaillese, leading to Rossel's disenchantment and his resignation on May 10. He was replaced as commander-in-chief by Charles Delescluze, a civilian. At that, Rochefort reiterated his call for a military dictator—in contrast to the five-man committee [82]—and demanded that proof be shown before Rossel be charged with treason.[83] Delescluze meanwhile opened his term in office by suppressing ten Parisian newspapers; and though *Le Mot d'Ordre* was not among them, Rochefort must have realized that his turn was coming, especially with Félix Pyat on the Committee of Public Safety!

Although Rochefort may have been considering his chances of escaping both the Commune and the Versaillese, there is no evidence as to when he began contemplating flight. Indeed, even if he had been thinking of it for some days, he must have been troubled by the risk of falling into Versaillese hands if he got beyond the capital. He later claimed that the decision to flee was spontaneous and based on a rumor that Raoul Rigault had issued an order for his arrest.[84] Whatever the truth of the matter, Rochefort remained in Paris for ten days after Delescluze suppressed the ten newspapers. They were significant days, suggesting the utter desperation at Communal headquarters. On May 13, the Commune ordered the destruction of Thiers' home on the place Saint-Georges;[85] on the sixteenth, the Vendôme Column was pulled down—a statue of Napoleon I was at its top—as part of a political ceremony;[86] and on the nineteenth, the Commune revealed its intention to start shooting hostages.

Rochefort had observations on all these decisions. Asked by a number of readers to say clearly whether he approved the destruction of Thiers' home and the confiscation of his furniture, Rochefort compared the incident to Vinoy's suppression of *Le Mot d'Ordre:* "The property of which I speak was *Le Mot d'Ordre.* While admitting that the axiom 'an eye for an eye, a tooth for a tooth' might not be to everyone's taste, it is well to remember that it was not the Commune which started [the destruction], but rather the noble Thiers, by suppressing six newspapers at one swoop, who gave us the sad example of demolition."[87] Nor would he condemn the destruction of the Vendôme Column, built as it was in the Empire style ("the most insupportable of all styles") and in honor of the most insupportable of governments.

As for the decision to begin shooting hostages, he had never opposed the law providing for reprisals and limited himself in the final issue of *Le Mot d'Ordre* to saying that, since crime has its degrees, the hostages should be chosen for execution depending upon the degree of their treachery and not arbitrarily chosen.[88] When these words hit the street, Rochefort was in flight. As an explanation, he sent a brief note to the publisher of *La Politique,* asking that it be printed: "I should be very much obliged to you if you would be good enough to announce to your readers that, under the circumstances presently facing the press, *Le Mot d'Ordre* believes it to be dignified to cease appearing.[89] His flight was not a protest against the Commune in principal, but a judicious escape from the wrath of Félix Pyat and Raoul Rigault.[90]

Having neither passport nor identification card, Rochefort could not legally leave Paris; nor could he hope to slip out unidentified, even though he had already shaved his beard because of an infectious ski disease, erysipelas. Luck, however, was with him. When he approached the guards at the Porte Est on May 20 and gave his name, they passed him through without incident.[91] His escape was doubly judicious, for on the afternoon of May 21, the Versaillese penetrated Paris from the west, opening the final week of fratricide. His escape does, in fact, raise the question, probably unanswerable, of whether Rochefort feared the Versaillese more than the Communards, or if he knew that his particular game was up and was fleeing from both without distinction. Whichever the case, he escaped the most frightful street fighting and savage reprisals Paris had ever known. Between 17,000 and 20,000 Parisians fell during the "Bloody Week," and the end of their military resistance opened an era of legal reprisal that left France bitterly divided for generations.[92]

Bitterness and the desire for revenge after 1871 did not, of course, grow only from the Commune. The National Assembly, having accepted the necessity of a harsh peace with Prussia, still had to experience the agony of ratifying the terms put into definitive form —the Treaty of Frankfurt. Jules Favre signed the convention on May 10 at the Hôtel du Cygne in Frankfurt and brought it back to the Assembly at Versailles. Protests against its harshness were again heard in the Assembly, but the realists overwhelmingly voted to accept the treaty, 433 to 98. The two governments' ratifications were exchanged in Frankfurt on May 21, the very day that marked the beginning of the Bloody Week in Paris.[93]

Rochefort's memoirs reveal little about his family, and the evident rifts within the family precluded much correspondence. Except for his children, whom he adored, a rigid coldness between him and his family existed for years. The most plausible explanation is Rochefort's political and religious radicalism, which his Legitimist family found embarrassing and irritating. During the Commune, Rochefort's elderly father died in Paris. Some newspapers, in noting the death, indicated that he had been shabbily treated by his son. Jean Destrem, Rochefort's legal administrator, wrote in his 1871 brochure that these charges were absurd. On the contrary, Destrem claimed that Rochefort gave his father a monthly pension of 400 francs.[94] Perhaps he did, but further evidence is lacking.

The matter was not allowed to die, probably because the question of Rochefort's public guilt aroused an interest in his private guilt. Rochefort's father died in the parish of St. Eloi, and his parish priest, the Abbé Denys, wrote a long letter on the subject, which was published in the *Autographe,* July 15, 1872, and then republished by *Le Figaro* on August 27, 1872. Abbé Denys charged that Rochefort had retaliated against family disapproval by letting his father live in poverty. When he learned he was dying, the old man had called for Abbé Denys on April 8, 1871, and received the last rites of the Church. Subsequently, Rochefort had insisted on a civil burial for his father despite the old man's obvious desire for a religious ceremony.[95] By the time this story was published, Rochefort was a state prisoner, and those who thought him guilty of sedition saw this betrayal of his father's wishes as proof of a depraved character.

CHAPTER IV

Rochefort the State Prisoner
1871-1874

The arrest of Rochefort has given me a moment of gaiety. It is not he whom I wish to see punished; rather I should like to see drowned in filth—with his stupid person—all the cretins who swooned before his style! When I think of the gigantic stupidity of my country, I wonder if it has been sufficiently chastised.

GUSTAVE FLAUBERT [1]

ROCHEFORT asserted that he fled Paris in haste, having time to warn only one of his collaborators on *Le Mot d'Ordre,* his editorial secretary Eugène Mourot. After leaving the city without any difficulty, the two boarded a train bound for the frontier. It was May 20, 1871, a day that Rochefort remembered as unseasonably hot. At Meaux, only forty-four kilometers from Paris, all passengers were asked to disembark for an examination of passports, documents that neither Rochefort nor Mourot possessed. The French police agent at the station apparently expected to find Rochefort on the train and informed him that he had an order for his arrest. When news of the arrest was telegraphed to Versailles, it was ordered that the two prisoners be kept under constant surveillance.[2]

The swiftness of the arrest lends credence to evidence that Rochefort was betrayed, though Rochefort himself seems to have believed that he had simply been spotted by a secret agent as he boarded the train to escape. The betrayal theory was not published until three years later, written by Jules de Gastyne after an interview with a Parisian policeman named Delachapelle. In brief, Gastyne argued that Rochefort had been betrayed by his former associate on *La Marseillaise,* Paschal Grousset, who had been elected to the Commune. Grousset had grown increasingly intemperate as a member of the Commune, until he was known as one of the extremists eager for the creation of the Committee of Public Safety.[3] At the same time, Grousset had developed a grudge against Rochefort, for reasons Gastyne did not know, and had sought to have Rochefort arrested as the most "dangerous friend" the Commune had. In fact, Rochefort had published a jibe at Grousset in *Le Mot d'Ordre* after a public announcement of Grousset's assignment to the Commune's office of foreign affairs. Knowing of Grousset's inexperience, Rochefort found it hard to take the appointment seriously.[4]

In any event, Gastyne asserted that Grousset obtained an order for Rochefort's arrest and that Delachapelle was the policeman charged to carry out the order. Then, in order to avoid popular resentment over the arrest, Grousset warned Rochefort to flee, after which he presumably tipped off a Versaillese agent of the probable flight.[5] Perhaps this stretches the imagination. Yet it could account for the swiftness of the arrest. Rochefort would ultimately find Grousset a fellow prisoner on New Caledonia, but at that time the Gastyne revelation had not been published. As fellow victims of the Versaillese, they were easily comrades, but nothing more. A police informer correctly surmised that "Grousset is too communard for Rochefort and Rochefort too little communard for Grousset."[6]

Rochefort and Mourot were taken from Meaux to Versailles handcuffed and under heavy guard. The excessive security measures convinced Rochefort that he was being taken to Versailles to be shot. En route, at St.-Germain, the police were augmented by mounted troops commmanded personally by Colonel de Galliffet, and the

Henri Rochefort, a portrait by Gustave Courbet.

Napoleon III, the Flandrin portrait.

The Empress Eugénie, the Winterhalter portrait.

The Duc de Morny, engineer of the *coup d'état* of December 2, 1851.

A cartoon from *Le Charivari*, January 11, 1870:

—"Impossible, dear M. Rochefort, you have my hair!
— Dear M. Crémieux, I was just going to reclaim yours."

—Pas possible cher M⁻ Rochefort vous avez mes cheveux!
— Cher M⁻ Crémieux j'allais réclamer les vôtres.

A cartoon from *L'Éclipse,*
February 9, 1871, showing
an imaginary Rochefortean
metamorphosis:

Our deputy Rochefort,
As you see, looks very much
Like a bunch
Of grapes, savory fruits,
From which come
A wine clear, red and generous.

Rochefort's arrest in Paris during the disturbances of February, 1870.

The trial of Prince Pierre Bonaparte, in the High Court of Justice at Tours, April, 1870.

Gambetta proclaiming the Republic in front of the palace of the Corps Législatif, September 4, 1870. Members of the crowd are cheering the Republic, Gambetta, Trochu and . . . Rochefort.

Louis Jules Trochu, General and
President of the Government of
National Defense.

Gustave Flaubert, caricatured by
E. Girard.

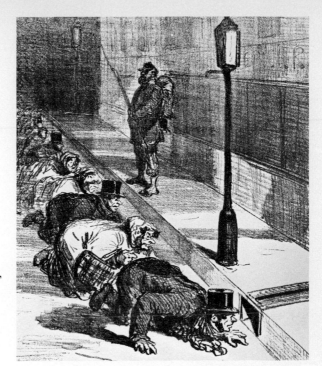

Privation during the seige of Paris,
1871: "The queue for rat meat."

A cartoon from *Punch*, October 18,
1873, showing President Thiers
listening to the appeal of "France":
"Between Two Terrors ('White'
and 'Red')."

Général Boulanger: he was a "Man on Horseback."

Ferdinand de Lesseps, from *Vanity Fair,* November 27, 1869: "He suppressed an isthmus."

Émile Zola, a portrait by Édouard Manet.

The duel between Col. Henry and Col. Picquart, at the height of L'Affaire Dreyfus, 1897.

Rochefort's arrival at the prison of Sainte-Pélagie, from *L'Illustration*, February 26, 1898.

The arrival of President Loubet and his family at the Grand Prix de Paris at Auteuil, June 11, 1899.

On the same occasion, the arrest of the President's assailant, Baron Christiani.

The opening of the Pont d'Alexandre III in Paris, 1900.

Rochefort peering through the October 30, 1901, issue of *L'Intransigeant*.

procession rode into Versailles to be greeted by a shrieking mob, largely women, who were shaking their fists and howling for Rochefort's death. One image remained with him the remainder of his life: a man in a cinnamon frock coat waving a red umbrella—straight out of Daumier—yelling "It's Rochefort! Skin him alive!" [7] Despite this popular hostility, Rochefort reached the Versailles prison alive and intact and settled down to await his trial.

Rochefort wanted little of the prison food and gave much of it to a guard, who in turn brought him an occasional delicacy deliberately wrapped in a late newspaper. Thus Rochefort learned of the fall of the Commune and that his prison contained other notables, Paschal Grousset and Gustave Courbet among others. The prison confessor, the Abbé Foley, visited Rochefort every day, fruitlessly concerned about Rochefort's salvation, but bringing valuable news of the outside world. If Foley could not offer Rochefort hope for eternal salvation, he did inspire in Rochefort hope for a more immediate kind. Public passions, Foley believed, would soon subside, and if Rochefort would employ every means to delay his trial, the penalty would surely be lessened.

The distinguished attorney Charles Lachaud, who would defend Gustave Courbet in July of 1871, declined to defend Rochefort, but nevertheless visited him in his cell and promised to advise whomever Rochefort managed to retain. The competition was not keen among those who already had legal reputations, and Rochefort was ultimately forced to retain the relatively unknown Albert Joly. Which of the three really devised the defense strategy remains unclear, but certainly attempts were made to invoke the intervention of well-known Republicans on Rochefort's behalf. [9] Rochefort would later deny that he had approved such tactics, placing the responsibility upon Joly; and the denial would lead to a public scandal late in 1880. But one must suspect that as Rochefort's life was in real danger in 1871 he was not so high-minded that summer as his later memory would have it.

The first Republican to be invoked was Gambetta. The letter denied that Rochefort had supported the Commune and that he had pointed out Thiers' house to the mob on the day of its destruction. Gambetta was asked to see Thiers about the case, and Rochefort offered to go into exile for an unlimited time to avoid a prison sentence. He promised that during his exile he would devote himself to a history of the Second Empire rather than to opposition.[10]

Less than two months after Rochefort's imprisonment a new parliamentary election was held, on July 2, 1871, to supplement the February elections for the National Assembly. The result was clearly a Republican victory and a tribute to Thiers. Nearly a dozen Royalists were returned, but the Republicans captured almost a hundred seats, including a seat from Paris for Gambetta. The Monarchists still held their majority, but their divisions deepened four days later when the Legitimist pretender, the Comte de Chambord, announced that he would not give up the "white flag of Henry IV." [11] His intransigence gave the Republicans new hope that they would eventually prevail.

Even before the shooting ceased in Paris, a member of the National Assembly, Haentjens, proposed that a commission be established to investigate the causes of the Commune. Three weeks later, June 13, 1871, the Assembly did create a commission of thirty-one members, but to examine first the acts of the Government of National Defense. Presided over by Comte Daru, the commission reflected the monarchical majority in the Assembly and was predisposed to view the Commune as a socialist conspiracy engineered by the Internationale.[12] Nevertheless, the commission heard and published an immense amount of testimony, which is a valuable source of information about the charges and countercharges of that troubled era.

Even though that testimony did not bear directly upon Rochefort's trial, it may have somewhat affected Thiers' eventual decision to be relatively lenient. General Trochu, as we already know, insisted that Rochefort had behaved properly and loyally as a member of the Government of National Defense.[13] Edmond Adam sought to show that Rochefort was not like the other radicals: "Rochefort is a man of pure whim. . . . He conducted himself well during the siege.

He left the Government without a fuss and caused it no embarrassment. I am with those who were very happy with him. Rochefort is not a conspirator, he is not the leader of a party, he is, I repeat, a *fantaisiste* [and] he lacks prudence." [14] Another Republican, Claude-Anthime Corbon, who had been mayor of the Fifteenth Arrondissement under the Government of National Defense, evaded leading questions designed to show that Rochefort had been friendly to members of the Internationale by insisting that Rochefort had clearly represented himself as a member of the Government rather than the Central Committee.[15] Finally, an army officer familiar with the conduct of political prisoners being held for trial testified that Rochefort was subdued and had little to say: "He is quite sick, he is very nervous; there is something quite feminine about him, and the doctor says that a few years from now he can be carried off by a chest ailment." [16]

The specific charges made against Rochefort in the indictment related solely to events during the Commune and were hastily and inaccurately drawn up. Thus, as in so many other cases after the Commune, Rochefort's guilt was real, but the slapdash prosecution bared the slight concern for justice and a thirst for vengeance. During the investigation leading to the indictment, for instance, police informers testified that Rochefort had been seen carrying off works of art from the Louvre and bronzes from Thiers' house at the time of its destruction. Autographed portraits of Garibaldi and Mazzini were found in Rochefort's home and introduced as evidence of Rochefort's seditious nature.[17] The trial did not hinge on such ridiculous evidence alone, but the aura of shabby reprisal was only too evident. Thiers had little part in the trials of political prisoners, who came before courts-martial, a fact that alone enhanced the probability of arbitrariness. But Thiers, who was advised by a parliamentary Pardon Commission, did have the power to pardon the accused.[18]

Once the charge of looting was added to Rochefort's indictment, he sought a substantial character witness for his defense. His choice was General Trochu, to whom he wrote on September 1,

1871, claiming that it was a matter of honor for Trochu to speak out. In the first place, he reminded Trochu that he, Rochefort, had controlled the Parisian masses on September 4 of the previous year; and had he been ambitious for power, the presidency of the Government of National Defense could easily have been his. Instead, he had insisted that Trochu be given the post, that he had even suppressed *La Marseillaise* to avoid undesirable agitation since the requirements of defense came first, and he explained his resignation from the Government of National Defense as a protest against armistice negotiations.[19] In fact, Rochefort had had nothing to do with Trochu's nomination, which the general very well knew; and *La Marseillaise* had been suppressed in July of 1870, long before Trochu assumed the presidency of the government. The claims were ill-chosen as the justification for a character reference.

Trochu published Rochefort's appeal along with his answer to it. He began with a lengthy—and accurate—review of the events that had led to his nomination as president of the Government of National Defense on September 4. Rejecting Rochefort's claim to have "insisted" on that nomination, Trochu added:

> I saw you that day for the first time, and I saw you for the last time on the eve of October 31. During the interval, that is, during the time you had a seat at the Hôtel de Ville, I found you very actively engaged with the defense, without any apparent personal ambition, and more moderate than your notoriety would have led me to expect. Several measures of a conservative character, which I proposed, were supported by you. One of your acts particularly touched me: Along with one other member of the government, whose name I do not remember, you refused any payment for your participation in public affairs. But I subsequently learned that, after this public refusal, for it had been made in the council, you *secretly* asked for the payment in question, a circumstance which gravely compromised your character in my mind. I do not recall having seen you at the Hôtel de Ville on the thirty-first of

October in the midst of the common dangers. The next day you gave your resignation. But I refuse to acknowledge that it had as its cause, as you claim, the armistice negotiations that M. Thiers was then pursuing at Versailles. You knew as all of us that the idea for this armistice came from the outside, that the government, on being informed, had deliberated on it, that it unanimously —you being present—pronounced for an ultimatum which was *an armistice with the provisioning of Paris, an election in all the departments, and the meeting of a National Assembly.* . . . Finally, during the bloody reign of the Commune, I was shown articles taken from *Le Mot d'Ordre* which belonged to you. They were of the most abominable character. One of them provoked the mob to the destruction of M. Thiers' house. It has fixed you in my mind." [20]

Clearly General Trochu was no help. But Albert Joly had delivered Rochefort's appeal to Gambetta, who now transferred that appeal to Thiers.[21] Edmond Adam, now a member of the National Assembly from Paris, was received by Thiers at a private dinner for the purpose of discussing the Rochefort case. Edmond Adam was not an extremist. Well known for his loyalty to friends, he continued to risk contamination by calling Rochefort "my friend." Thiers frankly told Adam that most of the ministers favored shooting Rochefort, though Jules Simon was opposed to all the blood-letting. Thiers' private secretary, the learned and austere Republican Jules Barthélemy-Saint-Hilaire, who had more than a little influence on Thiers, revealed in a remark the President's decision to spare Rochefort's life: "They tell me that [Rochefort] is too fond of gambling, suppers and women. All that is waste of time: a sojourn in New Caledonia will do him good."[22] Thiers overrode the opinion of his ministers. "He was mixed up in the destruction of my house," Thiers told them; "if I let him be shot, I shall incur all the odium of personal revenge."[23] The verdict, in short, was determined before the trial, as Rochefort came to realize.[24] A year later, Rochefort would write to Mme. Edmond Adam: "You tell me that Thiers saved my life. I agree, and it is impossible for me to forget it." [25]

The court-martial convened on September 20, 1871, with Eugène Mourot also present. The charges against Rochefort were: publisher of false news published in bad faith with intent to disturb the public peace; accessory to attempts to incite civil war; accessory to provoking pillage and assassination; offenses against the head of the government; and offenses to the National Assembly. Rochefort tried to defend his articles in *Le Mot d'Ordre* by insisting that, while some of the things he had written were violent and even overdrawn, he had basically worked for conciliation. The court observed that if this were so, it would have taken highly intelligent readers to see conciliatory intentions in his particular use of words. To the charge that he had goaded the mob to take vengeance on Thiers, Rochefort replied that he had not intended his article to be interpreted as an encouragement to destroy Thiers' house; moreover, that as a journalist he was aware how repeatedly one has to preach something to get action, and he had mentioned this matter only once. Throughout his life, Rochefort believed that he had defended himself skillfully against "empty" charges.[26]

The verdicts were returned on September 21. Rochefort was sentenced to deportation for life, to be held in a fortified place. Mourot, only twenty-three at the time and clearly subordinate to Rochefort, yet affiliated with the Internationale, was condemned to simple deportation. He had signed three inflammatory articles in Le *Mot d'Ordre,* but his police dossier reveals that, since they were in Rochefort's style, even the police had doubt that he had actually written them. Mourot, in short, was guilty by association. Sent to the Isle of Pines, he was not pardoned until June 5, 1879.[17]

Rochefort remained for a few weeks after sentencing in the Versailles prison, where he was allowed to have visitors. His immediate concern was to provide for his children, whom Edmond Adam had sent to England in custody of Rochefort's sister Emilie after his arrest. On September 28, Rochefort wrote to Adam asking him to make arrangements for the care of the children, who were then brought back from England by Emilie. A *conseil de famille* was appointed, headed by Jean Destrem as legal administrator, and Noémie and Henri were kept by their Aunt Emilie, while Octave (Bibi) was taken by Mme. Adam.[28]

The separation of the children into two homes may have been a necessary expedient; but it may also indicate that they were born to different mothers. (There remains a birth certificate for only one child, Noémie, born to Marie Renauld.) Mme. Adam had earlier indicated an exceptional fondness for Octave. She noted in her journal on October 18, 1870, that Rochefort and Bibi had come for dinner. "He [Bibi] thinks, he talks like a man of forty; at eight [he was actually ten] he is more aged than his father."[29] The two came again for dinner on October 30.[30] Then on February 11, 1871, with Rochefort and Edmond Adam destined for Bordeaux and the National Assembly, she made a curious entry in her journal. It happens to be one of the few passages she altered in the second edition of the journal:

I sent for Octave-Bibi Rochefort. I am too alone and must have a child to love. Rochefort, who is clearly elected a deputy from Paris, leaves for Bordeaux; I beg him to leave me his son.[31]

I sent for Octave-Bibi Rochefort. I am too alone and must have a child to love. Rochefort is bringing his son and promises me to leave him with me during his stay in Bordeaux, where he presumes he will remain only a few days, the time to give his resignation if the capitulards decree peace. Rochefort is elected deputy from Paris. Adam, who was on the list of *Le Mot d'Ordre,* is also elected. He owes his election to our friend and to me.[32]

Meanwhile, friends were making further efforts to modify Rochefort's situation. Victor Hugo took it upon himself to call on Thiers, who received him on the afternoon of October 1. The interview was cordial and, to Hugo's satisfaction, achieved results. Given the "savage" temper of the "Commission of so-called Pardons," Thiers felt that a commutation for Rochefort was impossible. On the other hand, Thiers promised that Rochefort would not be sent abroad, but would be held in a French fortress. Hugo urged that it be a pleasant place where Rochefort could see his children freely and could work on a history of Napoleon III. He assumed that an amnesty would be granted in six or seven months.[33] Hugo brought this encouraging news to Rochefort at Versailles, who thereafter assumed that because of his health he would not be deported. He understood that no further promises had been made.[34]

But when Rochefort was transferred from Versailles to a French fortress, he found himself in the company of prisoners sentenced for deportation, a circumstance that caused him understandable anxiety. He was one of twelve confined in leg irons in a special prison railway car for the two-day trip to La Rochelle. From there he was sent to Fort Boyard on the Isle of Aix off La Rochelle, where his name was entered in the jail book on November 9, 1871.[35] He was at first refused permission to see his two elder children, whom Emilie brought to reside nearby; but when he organized a noisy protest by other prisoners on his behalf, the prison director relented.[36]

Most of the prisoners at Fort Boyard were confident that a general amnesty would be soon forthcoming; but as the months went by, first one and then a second frigate called at the island to pick up deportees. The second group to leave, which included Paschal Grousset, was sent to New Caledonia. Rochefort, on the other hand, was transferred to the citadel on the Isle of Oléron, only an hour by small boat from Fort Boyard. This transfer, on June 22, 1872, was the best evidence he could have had that Thiers meant to keep his promise about deportation. Yet Rochefort's friends had hoped that he would be sent to the south of France. Hugo had suggested Nice, and Gambetta had preferred Isle Ste. Marguerite, just off Cannes. Gambetta's secretary had promised Destrem that "[Gambetta] will make every effort to have Rochefort sent to Fort Ste. Marguerite. . . . In the meantime, and to improve the prisoner's present situation, he begs you to let us know the name of the director of Fort Boyard." [37]

Indeed, the citadel of Oléron was far from the Riviera! It was in fact a real dungeon. Rochefort found himself in a cavelike room, damp from seawater, with straw provided for beds. Roughly fifty prisoners shared the space with huge water rats, which came out at night to frolic over the sleeping bodies. An invasion of fleas was the final degradation for Rochefort, who had simply had no experience with such horrors. After several days, he was removed to the citadel hospital. Although, of course, his frailty had long been recognized, he was not above exploiting this reputation. A few weeks before his transfer to Oléron, he wrote of continuous stomach trouble and of being in the infirmary, adding, "I am going to play as sick as possible." [38]

His other concern was writing, for writing meant money. The profits from his newspapers had virtually been exhausted, and though he had given instructions for the sale of his personal possessions, he knew his creditors might devour much that could be realized from the sale. A catalog of his possessions had been published and their value roughly estimated by a police informer: "Rochefort was an amateur of some learning in matters of painting. . . . The books are few in number, but interesting and mostly well bound. The value of the objects can be estimated at about 40,000 francs." [39] A former manager of *Le Mot d'Ordre* had thereupon filed suit for 5,776 francs for having covered some of Rochefort's debts.[40] Destrem was in charge of affairs, but the legal entanglements also kept Albert Joly involved, and evidently he and Destrem could not agree on details. From the partial correspondence that remains, one can see Rochefort's temper rising and can note his dislike of Joly as "an insupportable maker of trouble." [41]

To get ready money meant returning to writing. Otherwise his children would become financial wards of the Edmond Adams. The only literary form suitable to his situation was the novel, and he began—amidst his fellow prisoners—to sketch out a work to be called *Les Dépravés,* which he hoped to have published episodically in the radical *Le Rappel.* Whether for reasons of health or literature, the prison authorities transferred Rochefort once again after nearly two months, this time to the citadel of Saint-Martin on the Isle of Ré, also off La Rochelle. Here, beginning on August 20, 1872,[42] he enjoyed a single room and relative comfort. His children also moved to the island and were allowed to visit him for an hour or two every day.[43] Beginning in August and continuing well into 1873, much of Rochefort's correspondence with Destrem was about publishing details—that is, until Thiers' fall from power removed Rochefort's protector and resurrected his anxiety about deportation.

In the autumn of 1872, Rochefort's ex-mistress, Marie Renauld, fell dangerously ill, evidently suffering from paraplegia of the spine.[44] Rochefort learned this from the Abbé Foley, the chaplain he had known in the Versailles prison; for evidently Mlle. Renauld, of whom we know very little, had lived in Versailles for some time. Foley wrote of her extreme need for money and advised Rochefort to write to Thiers for authorization to go to Versailles to marry her and thus legitimize the children. "It is my intention to legitimize them," Rochefort wrote to Destrem, "but not to write M. Thiers." He felt it would be far better to have her brought to La Rochelle.[45] Quite clearly the children were Rochefort's concern: "The children's mother is, and always will be, insupportable." [46]

Marie, meanwhile, had been transferred from her home to a convent where she could receive continual care, and Rochefort finally realized that she could never make the trip to La Rochelle. He put the matter in Joly's hands, giving him authority to make the arrangements necessary for a wedding in Versailles, but advising him that birth certificates for two of the three children would probably be unobtainable.[47] The government responded immediately, and two police agents were detailed to escort Rochefort to Versailles, where he was lodged once again in the prison. "I thank you for the authorization," he at once wrote to the Minister of the Interior. "It is my wish to be returned to St.-Martin de Ré on the same day as the ceremony, so that it cannot be said that I was brought to Versailles for any but the true reason." [48]

What, indeed, had been the "true reason"? A desire to legitimize his children was quite understandable, but he had also written earlier that he would *never* request official permission to go to Versailles.[49] Hostile to religion in general and Catholicism with a vengeance, he intended to have nothing more than a civil marriage to be performed by M. Rameau, a Left-Wing deputy also serving as mayor of Versailles. But he not only permitted a religious marriage, too, but confessed himself to the Abbé Bourgeois and received absolution as a preliminary to the marriage.[50] Finally, while we may be unsure as to which of Rochefort's children had actually been born to Marie, it is unlikely that all three were hers; yet all three were listed as hers on the register. A number of newspapers covered the November 6 wedding, and each paper had an opinion about the children. *Le Figaro, Le Pays,* and *Paris-Journal* all stated that only Noémie was Marie's child.[51] More radical papers, *La Cloche* and *Le Rappel,* for example, accepted without question that all three were hers.[52] Rochefort merely referred to her as "the mother of my children" in his memoirs; yet in his letter requesting official authorization to make the trip to Versailles, he explained that "I do not want, following either my death or that of the mother, this child to be condemned all its life to an irregular position."[53]

The ceremony itself was a cruel affair, and fortunately the children were absent. Marie was obviously dying—and knew it—and she spoke her words in a weak voice. Rochefort apparently wept throughout the ordeal, and when it was completed asked to be taken to his cell. The bride, now in tears, cried out something to the effect of, "Oh my God, we shall never see each other again!"[54] And so it was. Rochefort remembered that she survived the marriage by only two months.[55] In fact, she died five and a half months later and was buried in the church of St. Louis de Versailles.[56]

Public curiosity about the Rochefort marriage did not subside easily; there was doubt about his motives. Had he been morally stricken by the illegitimate status of his children, as well as solicitous for Marie's religious scruples, as he claimed?[57] Or by appearing as the devoted father and the respecter of religion, did he mean to appeal for public sympathy, as one editor charged?[58] Whatever he intended, the marriage had one result that he most certainly did not anticipate. It called attention to the fact that he had not yet been deported, and that he was evidently enjoying privileges unavailable to ordinary prisoners. As one journalist put it, "If Rochefort had not belonged to the aristocracy of disorder, would he have been granted permission to come to repair an oversight dating from a happier time?"

This journalist, Jules Richard, devoted a long column to the Rochefort phenomenon. He claimed that *La Lanterne* revealed Rochefort to have no political ideas, no social formula, no sense of history—that there had never been any new insights in it. Moreover, when Rochefort was in the government, he was also nothing and was completely bored with the vast details necessary to good government. "Every time I saw Rochefort, whether at *Figaro* or elsewhere, I always found him frantic to escape from a formidable bore, suggesting both a permanent anxiety of mind and very violent stomach upsets. . . . He sought pleasure in every form, tracked down all the emotional thrills. He gambled at roulette, at the tracks, at cards, in the stock market; suppers, girls, theater, and journalism. . . . The dominant feature of his character was vanity, and what vanity! Rochefort has never had what one calls principles nor even political or social opinions; he has always had an attitude and instincts. . . . Rochefort without political education, ignorant of history and philosophy, vaudevillist and boulevardier, has been the most powerful agent for destruction in our century.[59] Richard called Rochefort a nihilist. But "aristocrat of disorder" really suggests *frondeur*.

Relatives and friends of men already deported were openly critical that an exception had evidently been made for Rochefort. Some of them assumed that Rochefort's deportation might lead to an early general amnesty and thus were eager to see him packed off.[60] But Rochefort's friends had confidence for good reason, for one of Gambetta's assistants on the *République française* wrote to Destrem to reassure him about Rochefort's fate. "M. Rochefort will not leave France. You may discreetly repeat this good news to friends of our poor prisoner."[61] Probably Gambetta had wind, as Edmond Adam did, that Thiers was considering moving Rochefort to the Isle of Ste. Marquerite off Cannes, a move that Gambetta had recommended earlier. This would apply the letter of the condemnation, while avoiding the unpleasantness of a penal colony in the tropics.[62]

Rochefort did his own cause no good, however, by plunging into publication despite known government opposition. By the beginning of 1873, he had finished his novel, *Les Dépravés,* and was commencing a second, to be called *Les Naufrageurs.* Around this time, a police informer named Bridoux managed to make the acquaintance of Destrem and became a frequent caller at Destrem's home. Destrem was apparently unaware of what riches he fed into the Rochefort dossier. Through this acquaintanceship, the regime learned that Rochefort deliberately meant to ignore its suggestion, because he placed no stock in the threat to send him to New Caledonia. He would not sign the installments of *Les Dépravés* to appear in *Le Rappel,* but he realized that every reader would know the writer. The political stand-off between Thiers and the Assembly seemed to be reaching a crisis, and Rochefort was confident that the Chamber would soon be dissolved and that a Republican chamber would be elected. In that case, he should have nothing to fear.[63]

Monarchical divisions, in fact, were leading to Republican electoral success in 1872, and Gambetta, confident of a Republican victory, campaigned up and down the country for actual dissolution of the National Assembly and new elections. Thiers, while opposing radical Republicanism, formally indicated his preference for the Republic on November 13, 1872, leading the alarmed monarchical majority in the Assembly to attempt to reduce his authority. Yet they hesitated to overthrow him until negotiations for evacuation of French territory were completed. Thiers had, in fact, been astoundingly successful in raising money to pay both the indemnity and the daily occupation costs to Germany. Under the Treaty of Frankfurt, the final installment was not due until May 2, 1874, but on March 15, 1873, Thiers reached an agreement with the Germans for the last payment to be made the following September and for an end to the occupation. Considering that the occupation costs amounted to considerably more than the indemnity, he had achieved a remarkable economy. But March 15 also marked the end of his financial usefulness to the Assembly.[64]

In the meantime, Rochefort and Destrem were having troubles over the publication of *Les Dépravés*. Although *Le Rappel* had accepted the manuscript, apparently a debate ensued as to the wisdom of publication. Some of Rochefort's friends were fearful that publication would lead not merely to his deportation but to the suspension of the journal. Destrem was in an agony, because Rochefort had offered him 5 per cent of the earnings, predicted to be no less than 50,000 francs, as payment for his services to Rochefort.[65] Finally, after much delay, the novel began appearing unsigned in *Le Rappel* in April. By that time, *Les Naufrageurs* was also finished, and Rochefort sought an outlet for it too.[66]

The anticipated political showdown came in the wake of a by-election in Paris on April 27, 1873. Barodet, a radical Republican standing for both dissolution of the National Assembly and a general amnesty, won a great victory over the Comte de Rémusat, a close associate of Thiers and a member of his cabinet. Thiers had, of course, backed his associate, but Gambetta had endorsed Barodet. Apparently Thiers' conservative Republicanism had been disavowed by the Republicans, and the monarchical majority in the Assembly seized the opportunity to interpret Barodet's victory as the natural outcome of Thiers' misguided faith in the Republic. Unable to agree on a crowned successor to Thiers, the Monarchists were determined to replace him with a president whose monarchical sentiments were steadfast: Marshal MacMahon. Given what amounted to a no-confidence vote on May 23, Thiers immediately resigned office. A new president was elected the same evening, the Left abstaining from the voting.[67]

Radical Republicanism may have won a victory over conservative Republicanism, but the Right was the immediate beneficiary; and Rochefort's confidence vanished.[68] He began preparing for the possibility of deportation, which his friends and family not only believed to be inevitable but from which they thought he would not return alive. Destrem was given the furniture belonging to the late Mme. Rochefort in payment for his legal services to Rochefort, but he was saddened by the thought that Rochefort's deportation would postpone indefinitely grander financial rewards from their association. Accordingly, he labored on in his humane task, calling on Victor Hugo for renewed efforts,[69] and on Edmond Adam for renewed intervention. Adam, however, not only told Destrem that nothing more could be done, but wrote Rochefort to prepare for imminent departure.[70]

Destrem's final attempt was a public letter in which he sought public pity for the probable deportee. Having seen Rochefort twice on the Isle of Ré in 1872 and for ten days in March of 1873, Destrem focused on Rochefort's bad health. He claimed that bad health had been the reason for not transporting Rochefort to date and that that health was deteriorating: he reported that Rochefort had frequent pain around the heart and palpitations after climbing stairs or walking any distance.[71] It was difficult to muster public sympathy for a man out of circulation for nearly two years, a man whose character was sufficiently dubious as to preclude a spontaneous public demonstration for an innocent victimized by wolves. The more radical the Republican, the more likely he was to condemn the deportations in principle; but many of the Republicans were only mildly concerned, and then for the principles at stake rather than the men.[72] Destrem's appeal, therefore, evoked some response from the radicals and the artists of Paris but met indifference elsewhere.[73]

Victor Hugo, having succeeded for Rochefort once before by going to the President, tried once again. This time he approached the new premier, Duc Albert de Broglie, rather than President Mac-Mahon. Both Broglie and Hugo were members of the French Academy, and Hugo's plea was for "one of the most celebrated writers of our day." He asked that because of health, Rochefort be sent to Ste. Marguerite: "This is a matter of a writer, and of a writer of original and rare talent. You are both Minister and Academician, and here your two duties are compatible and complementary. . . . I ask you, Monsieur and dear colleague, in this critical moment to protect M.

133

Henri Rochefort and to prevent the departure which would be his death.[74]

Broglie replied that under no circumstances would Rochefort be deported unless medical authority deemed he was fit for the voyage to New Caledonia. Beyond that "you will no doubt agree that the intellectual qualities with which M. Rochefort is endowed increase his responsibility and cannot serve as grounds for lessening the punishment due the seriousness of his crime. Those poor ignorant or misguided ones who have been attracted by his words, and who leave behind them families shackled to poverty, should have more claim on indulgence."[75]

The Edmond Adams, having no confidence in last-minute appeals, had meanwhile taken Octave for a final visit with his father. Rochefort saw all three of his children on board the *Virginie* before sailing for New Caledonia on August 10, 1873. He asked Mme. Adam to be a mother for all three,[76] lending further credence to earlier speculation by Destrem and the informer Bridoux that she had been a mistress of Rochefort.[77] His physical discomfort, by the time he boarded the *Virginie,* was so great that the emotional stress of the departure was lessened. This frigate, built in 1848, had been recommissioned for transporting prisoners. Anchored in deep water off the Isle of Ré, she received her cargo by small boat; this short trip was long enough for Rochefort to exhaust himself from vomiting.

He was given a clean cabin with barred windows and a privacy not enjoyed by other prisoners; but loneliness soon added to his depression. Continuing seasickness made it difficult for him to eat or drink, and he began to despair for his life. The captain then urged him to invite three or four friends from St. Martin de Ré to live with him in the cabin, which he did. Ste. Catherine, Brazil, was the first port where mail could be sent and received. After more than forty days at sea, he remembered only three on which he had not vomited, but he added that he was well treated by all on board.[78] From Ste. Catherine they rounded the Cape of Good Hope and made for New Caledonia, entering the port of Noumea on December 10, 1873. The voyage had taken exactly four months.[79]

In the meantime, Rochefort's personal possessions had finally been sold, at a two-day affair at the Hôtel Drouot beginning September 26, 1873. The proceeds were astoundingly meager, around 3000 francs, partly because the sale was eclipsed by others of greater public interest and partly because of his close associates only Destrem turned up. Perhaps, as one observer claimed, the sale was insufficiently advertised, but public indifference was undeniable.[80]

The colony of New Caledonia contained more than one area marked out for prisoner settlement, but prisoners were restricted to their area of assignment. Rochefort was lucky to be delivered to the Ducos Peninsula, the settlement closest to Noumea, where it was easier to obtain news and necessary commodities. Indeed, the proximity to the port raised markedly the possibility of escape, about which those on the Isle of Pines, for instance, felt much less hope.[81] News of Rochefort's arrival preceded him, and he found that Paschal Grousset and Olivier Païn had been working to enlarge their mud-and-straw hut to accommodate him. For the first few weeks he worked at a garden; but the soil was so poor that even most of the colonists' food had to be imported from Australia. Rochefort bought a few chickens, but they did not flourish and produced only about two pigeon-sized eggs a week among them. And the prisoners had little luck fishing among the coastal rocks. Mosquitos were the only abundant creatures.

Fortunately Rochefort had brought some money with him, which made it possible to order supplies from Noumea; and Edmond Adam sent him a draft for 1500 francs to make life more bearable than that endured by ordinary prisoners. If the insects and heat were burdensome, the climate did enable him to recover from the respiratory ailments of the French west coast; and the simplicity of the life, the beauty of the nights, always remained a pleasant memory for him.[82] In February, he got news from both Destrem and Mme. Adam that his second novel, *Les Naufrageurs,* had begun to appear in *Le Rappel* and was well received.[83] This meant more money, and money now meant more than support for his children: it might buy his escape.

The plans for that escape and whose responsibility they were have always remained somewhat obscure—each participant in the plot was inclined to enlarge upon his particular role. The matter would, in fact, be unimportant had it not led to more rumors about Rochefort's unprincipled behavior in private affairs. This much seems clear: the best hope of escape was to establish a secret understanding with one of the masters of British trading ships that frequently called at Noumea on their way to Australia. Rochefort thought that the anticipated royalties from *Le Rappel* would give him enough money to finance an escape; and he found an intermediary at the store in Noumea from which he bought supplies, a deportee employed there named Bastien Granthille. (Some deportees were not confined by their sentences.) Granthille had two trusted friends, Jourde and Ballière, whom he enlisted, either because they were already associates in an escape plot or because Granthille felt he needed physical assistance to insure the escape of the frail Rochefort. Finally, Pachal Grousset and Olivier Pain were to be included, making six plotters in all.

Though Rochefort had little money with him, he authorized Granthille to offer a captain as much as 40,000 francs for the escape of the six, claiming that royalties were owed to him for that sum; but he instructed Granthille to begin the negotiations with an offer of 10,000 francs. Ballière later insisted that the initial offer was enough to obtain the help of Captain Law, who commanded the *P.C.E.*, a coaler bound for Newcastle in Australia. Rochefort later claimed that the 10,000 was for him alone, and that he had to pay 5000 francs for each of the other five escapees. In any case, the six got on board. Granthille, Jourde, and Ballière rowed under cover of night to an offshore rock, to which the other three had swum, and then to the *P.C.E.*, whose ladder was down to receive them.[84] The escape date was March 20, 1874, three months and ten days after Rochefort's arrival in New Caledonia.[85]

Seven days later they were in Newcastle to begin the financial squabbling that marred their relationship. Out of the welter of the subsequent charges and countercharges, one may surmise that Rochefort, in desperation to escape from New Caledonia, had offered his 40,000 francs to be used equally by all to return to Europe. Once in Australia, his egalitarian enthusiasm flagged. A few of the escapees had put their meager financial resources into the escape preparations and were penniless. They anticipated sizeable reimbursement from Rochefort's initial offer, but since he gave them much less, and even that grudgingly, they remained grieved for many years and did him much harm in radical circles. Years later one of them wrote, "The entire social theory of the aristocrat of *L'Intransigeant* is contained in this dilemma: 'No money, no friend.' " [86]

To get the necessary money, Rochefort, Grousset, and Ballière sailed on to Sydney, provincial capital of New South Wales, where a telegram requesting 25,000 francs was sent off to Edmond Adam. Adam promptly raised the money from various friends of Rochefort and had it telegraphed to Sydney from London, since it was politically impossible to send it from France.[87] The news of the escape, telegraphed to Paris by the French Consul in Sydney on April 1, 1874, only became public as a result of Rochefort's appeal for money. Since the government denied the news for a time, the newspapers could do little but speculate as to whether the escape was fact or rumor. By the ninth and tenth of April, most newspapers had concluded that the escape was evidently real, though no details were known.[88]

Rochefort's plan was to return to Europe via San Francisco and New York. On April 11,[89] he and Olivier Pain boarded the first available steamer, which took them as far as the Fiji Islands. There they remained a few days to pick up a second ship bound for Hawaii, where evidently they were received by the King. From there they went on to San Francisco where they landed on May 20, 1874. Newspaper reporters overwhelmed them, giving them no peace as they sought to buy clothes and a few souvenir prints of "Yo se mit" valley. The following morning they gratefully escaped on the train bound for New York, stopping for a day of rest in Salt Lake City. Rochefort attended a service in the Tabernacle, whose architecture struck him as "anti-artistic." By the time the two got to "O'Maha," the curious were lined up along the tracks to catch a glimpse of the escapees. At Chicago, a journalist from the *New York Herald* boarded the train to ask Rochefort to write an article to be published in both French and English in the *Herald*. Rochefort accepted this offer.

He finished the article in New York at the Central Hotel on Broadway and turned it over to the translators, but he soon found that his prose was very difficult for Americans to translate.[90] The article, which was about the Commune and life on New Caledonia, was published by the *Herald* on May 31, 1874, and was soon republished in Brussels. A week later, Rochefort delivered a lecture in French at the New York Academy of Music before a small but enthusiastic audience. Aside from describing his imprisonment, he dwelt on a comparison of the constitutional safeguards in Hawaii with those in the French Republic, clearly showing more enthusiasm for those of Hawaii. John Swinton, a leading American radical, presided at the meeting and managed to make a flamboyant and wildly uninformed introduction for the speaker, predicting that "Rochefort's constructive genius will be found to be equal to that of Cavour." [91]

Rochefort's speech made it quite clear that his sympathies then lay entirely with the Communards, and the 3,222 francs that he netted from it were presumably to be used to aid deportees from New Caledonia.[92] His sincerity, however, was already questioned by some radicals. The Bakuninists of the Jurassian Federation, for example, had already opened a subscription in the spring of 1874 for men deported to New Caledonia; and in their publications they contemptuously wrote Rochefort off as self-seeking.[93] He had other opportunities to speak in the United States and Canada but declined them in favor of a swift return to Europe.

During the crossing Rochefort once again suffered from seasickness. But even his happiness at reaching land was short-lived. Disembarking at Queenstown (Cobh), he had to be protected by the police from an Irish crowd bent on stoning him. As a Communard, he was held responsible for the murder of the Archbishop of Paris. Unfriendly crowds gathered at railway stations to insult him on his way to Cork, where he took ship for London. Those who witnessed his arrival there on June 18, 1874, reported that he seemed ill and had been frightened by the possibility of being lynched in Ireland.[94] He went into virtual seclusion for a time in London, uncertain about his reception there. When a group of French exiles proposed a banquet in honor of his return, he declined their invitation in a manner that not only offended them, but that confirmed their doubts about his integrity. No matter how modest the gathering might be, Rochefort claimed, the press would see it as "an incendiary and Saturnalian demonstration." Ordinarily he would not care, but given the progress of the Republicans in France, the exiles should do nothing rash which might lend weight to Rightist arguments against the Republic. "It seems to me that it is time to be as clever as our adversaries and to cease being dupes for their benefit." [95]

The French police maintained a number of agents in London, some of whom had evidently infiltrated the ranks of the exiles. Their reports, while not always reliable, were consistent at least in reflecting radical opinion that Rochefort was putting on aristocratic airs and that he could not be relied upon. "Rochefort is not a revolutionary," Félix Pyat told one informer; "he is a boy who stands next to the revolution in order to advance himself, but he has none of its principles; he has only hatred of governments. . . . I would use him if I needed, but there is a chasm between us." [96]

Félix Pyat and his friends were no doubt right in suspecting that Rochefort was snubbing them; it is also true that the Monarchist position in France was deteriorating, as Rochefort pointed out. The previous year, August 5, 1873, to be exact, the two Royalist pretenders had met at Frohsdorf. The Orleanist Comte de Paris agreed to recognize the principle of legitimacy and hence the right of the Comte de Chambord to the throne. Subsequently, Chambord indicated that he would reign as a limited, rather than an absolute, monarch. The compromise might have survived had he not insisted on the old Bourbon white flag in the face of Orleanist demands for the tricolor. Because neither side would give way on the issue, an immediate restoration was impossible. President MacMahon, who was devoted to the tricolor, was, as a result, really holding the fort for the Orleanists, and he made cabinet changes in their favor at the expense of the Legitimists. This Royalist rift became the more evident in the spring of 1874 when a coalition of Legitimists and Republicans brought down the Orleanist cabinet. As the Royalists had no long-term hope of cooperating to form a stable government, the Republicans were right to anticipate that their day was coming.[97] Some of them, especially those among the exiles, supposed that a Republican majority in the Assembly would soon vote a general amnesty—if that majority could only be voted into office.

Perhaps this hope of early amnesty contributed to Rochefort's inclination to snub other exiles, but he was also busy arranging to lodge his children in London. "Your children departed," Edmond Adam telegraphed on August 14. "They will arrive Charing Cross this evening 6:30."[98] Thus life could be somewhat normal again, and Rochefort acknowledged that he had never been so happy.[99] He could even find it amusing, when taking his children to Mme. Tussaud's, that his statue, once among those of Thiers, Gambetta, Favre, and Trochu, now stood next to that of Mme. Lafarge in the Chamber of Horrors.[100]

CHAPTER V

The Leisure of Exile
1874-1880

They latch on to anything. They name dukes and marquises to embassies. We read every day: M. le Duc de etc., amusing names to make the great powers believe that the old world is not dead—but it is.

ROCHEFORT [1]

ROCHEFORT did not remain long in Britain, but long enough to revive *La Lanterne*. The French government had anticipated its revival even before Rochefort reached London, and the Ministry of the Interior issued a notice that the paper could not be legally imported.[2] The new *Lanterne* was produced in two formats: one edition was printed on sheets that could be inserted in British newspapers imported into France; the other was a photographic copy that was small enough to be sent by carrier pigeons or hidden in hatbands. The printing was done in London, Brussels, and Geneva, Rochefort having sent Olivier Pain abroad to negotiate with foreign printers.[3] The French police suspected that some of the railway conductors on the Nord line between Brussels and Paris were bringing in

141

copies,[4] and they threatened to cut off traffic from Britain by forbidding entry of those journals found to be concealing sheets of *La Lanterne*.

The first issue of the new *Lanterne* sounded like the Rochefort of old. He opened with a brief résumé of all the "fairy stories" concerning him:

> It was a beautiful morning in April. I had just killed my father; two of my children, tied to their beds, were writhing in the convulsions of hunger, while, merrily at the table with its silver plates stolen from the Ministry of Foreign Affairs, I drank from some sacramental vases a small Moselle wine which I recommend to you. I was inclined to go out to buy some holy vases lifted the evening before from the altar of Notre-Dame, but the business crisis had hit me hard. I had trouble getting a hundred thousand crowns for the bronzes taken by me from M. Thiers' house. The six hundred thousand francs that I had requisitioned from the Bank had, of course, been dissipated in orgies, and I was considering getting myself afloat again through the sale of some pictures from the Louvre, when I received through the mail a letter containing a thousand-franc note with these few words: "This is how the Bonapartes get even." It was from the Empress Eugénie, who, learning of my poverty, undertook to extend relief.[5]

But distributing *La Lanterne* from London proved too much for Rochefort, and he left for Switzerland in September of 1874, traveling through Belgium, Alsace-Lorraine, Basel, to Geneva, where he arrived on September 15.[6] His reasons for moving to Switzerland are not absolutely clear but seem related to the difficulty getting *La Lanterne* into France from across the Channel. Certainly he knew that smuggling was easier along the Belgian and Swiss frontiers, but Belgium was out of the question as a residence for Communards. Belgian authorities could not prohibit the publication of a journal in Belgium, but they could prevent the editor from residing in Belgium and had every intention of applying the prohibition to Rochefort.[7] Rochefort probably concluded that in the long run Switzerland offered him the greatest opportunities; and he knew that the French exiles there enjoyed as much security as those in Britain.

Almost at once Rochefort found himself embroiled in a public quarrel that led him to send a challenge to a duel. Henri de Pène, the Monarchist editor of *Paris-Journal,* noted that both Rochefort and he had refrained from publishing their journals during the siege of Paris, each of them thereby sacrificing 100,000 francs, but that Rochefort had continued to mourn their loss and to cite it as a measure of his patriotic virtue: "In this way, he associates himself with the world of the courtesans, where the best of them regard themselves as voluntarily rehabilitated when they leave a gray-haired millionaire for a young lover from whom they accept only the bare necessities. The well-known patriotic sacrifices about which M. Rochefort so naively prides himself are of that order."[8] Unamused by the analogy, Rochefort sent off a challenge. De Pène, unaccustomed to refusing challenges—he had been seriously wounded in a duel in 1858—this time refused, saying that Rochefort was mad and that he would not fight a madman.[9]

Soon after his arrival in Switzerland, Rochefort paid a call on a fellow victim of Versaillese justice, the painter Gustave Courbet, who then lived in Vevey. In 1871, Courbet had received a mild sentence from an indulgent military court, which recognized that while he had supported the Commune and briefly sat in its council he was politically naïve and harmless. Unfortunately he had been associated with the movement to remove the Vendôme Column, though he had not voted for its destruction. Nevertheless, shortly after Marshal MacMahon assumed the presidency in 1873, a bill was passed obliging Courbet to pay for the reconstruction of the column. This vindictive and childish piece of legislation forced him to flee the country to avoid complete ruin.[10]

Rochefort and Courbet, with their mutual interest in courts of law, attended a court session in Vevey where a female abortionist was being tried. Even though seven fetuses had been discovered in her home, she received a soft sentence of six months in prison. Courbet loudly remarked that they could have at least given her one month for each fetus.[11] He also had planned for some years a portrait of Rochefort, and this visit enabled him to make his first sketches toward that project.[12] The portrait was completed, but we cannot be certain how much of it was Courbet's work since he often allowed students to complete his pictures during these last few years of his life. Rochefort wrote to one of his lady friends that Courbet had given him the air of a Portuguese diamond merchant.[13]

In France meanwhile, the constitutional commission of the National Assembly continued its work late in 1874 with the deepening realization that the rifts within monarchical ranks made a republic the only possible form of government. Toward the end of the year, therefore, the commission proposed a constitutional compromise, hoping to please both Republicans and Royalists: a bicameral Republic, the lower house to be elected by universal suffrage, the upper house to be elected by a highly restricted suffrage. Sensing the probability of a greater victory, the Republicans joined with the extreme Right in defeating the proposal. For a few weeks there was deadlock, until one of the members of the commission, a professor named Edouard de Laboulaye, told the Assembly: "You can form a government with the Republic. If you do not accept it, you cannot form any government at all. If we do not constitute one, our mandate will be finished; it would be necessary to leave it up to the Nation."[14] There would have to be new elections, in other words, and the Royalists knew that national sentiment was increasingly Republican.

On the following day, January 30, 1875, Henri-Alexandre Wallon put forth a new resolution: "The President of the Republic is elected by a majority vote of the Senate and Chamber of Deputies sitting together as the National Assembly. He is named for seven years and eligible for re-election."[15] Again the Right was opposed, but enough members modified their views to carry the motion 353 to 352. The Republic was made by one vote, and on February 25,

1875, the completed constitution was formally adopted. To get their Republic, the Republicans had had to accept a conservative Senate; and some of them no doubt, with the memory of the Commune, were quite willing to have a senatorial barricade against popular passions.

But the compromise infuriated the more Leftist Republicans by apparently equating the smallest municipality in France with Paris: The new Senate was to have 300 members. Seventy-five of them were to be appointed for life, the first group by the existing National Assembly, their replacements thereafter by the Senate itself. The remaining 225 Senators were to be chosen by electoral colleges in each department and colony; and the electoral colleges were to include the local deputies popularly elected to the Chamber, the departmental councilmen, the arrondissement councilmen, and one delegate from each municipal council within the department. The system included roughly 42,000 electors for all of France, and the minimum age for a Senator was set at forty. Gambetta called the Senate the Grand Council of the Communes. Rochefort called it the Grand Council of the Orleanists,[16] complaining that the system would simply represent the municipal councils, "seven-eighths of which are composed of peasants who represent the least enlightened part of the population." He predicted that the system would provide the Bonapartists opportunity to dominate the Senate.[17] Apparently the Bonapartists did not agree, for one of their leaders, Raoul Duval, argued as passionately for universal suffrage as did the Leftist Republicans.

In the spring of 1875, *La Lanterne* began to recover some of its 1868 verve. Indeed, the targets were the same: conservatism in general and the chief of state in particular. "Veuillot [the conservative Catholic editor] is amazed. He has just been fined three hundred francs for false news. For twenty years he has not printed any news which was not false, and this is the first time he has been sentenced. Hence his astonishment."[18] Another example: "M. Buffet [Orleanist Minister of the Interior] does not only cover his bureaucrats, but is in the process of covering all France, with portraits of Marshal

145

MacMahon. This Minister of the Interior has just emerged from inaction [he had been president of the National Assembly] to send by the bale the picture of our president to every town hall in France. It is equestrian and bears the legend *Forward!* Probably there is a typographical error; it should be *To the Rear!*" [19]

The Swiss edition of *La Lanterne* was published in two formats. One was a regular edition similar to the 1868 format, running about sixty pages an issue and bound in bright red-orange. A smaller size, two by four inches and averaging thirty pages an issue, was published for export to France. Sales were evidently very disappointing, often not covering publishing expenses; a principal factor was the high cost of getting the French edition distributed to subscribers. [20] Rochefort worried about paying back the 25,000 francs that Edmond Adam had raised for his escape, for the royalties from his novels had by no means covered the debt. Through Destrem, he asked his sisters to borrow the money to clear up his indebtedness, yet he would not allow Destrem to give the sisters his Swiss address. But they disapproved of him and his children and refused to help. Three impossible old girls was his outraged verdict! [21]

Rochefort contemplated abandoning *La Lanterne* to become a paid writer for another journal, but meanwhile he kept up the assault in the hope of greater fortune. In one issue he turned to a theme that had occupied some French intellectuals in the wake of military defeat: Had French morale been corrupted by the music hall gaieties of *la vie parisienne?* "*Le Figaro,* whose patriotic strings vibrate at the least breath like those of an Aeolian harp, has just indignantly informed its subscribers of the new operetta by Hervé, *Alice of Nevers.* Not only do they accuse this mad composer of insulting common sense, but they are not far from attributing to him a deleterious influence on the recent events. . . . This strange man composes riots for the piano and constructs barricades in B-flat. . . . I was in Paris during the Commune, and I do not ever recall hearing the National Guard band play tunes from the *Petit Faust.* Instead, I remember that, if theatricals by Hervé formerly had great success, it was all those boulevard fops and the sophisticates of the Jockey Club who made it possible. The people never understood one word of their incoherences." [22]

Who could have read the following article without memories of Rochefort's abuse of the former Empress, by then the Widow Bonaparte! "Wednesday, July 7th: The MacMahonian buffoonery becomes more involved. After the military trip by the Marshal, the departments of the Midi, already so tried, are threatened by a feminine circuit directed by his wife. They are presently considering in the Privy Council whether this Duchesse de Gerolstein will go to inspect the ruins recently honored by her husband's visit, to carry to those flooded out consolations along with flannel waistcoats. It is not well enough known that this noble woman, whose great grandmother was close to Dubarry, which is always a recommendation, aspires to play Catherine II on the republican throne which the Versailles Assembly has padded for her husband. It would be most regrettable if this pseudo-presidential trip were to be cancelled. In the midst of the horrors of the flood, the arrival of Mme. Mac-Mahon would obviously make for a pleasing diversion." [23]

Whatever the amusement value, the sales of *La Lanterne* did not improve in 1875. Rochefort thus began to negotiate with various French publishers in the hope of collaboration. The law was a problem, as the Act of May 11, 1868, made it a crime to publish political articles written by anyone condemned for illegal political activity. French editors thus hesitated to run the risk but were tantalized by the opportunity to employ Rochefort's notorious talents. Because of the compromise nature of French governments after 1871 and their inherent instability, the authority of the courts was rather too quickly invoked to bolster the regime against its enemies; naturally, under such circumstances, verdicts were seen as especially politically inspired. Moreover, in the aftermath of revolution and civil war, governments easily justify themselves as guardians of order. This was especially true of the MacMahon regime, which claimed to be reestablishing what it called the "moral order," a phrase that would have been vulnerable to satire under the best of circumstances and was defenseless in that day when the courts could rarely demonstrate an administration of absolute justice. Societies suspected of hostility to the regime were prosecuted and dissolved, and the press was watched for signs of opposition with an intensity that was supposed to have disappeared with Napoleon III.[24]

In negotiations with *Le Rappel* during 1875, Rochefort considered evading the law by signing simply the name Henri, or perhaps using the name *Le Lanternier*. "Even the law permits a deportee to write," he noted, "but not to sign."[25] Pain and he, meanwhile, worked at a book in the hope of income. Called *Voyage aux Antipodes (Aller et Retour): Impressions de Deux Parisiens en Océanie,* it appeared first in January, 1876, in Geneva in serial form at fifty centimes an issue. Sixty installments were projected, all of them to be illustrated with engravings. The same material in different forms appeared later that year in France, some of it serialized in *Le Rappel* beginning on April 17, 1876, some of it in pamphlets at ten centimes a copy.[26]

The National Assembly came to an end on the last day of 1875 in order to begin preparation for elections under the new constitution. About ten days before the final session, Alfred Naquet moved unsuccessfully for an amnesty for the Communards on New Caledonia. The issue was extremely touchy, even more so because the Law of June 17, 1871, asserted that an amnesty could be granted only by the Assembly. The right of pardon was given to the Executive except in cases involving the Commune, when that power was exercised jointly by the Executive and a fifteen-man legislative committee. Amnesty and pardon meant different things, for to pardon is to forgive an individual for his crime, while amnesty refers to wiping the slate clean. The deed is what is amnestied, not the doer. An amnesty bill was first introduced on September 13, 1871, by Henri Brisson, which had the support of forty-eight members including Gambetta, to include all those condemned for political offenses in the past year. Brisson's motion, along with further proposals, were referred to committee, where they received the burial of postponement.[27] Without much doubt, the Republic after 1871 was too weak to risk favoring an amnesty; but if the Monarchists were thus placated, the resentment of more radical Republicans and Socialists deepened against those Republicans in power who had to compromise on the issue.

It has been reliably suggested that the monarchical majority in the Assembly was even more dead set against amnesty in 1875 than it had been in 1871, and that it was increasingly vindictive as its strength waned and the chances of monarchy diminished. All that the Republicans in the National Assembly could do was hope that the committee on pardons would ameliorate the plight of the Communards. Probably most of the condemned were more concerned about becoming freed than the form in which freedom was obtained, but there were those who said they would insist on an amnesty and would not accept pardon. The issue was somewhat academic considering both the pace and the inclination of the committee on pardons. By mid-1874 it had reviewed 6000 petitions and rejected two thirds of them. Only 350 got full pardons; the remainder had their sentences reduced.[28]

After the dissolution of the National Assembly, Alfred Naquet took himself off to Geneva to talk to Rochefort about the coming elections.[29] As a result, Rochefort produced a printed campaign letter, dated from Geneva on January 6, 1876, which was mailed to a number of Republicans apparently selected by Naquet. "My dear Compatriot," it began. "Being proscribed and denied all my political rights, 1 hope that my frankness [on matters of candidates and the Naquet amnesty bill] will not be criticized as an electoral maneuver. Yesterday, our enemy was the Center Right. Today, it is the Center Left. It is possible that parliamentary alchemy can detect some difference between M. Buffet and M. Dufaure; *I* perceive none. . . . If a deal is sometimes a necessity, it cannot become a rule of conduct. . . . Alongside those deputies who negotiate for the Republic, we must have some deputies who stand for it. In the name of what principles are you defending it if you abandon them all? . . . The attitude taken by M. Alfred Naquet and the intransigents has had the valuable result of showing just how far off the road [the other Republicans] have already strayed." He ended by urging the election of men dedicated to an amnesty bill.[30] What is more, he had introduced the name *intransigeants* to describe right-thinking Republicans; he was but a step away from calling the others opportunists.

The elections of 1876 confirmed the national drift toward republicanism, evident already for several years; but the restricted method of election to the Senate prevented popular sentiment from being registered. Thus, while the Republicans carried the Chamber of Deputies easily, winning 371 of the 514 seats, the Monarchists won a clear majority in the Senate. What is more, most of the Republicans elected to the Senate were considered conservative—strongly opposed to an amnesty bill. In the campaign for the Chamber, only the radical Republicans made an issue of the amnesty question, a number of them winning seats from Paris. But most of the more moderate Republicans either avoided the issue or sidestepped it by opposing an *immediate* amnesty. Gambetta and Brisson, zealous for amnesty in 1871, were in the latter group in 1876, which swept the provincial field at radical expense. Thus, if the Republic was safer, an amnesty was far from guaranteed.[31]

With this in mind, two radical members of the Paris Municipal Council, Sigismond Lacrois (Sigismond Krzyznowski) and Yves Guyot, founded a new paper, *Les Droits de l'Homme,* frankly a Communard sheet with a number of the proscribed as collaborators. Rochefort, realizing this was his best opportunity to abandon *La Lanterne,* accepted their invitation to collaborate, with the understanding that he would sign his articles with an X. *Les Droits de l'Homme* began publication on February 11, 1876; *La Lanterne* ceased a few days later on the nineteenth.[32] In his first article, Rochefort used a label that was to stick to the moderate Republicans. Commenting that the French might think that, in addition to the Republicans, there were only three other political parties in France, he claimed there was in fact a fourth, the Opportunists. "The Opportunist is that sensible candidate who, deeply affected by the woes of the civil war and full of solicitude for the families which it deprived of support, declares that he is in favor of an amnesty, but that he shall refrain from voting for it until *the opportune time. . . .*

At the opportune time is a term of parliamentary slang which means Never!" [33] He signed the article X.

In March, the President formed his new government, selecting Dufaure as Prime Minister. The cabinet was heavily Left Center, essentially "Thierist," meaning considerably to the right of the majority in the Chamber. This new regime toyed with solving the amnesty question by greatly extending the pardons granted. Rochefort responded by announcing that he would not accept a pardon in lieu of amnesty,[34] and following this with a commentary later: "I understand, to a certain extent, M. Dufaure's annoyance with a man who, stuck in an iron cage, as under Louis XI, and shipped off to New Caledonia, meaning off to death, in the hold of a ship, who has the ingratitude to shun the 'clemency' of the Marshal. The government revealed the degree of its fury by having this foolhardy person and his accomplices sentenced to two years in prison for escape, which is most comical since it was necessarily pronounced *in absentia.*" [35] (In fact, those extra two years had been tacked on almost two years before to the day by the Noumea Court Martial, May 26, 1874.[36])

President MacMahon's actual move was a recommendation on June 27 to the Minister of War: "I think that we ought to let all the acts connected with the fatal insurrection of 1871 fall into oblivion." This was not a decree of amnesty, true, but it suggested to many of the Republicans that the President might be on the verge of usurping the parliamentary prerogative to grant amnesties.[37] This sidetracked the main amnesty question into a Republican defense of parliamentarianism against suspected Executive high-handedness, frustrating the hopes of those exiles who had been anticipating a quick amnesty after the elections. Rochefort delivered himself of an especially intemperate blast which won his publisher a 3000 francs fine and three months imprisonment. "Physicians have named 'hospital gangrene' a kind of typhus which quickly invades rooms crowded with wounded and transforms the slightest scratch into a mortal sore. The sick man, without apparent cause, suddenly loses his strength and dies just when everyone believed

151

him cured. I allow myself to point out to the political doctors an analogous disease resulting from the cohabitation of deputies in a confined space, that one could call Assembly gangrene." [38]

To underscore the legislative prerogative on amnesties without actually granting a general amnesty, the Republicans pushed a compromise bill through the Chamber in the autumn of 1876. All further cases having to do with the Commune were removed from the jurisdiction of military courts, and the usual ten-year statute of limitations was to apply to all cases relating to the Commune except those involving murder, arson, and theft. The controversial aspect of the bill lay in its wording, for it was intended as a warning to the President not to exceed his constitutional authority. As the committee reporting on the bill put it, the measure was desirable as "a legislative resolution which would insure more clarity, above all more permanence, to the general declaration [made] by the executive." [39] Prime Minister Dufaure, having opposed the bill as insulting to MacMahon, resigned office on December 3, and ten days later Jules Simon succeeded in forming a government—a government more clearly Republican. Yet he said not a word about the amnesty question in his opening speech as Prime Minister.[40]

During this time *Les Droits de l'Homme* was numbering its days through an inability to avoid costly lawsuits, an inability common to polemical sheets that do not live by literary quality alone. Rochefort maintained that the government sought to destroy such journals by aiming at their financial belly,[41] but fines levied for such imprudences as "Assembly gangrene" accounted for only a part of the legal losses suffered by this particular journal. On November 16, 1876, for instance, Dona Maria Manuella Kirpatrick de Closeburn y Grevigne, widow of the Count de Montijo, a grandee of Spain, won a libel suit against a number of Parisian newspapers, *Les Droits de l'Homme* included. They had alleged that the plaintiff's two daughters, the Duchess of Alba and the Empress Eugénie, were illegitimate. The editors were fined and had to pay the plaintiff damages.[42] By the end of the year, *Les Droits de l'Homme* was in serious trouble for a Rochefort article insulting to President

MacMahon entitled "Pardon for Yourself."[43] This time the paper received a six-months suspension. The editor was certain that the execution of the sentence would soon be lifted and recommended that Rochefort continue to send copy regularly, but the end had come.[44]

The end had also come for hopes for an immediate amnesty, so much expected by the exiles after the elections of 1876. Rochefort went into a state of deep depression toward the end of the year, losing weight and suffering periodic fits of weeping.[45] Edmond Adam wrote him to abandon all hope of amnesty, and Rochefort was soon telling other refugees in Geneva that since MacMahon could not expect to be reelected in 1879 he would turn over the country to Napoleon IV at that time.[46] What Edmond Adam recognized were the bitter hatreds within the Republican ranks, immensely increasing the chasms that derived from different social and economic philosophies. The Monarchists were no more divided than the Republicans, and since the Right always wanted to prove that the Republicans were secretly sympathetic to the Commune, the amnesty issue was much too dangerous for the more moderate Republicans to embrace it. When Gambetta denounced extremists in a speech on October 27, 1876, along with the "criminal insurrection of the Commune," and said that he opposed the "street-corner clamoring of noisy windbags," he did little to endear himself to the radical Republicans.[47]

Part of Rochefort's depression no doubt related to his poverty and his consequent inability to provide money for his daughter's wedding. Noémie was engaged to an impoverished painter, Frédéric Dufaux, and the marriage had been postponed for lack of money. In April of 1877, Rochefort reached an agreement with an editor named Mervaud, who wanted to use the name *Lanterne* for a new Parisian journal and invited Rochefort to contribute articles. He received an advance of 20,000 francs and was thus able to provide for himself while contributing generously to Noémie.[48] Through a series of letters to Destrem, he managed to get the documents necessary for her marriage in Switzerland, particularly the birth certificate and the act of legitimacy.[49] The wedding, a civil ceremony, was announced for May 21, 1877, to take place in Petit-Saconnex near Geneva.[50]

Since he had already been condemned with *Les Droits de l'Homme* for using the signature X, Rochefort signed his articles in the new *Lanterne* with an X...y, which fooled nobody. He wasted no time in causing a sensation, this time with an article entitled "Jesus the Carpenter." The gist of it was that he had recently met an old Jew who showed him an antique table and remarked that before Jesus ran through the streets preaching his doctrine he had worked as a carpenter in his father's shop. The old Jew was certain that this worm-eaten table was Jesus's work. "Notice how solidly it is built. If that boy had wanted to apply himself a bit, he would have succeeded admirably in carpentry. But his parents could not keep him at it. He was always outside . . . talking with learned men about things which did not concern him. . . . When he was shown the cross on which he was going to die, he cried out at the first glance, 'It is quite badly planed; it must come from so-and-so's shop.' " Rochefort then went on to consider whether this relative ineptitude as a carpenter—for presumably Jesus bungled everything he was given to do—might not account for the vast discrepancies he had met in the Christian religion:

> The religion into which nearly all of us are born, the one which does not prove that we shall not die, is adjustable . . . into thirty-six different varieties. . . . [Reverend] Loyson, who calls himself a Christian, will speak on Sunday against [Bishop] Dupanloup who claims to be one. M. Dupanloup will then respond to M. Loyson's errors in the *Défense,* after which the government will put a stop to the fray by slapping the *Radical* with a severe sentence on the pretext that it has made fun of a "recognized" cult. We should like to challenge the government to make public whether that cult is that of the Roman Catholics, the Liberal Catholics, the Presbyterians, the Methodists, the Anabaptists, the Orthodox, of Peter, of Paul, of James, of

the Bishop of Nevers, of Loyson, of Pressensé, or of Mermillod, all of whom declare themselves in possession of the truth. I have also often thought that [the old Jew] was probably right, and that Jesus Christ would perhaps have been wise to remain in carpentry. He would have spared humanity so many discussions, so many onerous prosecutions, and some not bad autos-da-fé in which millions of not bad men have been reduced to ashes.[51]

In protest, Senator Kolb-Bernard published an open letter to the Keeper of the Seals on April 18, 1877,[52] and the editors of the new *Lanterne* soon came to realize that Rochefort was not an asset to their paper. Worse, he was also contributing some articles to *Le Radical,* also signing them X...y; and since the new *Lanterne* was evidently not making money, Rochefort's collaboration with a competitor was especially unwelcome. By the end of May, he had ceased collaboration with both journals and was sending articles to the revived *Mot d'Ordre.*[53]

These journalistic switches were ornamented with acrimonious letters and telegrams, which did nothing to enhance Rochefort's reputation in the newspaper world. Evidently a contract meant little to him in the face of a more lucrative offer, a fact that must have been especially galling to editors who found themselves in court as a result of publishing Rochefort's articles. Both the new *Lanterne* and *Le Mot d'Ordre* were cited in July for ignoring the law forbidding a sentenced person to write on political matters, and each was fined 5000 francs.[54] *Le Mot d'Ordre* suffered a second citation in August: the paper was fined another 5000 francs and the editor was given a two-months jail sentence for a Rochefort article that was especially offensive to President MacMahon.[55] In October, it was rumored that Rochefort was on the verge of another switch,[56] following which *Le Réveil* announced that an eminent and charming writer had been acquired whose articles would appear "exclusively" in *Le Réveil, Le Républican,* and *Le Peuple.*[57] *La Lanterne* insisted that Rochefort was bound to it by a long-term contract, but it soon admitted that it no longer had the collaboration of Rochefort.[58] On January 23, 1878, *Le Peuple* began publication of his novel *Les Dépraves,* which had earlier appeared in *Le Rappel,* but it interrupted publication on January 29; the few issues cost the paper a fine of 1000 francs.[59]

It is arguable that the press was more restricted under Mac-Mahon than it had been under Napoleon III. The press law of 1875, a Rightist device to control radicalism, was disliked by most Republicans; but when they proposed its repeal, Prime Minister Jules Simon opposed repeal simply as inopportune. On May 15, 1877, the Chamber voted for repeal 377 to 55, whereupon the angered MacMahon accused Simon of treachery and incompetence. The Republican Simon then resigned, and the President appointed the Royalist Duc de Broglie in his place. This crisis, known as *"le seize mai,"* developed into the first major Royalist attempt—since the promulgation of the constitution—to make a restoration possible. Seeing exactly what was at stake, the Republican majority in the Chamber challenged MacMahon by adopting a resolution supporting the principle of ministerial responsibility. The President answered by adjourning the Chamber for a month on the pretext of saving the country from radicalism. On June 16, he made public his intention to ask the Senate for power to dissolve the Chamber, power that the Senate granted him by a vote of 150 to 130. Dissolution meant new elections in three months.[60]

Probably the division of the Republicans into Intransigents and Opportunists lent some hope to the Monarchists, but the autumn elections of 1877 were again a clear Republican victory. The President then replaced the Broglie government with another conservative ministry, plainly in defiance of the national will. After a three-weeks struggle with the Chamber, the President gave in to the extent of bringing Dufaure back to power with a Center Left ministry, acceptable to the more moderate Republicans. The lengthy crisis, thus, ended in a victory of the Chamber Republicans over the Executive. But an amnesty seemed no closer by the beginning of 1878 than it had in 1876, as Dufaure publicly admitted his belief that an amnesty was impossible at the moment.[61]

This delay in a general amnesty was beginning to make Rochefort's private life in Switzerland uncomfortable for reasons other than politics. There were many stories of his cavalier treatment of women, some of the reports reaching the files of the police and some getting into print. In January, 1878, a Swiss-Romane newspaper, the *Gutenberg,* commented on Rochefort's barnyard morality, whereupon Rochefort challenged the editor, Leopold Sage, to a duel. Sage would neither fight nor retract.[62] How Sage obtained the information and why he printed it remains a question. One police informer, of doubtful veracity, reported that the gossip was spread by fellow exiles who were jealous of Rochefort's new earnings in 1877 and hated him for his exclusiveness and his comfortable living.[63] A more reliable informer thought the mess had something to do with a typesetters' union that had been unable to unionize the three Parisian newspapers for which Rochefort was writing toward the end of 1877. Presumably the union had asked Rochefort, as a champion of the common man, to intervene on its behalf; and when he ignored the plea, the typesetters took their grievance to Leopold Sage, who publicly asked why Rochefort would not defend the principles for which he supposedly stood.[64]

Of the "fleeting affairs" attributed to him by the police, one had more serious repercussions in Geneva. Rochefort would later write of becoming "associated" with a pastor's daughter soon after his arrival in Switzerland, though, as usual, he failed to mention her name.[65] She was Anne-Catherine Strebinger, his mistress for at least two years. Their bans were published in the town of Morges, the marriage proposed for May of 1878.[66] But the wedding never took place and thus serious doubts were raised, especially in Geneva, about Rochefort's real intentions.[67] Then in October of that year, he suddenly married a French woman whom he had not known long, Adèle-Marie-Jeanne Bouin de Beaupré. An older woman who was "neither witty, young, nor pretty," she was well-to-do and in search of a title.[68] As Rochefort failed to mention this marriage in his memoirs, it may well mean that the rumors then current about the marriage were true—namely, that she disappointed him by tying up her funds beyond reach of his whims and passions.[69]

Scandalizing the Swiss, however, was no substitute for scandalizing the French. The audience recently outraged by "Jesus the Carpenter" got a further dose from Rochefort's obituary for Pius IX: "The religious journals, besides being delighted by the Pope's death which furnished them copy, naturally attributed his extreme longevity . . . to Providence. We believe that it derived from the fact that Pius IX ate well, drank dry, and slept in an excellent bed. . . . If the inventor of that good joke about Infallibility, and of that spritely thing called the 'Immaculate Conception,' so fertile in obscene details, had gotten up at six o'clock every morning, . . . he would probably have died younger." [70] This contribution was signed with a star, Rochefort having by then dropped the X...y. The Comte de Mun immediately protested in the Chamber and asked that *Le Réveil* be prosecuted for the article. Rochefort answered by sending two seconds to challenge de Mun to a duel. De Mun's response to them was that he "had nothing to say to M. Henri Rochefort." [71]

Rochefort, meanwhile, was continuing his game of musical chairs with Parisian publishers. In the spring of 1878, we find him contributing to the revived *La Marseillaise;* in July, *Le Rappel* announced it was authorized to say that Rochefort was no longer associated with *La Marseillaise.* [72] Toward the end of the year, he toyed with Gambetta's *La Révolution française,* but actually returned to collaborate with *La Marseillaise.* [73] *Le Rappel,* meanwhile, began the serialized publication of an anticlerical novel by Rochefort called *L'Aurore boréale.* [74] *La Marseillaise* countered with a serialized history of Rochefort's life—to be written by one of his companions in captivity. [75] This playing one newspaper off against another, which had begun in 1877, was strictly for cash. Rochefort always demanded a large advance from an editor and did not hesitate to violate the spirit of his contracts, if not always the word, so that his journalistic career in those years was a frantic twisting and turning, negotiating and squabbling. Yet editors valued his collaboration as a matter of competition, all the while being very exasperated with him. [76]

The amnesty question was revived at the outset of 1879, as

a result of new elections to the Senate, January 5, 1879. Of the seventy-five seats contested, the Republicans won sixty-five, giving them a majority in the upper house for the first time. This encouraged the Republicans in the Chamber, led by Gambetta, to revive the issue of parliamentary responsibility, a concept they knew was anathema to President MacMahon and the Monarchists. Realizing that he no longer had the Senate with him and unwilling to accept parliamentary government, MacMahon resigned the presidency on January 30, bringing down the Dufaure ministry with him. The triumphant Republicans elected one of their own to the presidency on that same day, Jules Grévy; Waddington organized a new ministry on February 5, while Gambetta became presiding officer of the Chamber of Deputies.[77]

Those in exile who anticipated that a Republican victory would mean an immediate amnesty failed to take into account the legacy of hatreds dating from the Commune. Having focused their recent animosity on MacMahon and his threat to restore monarchy, the exiles may be excused for forgetting that there had been Republicans on both sides of the walls of Paris in 1871; and that those of them who fought in the parliamentary ranks to save the Republic after 1871 had been vilified as opportunists by those who, enjoying the leisure of exile, did not have to play the game of politics and could afford the haughty posture of intransigence. It is notable that influential parliamentarians like Gambetta were more solicitous for the exiles in 1871 than they were later in the decade, suggesting both the exigencies of politics and their pique over the envenomed darts hurled from abroad.

The Waddington amnesty bill, introduced on February 11, 1879, provided only for a partial amnesty by seeking to separate those who had been "misguided" from those who had been criminals. Rochefort surmised at once that he would fall into the latter category, and turned his wrath upon Gambetta whom he believed to be the absolute master of the Chamber and in a position to control such legislation. He saw Gambetta, surrounded by Jews and other adventurers, as "the chief of opportunism which he organized into a political party whose strength was as great as its unscrupu-lousness." [78] Rochefort thus struck at Gambetta even before the promulgation of the law. His article, in the form of a letter to a woman, facetiously invoking her aid, was published in *La Mar-seillaise* and then reproduced in a number of Parisian papers: "No doubt you know, Mademoiselle, that there is no longer any justice in France. . . . Those condemned in 1871 are no longer asked what they were during the Commune; they are asked if they are in good standing with Gambetta. When the answer is *yes,* they may benefit from the amnesty; if *no,* they are excluded. . . . I simply ask you to throw yourself at Gambetta's feet and assure him of my complete flatness. Physicists have invented the manometer and the ther-mometer. I dream of creating an abjectometer which will tell me the degree of baseness to which it is necessary to stoop in order to interest the great soul of the eloquent tribune in my lot." He signed the letter "An Excluded One." [79]

The partial amnesty passed both houses with substantial ma-jorities and became law on March 5, 1879. There had, of course, been many pardons granted before its passage; the new law reduced the number of men still in exile to something less than a thousand by mid-1879, Rochefort among them.[80] He took it very personally, writing to Destrem that "the partial amnesty is indeed partial, having been invented to bring Ranc* back and to leave me behind. . . . If it is necessary to act through friends in order to benefit from the amnesty, then it is pure favoritism." [81]

These Republican cleavages were naturally watched with some amusement—and hope—by the Bonapartists, now that the Royal-ists' chances seemed to have faded away. Nor were the Bonapartists above fanning the controversies that agonized the Republicans. When the radical *Le Réveil* editorialized that Rochefort had been excluded from the amnesty to be relegated to a life in exile because he had written *La Lanterne,* meaning that he was "a hostage of-

* Arthur Ranc was elected to the Commune without his consent, like a number of others, but he did not immediately resign as Edmond Adam did. His later resigna-tion did not save him from guilt by association.

fered by the government of the Republic to the Bonapartist party."
The Bonapartist organ, *Le Pays,* was quick to respond: "It is not
we who attribute the fall of the Empire to M. Rochefort. . . . [He is]
the victim of the Opportunists, who maintain him in exile because
they fear him. If he is excluded from the amnesty, it is not because
he wrote *La Lanterne;* it is from fear that *he will not write it.*"[82]
When we reach the Boulanger phase of Rochefort's career, that
prediction will seem prophetic indeed!

In 1869, when Rochefort was self-exiled to Belgium to avoid
prosecution for *La Lanterne,* he had stood for election to the *Corps
législatif* and had won a seat, which enabled him to remain in France
with impunity. By 1878, he had begun to reconsider this technique[83] but must have been deterred by the extraordinary penal risk
he would have been running. After his exclusion from the partial
amnesty in 1879, speculation revived about his possible candidacy
for the Chamber.[84] On October 15, a group of democrats in Var
wrote him an open letter of support,[85] but Rochefort declined this
invitation to stand for election.[86] Not only was the risk great, but
most everyone expected that the partial amnesty was a politic har-
binger of full emancipation. In other words, it paid to wait a little
longer. When a seat from Lyon fell vacant early in 1880, Rochefort
published a letter in the format of the old *Lanterne* to the Comité
de l'Alliance républicaine in Lyon favoring the candidacy of Blanqui for the seat: "The deputy Blanqui," he explained, "ought
finally to confront Gambetta; that is to say, the people confronting
the bourgeoisie, the eternally exploited face to face with the eternal
exploiter."[87]

Rochefort's recent marriage, meanwhile, offered him no comfort and little money beyond what his wife was willing to pay to
meet the expenses of maintaining their house. Perhaps this was a
small price to pay for being known as Madame la Marquise. But
the marriage cost Rochefort Mlle. Strebinger, about whom he
seemed to be depressed, and he talked openly in Geneva of how he
felt the marriage had been a stupid mistake.[88] Even the irregularities
of his first marriage kept pestering him. His two sons had reached an

age where they needed birth certificates, Henri because of approaching military service, Octave because his school required it. Destrem was once again pressed into service to see that the necessary documents were produced, including the acts of legitimacy. The fragmentary correspondence remaining on the matter indicates that Rochefort thought that even the birth dates listed on the marriage certificate had been erroneous in the case of the boys; and evidently Destrem believed that the documents on Octave in particular might prove embarrassing. But the details escape us, though they occupied Rochefort for some months.[89]

On May 23, 1880, Rochefort's son Henri, who was twenty or twenty-one at the time, was involved in a scuffle with the police during a radical demonstration in the Place de la Bastille. After being hit, probably with the flat of a saber, he jumped to his feet and fled from the scene, and the police were unable to catch him. Once he got the news, Rochefort composed an open letter full of rage to the Prefect of Police, Louis Andrieux, which he expected to publish in *Le Rappel*. When that journal rejected the letter, Rochefort turned to *Le Mot d'Ordre*. He claimed that Henri had arrived in Geneva with two saber wounds, one in the head and one in the stomach, that Henri just happened to be passing through the neighborhood where the demonstration was taking place, and that the incident was *deliberate* police vengeance on Rochefort whom they could not otherwise touch. "I have no expectation of obtaining justice from a government which has let your brother-in-law [Georges Koechlin] kill a man without punishment in a duel that was clearly unfair."[90] Therefore, Andrieux might expect to be challenged by Rochefort once an amnesty enabled him to return to France.

The Parisian press covered the incident rather thoroughly, the more moderate papers recognizing it as the ridiculous nonsense it was.[91] As for Koechlin, he had fought a duel the previous autumn with a man named de Liebenberg, for whom the outcome had been most unfortunate, but no charges had been filed. What the newspapers failed to recall, however, was that Prefect Andrieux, in his prior role as a member of the Chamber of Deputies, had been the reporter for the committee that had recommended only a partial amnesty in 1879. It is hard to believe that Rochefort had forgotten it when the minor street scuffle offered him an opportunity to charge the police with brutality and to challenge Andrieux to a duel as a consequence.

Koechlin, unwilling to let the matter ride until Rochefort should return to Paris, crossed into Switzerland at once to arrange a duel between Rochefort and himself for June 3, 1880. After wounding Rochefort in the duel, Koechlin saluted him and said, "Bonjour, au revoir." [92] But the press did not let the incident die, as histrionics make irresistible copy. One paper, recalling Rochefort's fragility and sensitivity, recommended to him a quiet life in place of an adventurous and agitated existence. A man unable to stand the sight of blood, of even a scratch or a prick, ought to give up dueling. The article did not claim that he was fearful or a coward but that, motivated by aristocratic notions of honor, he was foolishly brave. [93] Another journal got even closer to the heart of the matter: Reviewing the long list of Rochefort challenges and duels, the article concluded with an anecdote: "Someone once asked Rochefort if his duels had been successful. Yes, he answered, very successful. I have nearly always been wounded." [94]

The journals in Lyon, which was Andrieux's constituency, had great fun with the shirt that Rochefort wore during the duel. This bloodied item was taken by Olivier Pain to the office of the *Petit Lyonnais* for display and to be shown during a Blanquist political rally. "Henceforth," wrote the Center Left *Courrier de Lyon,* "Rochefort's name will figure in the socialist calendar. Saint Rochefort, pray for us." [95] A Legitimist paper carried an article called "Radical Relics." "We have been asked to announce the sale . . . of Rochefort shirts stained in his duel with M. Koechlin, to be found at the *Petit Lyonnais* offices. An assortment of Voltaire canes can also be found there. The shirts, quite authentic, are guaranteed; they arrived yesterday evening, sent immediately after the duel, and will be unpacked today, Place de la République, 51. Advice to collectors: Hurry!" [96]

The rather colorless Center Left Waddington government, which had granted the partial amnesty in the spring of 1879, gave way at the end of the year over minor issues to be replaced by Freycinet, whose views were much like Gambetta's. Neither man yet thought that the time was ripe for a full amnesty, though some of Gambetta's followers were beginning to press for it. There occurred in June of 1880, however, an incident that brought Gambetta up short. In a by-election in the Twentieth Arrondissement (Gambetta's own constituency) for a seat on the municipal council, the candidate he recommended was beaten by Alexis-Louis Trinquet, a deportee still on New Caledonia. Trinquet had been an employee of Rochefort on *La Marseillaise* in 1869 and, because he had been elected to the Commune in the supplementary election of April 16, 1871, was considered an extremist. He regained public attention in 1879 with a letter to President Grévy expressing his hope that the fall of MacMahon would lead to a general amnesty.[97] His election seems to have caused Gambetta to panic and to urge Freycinet to bring up an amnesty bill, which Freycinet did with considerable reluctance on June 19, 1880. The government was then embarked on an anticlerical campaign—a cause that tended to unite Republicans—to dissolve the religious teaching orders and secularize education, and Freycinet hesitated to raise another issue that might drive the more conservative to abandon the Republic.[98]

Too many in the Chamber were still reluctant to accept an amnesty bill, and Gambetta was forced to leave the presiding chair in order to make what proved to be the decisive speech: "It is necessary that you close the book on these past ten years, that you set the tombstone of oblivion on all the crimes and vestiges of the Commune, and that you say to everyone . . . that there is only one France and only one Republic." The bill passed in the Chamber three to one but ran into greater difficulty in the Senate where Gambetta had difficulty making himself heard. He succeeded only after allowing an amendment to exclude from amnesty those who were guilty of the most atrocious crimes—murder and arson. The bill became law on July 11, 1880,[99] making Rochefort free to come home. He was in Paris the following day.

CHAPTER VI

The Return of the Intransigent
1880-1885

*Whether he likes it or not, the aristocratic spirit pene-
trates all of his democratic words. Speaking of Gambetta,
whom he styled "the prince of the boors," one feels the
disdain of the well-born man for the grocer's son from
Cahors, as for all the plebeian manners of the parvenu.*

EDMOND DE GONCOURT [1]

WHEN the Chamber began considering its amnesty bill in June of
1880, Rochefort began making preparations for his return to Paris,
for he wished to launch a newspaper as quickly as possible after his
arrival. Police informers in both Geneva and Paris were aware of
his journalistic preparations and knew that the paper would be called
L'Intransigeant. And though Rochefort would later recount his surprise at the immense demonstration that greeted his arrival in Paris,[2]
he had taken some pains ahead of time to insure that a mob would
be on hand.[3] Both the business and demonstration arrangements in
Paris were entrusted to a promoter named Eugène Mayer.

From a number of reports by newspapermen and police agents,
we may be sure that Rochefort left Geneva on the very day the

amnesty bill became law, July 11, and that he boarded a train for Lyon accompanied by Olivier Pain. Madame Rochefort was not with him, and one unusually reliable agent in Geneva explained that she had been locked in her room by Rochefort's mistress and the maid, both of whom accompanied him to Paris.[4] They were welcomed in Lyon by a small committee of local Republicans. After spending the night in a hotel, they left for Paris the next day, where they were expected in the late afternoon at the Gare de Lyon. Rochefort's first Parisian dinner was to be at the home of Victor Hugo.[5]

As to the size of the crowd that had gathered at the Gare de Lyon, the estimates ranged from 100,000 to 200,000. In any case, the crowd was large and noisy, and the newspapers were ready to call it "absolutely revolutionary" and "ready for anything."[6] These reports were mistaken, as both the police and Rochefort recognized. Rochefort was an old Parisian favorite, a celebrity coming home, a man whose wit easily canceled out his sins as far as the public was concerned. Beside the friends, the admirers, and those previously amnestied, gathered the merely curious, who can be counted on to swell any public function or meeting; and one eyewitness noted that many of the curious were provincials who had come to Paris for the Bastille Day celebration. They gaped, stupefied by the spectacle of Rochefort's arrival, but they did not join in the enthusiasm.[7] Admirers certainly shouted "Vive Rochefort," but they were shouts of friendship and not seditious cries against Grévy or Gambetta.[8] Rochefort responded to the popular greeting in the first issue of *L'Intransigeant* while explaining its title: "We have refused to come to terms with Opportunism, nor has Opportunism come to terms with us. [Opportunism] limits its transactions to *le seize mai* and to the Senate."[9]

It was to be expected that conservatives would not extend Rochefort a friendly welcome, but the excitement of his reception tended to obscure the antagonism of many Leftists. Some of the radical journalists, of course, could not have been expected to be enthusiastic about competition from *L'Intransigeant,* and some of them had reason to doubt Rochefort's integrity. But many of the doctrinaire socialists believed that Rochefort had no program at all and that, while his support might come from revolutionaries who cared only to overturn whatever existed, he was in fact a bourgeois no matter what he might say. Others recalled his behavior during the Government of National Defense as ambiguous and unprincipled.[10]

Rochefort's attack upon Gambetta as the chief of Opportunism and the delayer of amnesty was an attack upon a Republican hero, and some of his associates at *L'Intransigeant* advised him to cool down, to stop appearing at so many public meetings, and to avoid at all cost letting *L'Intransigeant* appear too Communard. But he laughingly called these friends "dirty reactionaries": he was absolutely convinced that he could do anything at any given moment and had no doubts about the outcome of his fight against Gambetta.[11] Typical of his public utterances was a speech at a banquet for radicals at which he presided. He proposed unity among the socialist Republicans in the face of Opportunist cohesion where "party discipline approaches servility." He accused the Opportunists of being indifferent to "the people," and he charged that their regime was not far from that of Louis-Philippe: "They say to their friends 'Enrichissez-vous!'" Evidently he knew that he was accused of being a bourgeois, for he concluded by saying that "one is bourgeois out of sentiment, not by birth. . . . When one sincerely and courageously marches under the same flag against the same enemy, social classifications disappear." [12]

The Opportunists were seemingly vulnerable to such attack, because if they joined with the Left for the defense of the Republic, they allied with the Right in defending the social and economic status quo.[13] As a result, social legislation was notably lacking in the two decades after 1871. On the other hand, only recently has it been recognized that since French industry grew slowly and tended to be small-scale, France had no widespread "industrial problem" until the twentieth century. In the nineteenth century, Paris, Le Creusot, and the northern coal mines were far from being the whole country. Social legislation could only come with large-scale industry and the accompanying awareness of its problems. While one might argue that French politicians in the nineteenth century ought to have stimulated industrialization, they were, thanks to the political instability begun by the French Revolution, heavily occupied with form of government. French radicalism also grew out of the revolutionary tradition and its "idea of paradise around the corner." [14] This helps to explain why many radicals, like Rochefort, seemed to be programless—except for a simple-minded egalitarianism, which preached a return to goodness through revolution.

As for Gambetta, his services to the nation and to the Republic were too well known for Rochefort to write him off easily as a self-seeking politician of the July Monarchy school. One Leftist newspaper claimed that in making snide remarks about Gambetta Rochefort was using the impertinent tone of a marquis in Molière: "He accuses the deputy from Belleville of trying to forget, and of having forgotten, that he is the son of a merchant in colonial produce. . . . In his attacks, he also includes the name of M. Antonin Proust, forgetting that the deputy from Niort was one of the most ardent proponents of amnesty." They advised Rochefort to employ his verve more usefully for the Republic. [15]

Perhaps the sharpest criticism of Rochefort appeared in open letters to him, which were sold on the streets for ten centimes in July of 1880, entitled "A Rag-Picker of La Villette to Comte H.-V. de Rochefort-Luçay." The authors were unknown but were evidently Left Wing and did not regard him as one of them. They especially pointed out that he had not honored his electoral program of 1869 and advised him "to remove his mask." Rochefort tried to counter this propaganda with similar broadsides signed by "An Intransigent Rag-Picker"; but the point had been made that he was not the darling of all radicals. [16]

Let us be fair about one aspect of the problem. Many recently amnestied men needed financial help temporarily, and because Rochefort received an impossible number of requests for aid he inevitably earned enemies. [17] In August of 1880, he even decided to limit his public appearances at meetings organized to benefit those amnestied,[18] a decision that deepened resentments. Evidently he tried to give money rather than attend meetings, and on several occasions those organizing meetings used his name without his consent, angering the audience when he did not appear. Given his continuing attacks upon Gambetta, which many Leftists believed would weaken the Republic, it was easy for radicals to speculate that Rochefort was a secret Orleanist.[19]

In about November of that year, a weekly pamphlet appeared devoted to sketches of current celebrities. Its second issue included an article on Rochefort: *"Le lanternier* is a radical aristocrat. . . . If Rochefort waves a red rag, this flag must be made of silk. At the end of the Empire, he occupied a loge with M. Cochinat for the performance of Victor Hugo's *Lucrèce Borgia* at the Theater Porte-Saint-Martin. Rochefort had vainly presented himself in the Seventh Electoral District of Paris. In a place where one of the characters speaks of a certain quarter of Ferrara as inhabited by scum, [Rochefort] turned a scowling face to M. Cochinat and whispered: 'It is the Seventh District.' "[20] Whether or not this story was spurious, it was worthy of Rochefort and therefore believable and damaging to him. Indeed, for the first time in his career Rochefort was becoming the victim of the gutter press of which he had been reigning prince. Of course, unpleasant things had been written about him before 1880, but to be the target of a spate of published abuse from the Left was a novelty.

Small wonder that Rochefort seized upon an invitation to attend in Milan the unveiling of a monument to "the martyrs of Mentana," at which Garibaldi was to be present. It was at Mentana in 1867 that Garibaldi's attempt to seize Rome was blocked by the troops of Napoleon III. After the fall of the Second Empire, Garibaldi offered his sword to the new French Republic in its struggle against autocratic Prussia, an offer that Rochefort referred to in his short speech in Milan:

> Even if we had not come here, my friends from France
> and I, to pay tribute to the magnificent democratic and

anticlerical movement which invaded Italy, we should have come out of gratitude to the hero who presides at this ceremony. Attacked by Bonaparte's *chassepots,* he had, more than anyone else perhaps, the right to abandon us when, at the time of our disasters, everyone abandoned us. But his great soul knows not such meanness. He is one of those who does not hold peoples responsible for the follies and crimes of their governments. He knows that there are two Frances: Imperial France which supported every despotism; Republican France which defends every liberty. It was to the latter that he offered his glorious blood and that of his worthy sons, and he forgot Mentana to run to the aid of Dijon.[21]

What Garibaldi also forgot, along with Rochefort, was that Napoleon III did "something for Italy," and not the French Republic to whose aid Garibaldi came.

Rochefort ostensibly went to Milan to honor Garibaldi, but his real reason was to persuade Garibaldi to return to France with him in order to associate his name with the anti-Gambetta crowd, which needed its own hero. Olivier Pain, Blanqui, and Rochefort left for Milan on November 1, the ceremony was on the third, and they were back in Paris, without Garibaldi, on the sixth. For they found Garibaldi much too ill to make the trip. Their pilgrimage was, in fact, a fiasco. Rochefort's speech was placed near the end of the agenda, by which time the crowd was weary of words and was breaking up. In the distance a band struck up, completing the disaster. Blanqui made no attempt to speak, and the three of them refused to attend the official banquet and sulked in their hotel until train time. Back in Paris, Rochefort was heard to complain that Garibaldi was an Opportunist in his own country's affairs.[22]

Meanwhile, Rochefort had launched the first of those exposés, designed to discredit those who had governed France after 1871, for which *L'Intransigeant* became famous. In this case his target was old General Courtot de Cissey, a former Minister of War and a Life Senator. The old gentleman had taken as his mistress a woman with a most dubious past, Julie de Kaulla, a well-known member of the demi-monde during the Second Empire. She had married an army officer named Jung (later Brigadier-General H.-F.-T. Jung) and apparently became a spy, another profession open to her kind. After three years of marriage, she resumed her earlier calling; and since divorce was not yet legally possible in France, Captain Jung obtained a legal separation and was given custody of their two children. Whether Madame Jung ultimately became General Cissey's mistress in order to reach the inner military circles remains a question, though we may be certain that his interest in her was not conspiratorial.

On August 29, 1880, Ivan de Wocstyne, a journalist with a nose for dirt and a man of questionable reputation, published a story in *Le Gaulois* to the effect that Colonel Jung and his wife were in constant touch, that the wife was a German spy, and that she was Cissey's mistress. Jung at once brought libel charges against Woestyne and had little trouble demonstrating that he was involved in no intrigues. Woestyne was sentenced to six months in jail and had to pay Jung 5000 francs in damages. Though nothing whatsoever had been proven about Cissey, the government decided to relieve him of his command of the XI Corps at Nantes, although his retirement was imminent anyway as he had reached the age of seventy.[23]

Rochefort then plunged in. The former Minister of War was accused of having willingly given military secrets to a spy and having profited from their sale. "The Jung-Woestyne case," Rochefort wrote, "will at least have the result of showing the nation into what ignoble hands we have fallen, we other defenders of the Republic. And the Cisseys who keep Prussian spies at the expense of France, to whom they open their accounts and their ministerial files, accuse us, in papers as dirty as their souls, of treating with the Germans! . . . When M. Jung discovered what his wife was, he chased her permanently from his house; when the government knew what Courtot de Cissey was, it provided him with the highest of military functions."[24]

General de Cissey at once brought charges against Rochefort, and the case was heard November 25–27, 1880, the plaintiff in full uniform with a splash of the highest decorations. Rochefort had no evidence to back up his charges and his defense was ludicrous: "I have nothing to say in my defense: I believe that I have become aware of some serious facts, but, as they are unsupported by witnesses, they will appear to you to be fantasies. I shall, therefore, remain silent. I have always tried to do my duty, and I believed that I had the right to take a very close look at the conduct of the Ministers of War, after the Empire, after Sedan, after the campaign of 1870, which have left us with so many ruins and so much misery." This testimony was easily used by de Cissey's lawyers to show that Rochefort's motive had been revenge against the army. He was fined 4000 francs and made to pay de Cissey 8000 francs in damages.[25] Rochefort had considered raising a mob to be outside the Palais de Justice during the hearing in the hope of intimidating both court and government. Nearly a thousand people did watch him emerge after being sentenced, but only a few of them were militant radicals.[26]

In the aftermath, Julie de Kaulla-Jung, encouraged by her aged lover's success in court, brought charges against Woestyne, Rochefort, and several newspapers in the hope of a large settlement. But because of her reputation and career, she was unable to collect any damages even though she won the case in principle. The defendants were each fined 150 francs and were ordered to publish the sentences in their newspapers.[27] Rochefort regarded the entire business as a victory for himself, concluding that what he had had to pay de Cissey was so small that it amounted to the plaintiff's being beaten.[28] It is an interesting argument.

Albert Joly, the lawyer who had defended Rochefort before the court-martial in 1871, died on December 4, 1880, in Versailles. *L'Intransigeant* did not mention his death, nor did Rochefort attend the funeral. When he was publicly criticized for his indifference,[29] he responded that he did not attend the burials of Opportunists. This aroused his critic to write: "[Rochefort] has not forgotten that Albert

Joly, after having defended him as a lawyer, twice voted against amnesty as a deputy. He distinguished between his obligations to a client and his duties as a citizen." [30] Rochefort certainly ought to be grateful to Joly, the article concluded, for having gone to see Thiers and successfully obtained a change in the indictment, probably saving Rochefort's life. Rochefort's response was that he knew of no such conversation between Joly and Thiers. [31]

The Gambettists then entered the fray, stimulating a general press discussion of Rochefort's ingratitude. Joseph Reinach sent to *Le Voltaire* a letter of July, 1871, in which Rochefort asked for Gambetta's aid; this was the letter in which Rochefort volunteered to go into exile to avoid a prison sentence. [32] Rochefort immediately denied writing the letter. [33] Another journal then noted that Gambetta had contributed money for Rochefort's repatriation when he was in Australia, [34] while Joseph Reinach added more fuel by claiming that Gambetta had indeed tried to help Rochefort on at least three occasions: "following [receipt of] the letter which I published yesterday;" again in 1872 when Rochefort was trying to avoid deportation; and when he was in Sydney. Reinach was also furnished some correspondence by Joly's brother, which was turned over to *Le Voltaire*. These letters, which dated from June of 1871, showed quite unequivocally that Rochefort had readily accepted Joly as his defense attorney. There was a further letter of April 23, 1873, in which Rochefort thanked Joly for all his efforts and for the "marriage certificate which you have sent to me." [35]

Le Voltaire also published a letter from Alfred Duquet, a lawyer friend of Albert Joly's, who testified at great length about Joly's integrity. "In closing, I shall ask M. Rochefort a question. Since, according to him, Joly managed his defense badly, . . . since he was a heartless and conscienceless lawyer, why did he select him as the legal supervisor for the guardian of his children? why did he take him as a witness at his marriage? and why did he write, in 1873, the letter of affection, thanks, and gratitude?" [36] Rochefort's defense against this evidence was to insist that he was the victim of an Opportunist plot "reminiscent in all aspects of the tactics used

173

toward the end of the Empire." [37] He also sent his seconds to challenge Reinach to a duel for publishing an apocryphal letter. "I published in *Le Voltaire*," Reinach answered, "a letter written in your hand and signed with your name. You now declare that this letter is damaging to your honor. I can do nothing about that. Consequently I have no reparation to grant you." [38]

Other well-known journals added their support to the Gambettist side of the argument. *Le National* published Rochefort's letter to General Trochu of September 1, 1871, as evidence that Rochefort had indeed been seeking influential help at the time of his trial. [39] *La République française,* the paper of both Gambetta and Reinach, confirmed the authenticity of the letter that Rochefort denied having written. "In response to questions from several newspapers, we are authorized to declare that the letter from M. Henri Rochefort, published by *Le Voltaire,* was delivered to M. Gambetta, rue Montaigne, 12, at the end of July, 1871, by M. Albert Joly. M. Gambetta immediately made the request to M. Thiers which had been asked for by M. Rochefort." [40] Another Leftist journal retold the story of raising the escape money that brought Rochefort back to Europe, stating that Gambetta had helped Edmond Adam significantly. None of those contributing ever demanded repayment, "nor do they deny his right to disagree on politics and ideas. But it is hardly decent to overwhelm them with insults and slander." [41] Clemenceau, of *La Justice,* was also reported to disapprove of Rochefort's polemics against Gambetta. [42]

Evidently the squabble boiled over in the offices of *L'Intransigeant,* for Rochefort announced that he had fired one of his writers, Emile Dosquet. Dosquet publicly insisted that he had quit: "The profound disgust inspired in me by this heartless and faithless being's hypocrisy and egotism is the primary motive that led to my decision." [43] If the incident then died down, it did nothing to improve Rochefort's relations with the Left.

At the height of the controversy with Joseph Reinach, the Swiss maid in Rochefort's household committed suicide. Rochefort was in such an emotional state that he could not even be interviewed by the police, and he took refuge in a neighbor's home for several days. Ultimately he explained that he had sent the maid, whose name was Louise Gaillard, to the offices of *L'Intransigeant* to get five pieces of gold. On her way home she lost them through a hole in her pocket. Rochefort thought that as he had always treated her well she preferred death to being accused of theft.[44] The police investigation showed that she died either of gas or charcoal fumes sometime in the late afernoon of December 14 and concluded that it was obviously suicide.[45] While the police officially accepted Rochefort's explanation of her motive and closed the case, the death aroused the curiosity of secret agents, perhaps because of Rochefort's extreme reaction but more likely because there were already documents in Rochefort's police file that suggested domestic turmoil.

Moreover, that file contained the report of another suicide, that of Henriette-Marie Margueritte, a seventeen-year-old girl who worked in a charcuterie. She was found dead of asphyxiation on October 16, 1872, and she had left a note to explain that her mother had been a mistress of Rochefort, a relationship that had destroyed the Margueritte family. Although she was legitimate herself, she claimed that a younger sister had been the product of this adultery. Rochefort had deserted the mother several years before, and she now sold newspapers from a kiosk near the Madeleine. As a last request, Henriette-Marie asked that her mother be prevented from attending the funeral.[46]

Several weeks before the suicide of Louise Gaillard, Rochefort was known to be uneasy about his elder son, Henri, a flighty young man who kept company with some disreputable characters on the Left Bank. He had not yet been called up for military service, and Rochefort thought it might be well to enlist him in an African regiment.[47] The police had reason to believe that Henri slept with the Swiss maid and they knew of rumors that father and son had quarreled over her.[48] None of this, of course, proved anything about this rather simple girl's fate, nor did it necessarily account for Rochefort's extraordinary shock upon learning of her death. Nor did it necessarily have anything to do with Henri's own untimely end.

Rochefort had always posed in print as an ardent patriot and a champion of the common man. But his attacks upon General de Cissey and Gambetta made it clear that he could also be moved to seek revenge. In a new affair in the spring of 1881, he admitted for the first time that he was quite aware of the financial rewards to be won through scandalmongering and attacks upon the mighty. During dinner on the evening of March 13, he got news of the assassination of Czar Alexander II of Russia; and since he had met a number of Russian radicals in Switzerland, he went at once to Geneva to get their story directly. He found them delirious with their success.[49] In an article called "The Revenge of the Nihilists," he predicted that the bomb would do for Russia what William Tell's arrow did for Switzerland, what the scaffold of Charles I did for England and that of Louis XVI for France. "Liberty, among all peoples, has budded in the blood of oppressors."[50] Of course the Russian Embassy protested the article, and the subsequent session in court cost Rochefort 1000 francs, which he claimed was "cheap enough compared to the value of the merchandise."[51]

For several years, a committee of the Chamber of Deputies had been working on a new, liberal press law, hoping to sweep away finally the tangle of restrictive legislation that had plagued journalists during the nineteenth century. This new law, promulgated on July 29, 1881, eliminated the need to deposit caution money and to secure governmental permission to publish, and it took from the government and the courts all power to suppress newspapers and periodicals. Perhaps the most significant aspect of the reform was the disappearance of what were called *délits d'opinion,* that is, such offenses as inciting to hatred and contempt of the government or outrages against the government. Offenses punishable by law still remained, of course, but they amounted to *direct* provocations by editors to incite others to criminal action and to insulting or defaming the President of the Republic, heads of foreign states, accredited ambassadors, the courts, and the armed forces. These offenses were to be tried by jury rather than in correctional or police courts. The law has been rightly called a major contribution to the liberty of the subject under the Third Republic.[52] Editors especially appreciated it since it provided that in case of misdemeanor only the publisher could be jailed. In Paris especially, the law left jurymen open to blackmail by "the likes of Rochefort."[53]

Rochefort's next opportunity to attack the Opportunists grew out of French intervention in Tunisia in 1881, an incident of complex origin. When the Freycinet government took office in late 1879, the Minister of Public Instruction, Jules Ferry, proved to be the most prominent member. He had been a Republican opponent of Napoleon III in the *Corps législatif* and a member of the Government of National Defense. And he had earned the enmity of the Right by introducing the anticlerical legislation that drove religious orders from public education. Freycinet fell in the autumn of 1880 and was succeeded by Ferry instead of Gambetta; for the President of the Republic was personally antagonistic to Gambetta and refused to call him to form a cabinet. Yet Gambetta's great authority made it difficult for anyone else to govern. Ferry and Gambetta were old associates, but Mme. Ferry's refusal to receive Léonie Léon, Gambetta's mistress, imperiled their political association.

Ferry's decision to intervene in Tunisia in the spring of 1881 has always been clouded in controversy, though it is now generally agreed that by that date he had not developed that interest in expanding the French Empire for which he would later be celebrated.[54] Indeed, very few Frenchmen concerned themselves about overseas matters, save for some Navy people, missionaries, and the masonic lodges, which had inherited some of the Saint-Simonian traditions and thought it their duty to make exotic peoples benefit from the technical progress of "positivist civilization." When most of the French thought of expansion, they had in mind the recovery of Alsace and Lorraine.

The Tunisian affair, therefore, was rooted elsewhere—essentially in three widely separated situations: one financial, one naval, and one relating to the French position in Algeria. And the fact that one motive was financial immensely enriched the field for the scandalmongers. The government of Tunisia was a regency for the

Turkish government under Mohammed es Saddok Bey. He considered himself independent even though the Turks regarded him as their vassal. His regime was pitifully weak, unable to control tribes in the south and west; and the Bey himself was capricious and surrounded by venal officials. In the decade of the sixties, he borrowed heavily and irresponsibly from European bankers, until he had amassed the magnificent debt of 350 million francs. The three most interested nations, France, Britain, and Italy, then established a commission in 1869 to help the Bey (and European creditors) out of the dilemma. The debt was scaled down to 125 million francs, and the commission retained control of Tunisian finances.

A second financial aspect of intervention derived from the fact that Tunisian economic development required foreign capital. By the late seventies, an intense competition between French and Italian companies for concessions began to take on some serious political dimensions from the French point of view. Poor Italians had been settling in Tunisia by the thousands, and the French government began to suspect that their presence would eventually be used by Italy as a pretext for occupying Tunisia. The French Navy in particular dreaded the possibility of the Italians turning Bizerta into a powerful naval base close to Algeria. This takes us to the final situation troubling the French government: the general security of Algeria, which, comprising three departments, was regarded as an extension of France. Algeria was especially touchy in those years, because a number of Alsatians had settled there after 1871 rather than submit to German rule, and no French government dared to be found indifferent to their welfare. Kroumir tribesmen from southern Tunisia had conducted raiding parties into Algeria for a number of years, and the Tunisian government had repeatedly been indifferent to protests from the French Consul, Roustan, and from the Governor-General of Algeria, Albert Grévy, brother of the French President.

As early as the Congress of Berlin, 1878, the British had indicated that they had no interest in the area of "Carthage"; and in subsequent notes Britain made it quite clear that she would not object if France, in her civilizing work in Africa, should feel forced to do something about barbarism in Tunisia. No doubt the British hoped to placate the French, who had been irritated by British gains in Egypt through the necessity of regulating the debt of the Egyptian government. Bismarck, too, encouraged the French to deal with Tunisia, anxious to turn French eyes away from Alsace and Lorraine and willing to see tension heighten between Paris and Rome as a device to keep France isolated.

The Ferry government decided to move only after considerable hesitation, knowing it would face systematic opposition from the Right as a result of the recent anticlerical legislation, and from the extreme Left which wanted only Alsace-Lorraine and no side shows. The opportunity to block Italy, to help France emerge from the moroseness of defeat, and to demonstrate the vigor of a Republic to the monarchies of Europe seemed worth the risk of domestic opposition, and a new incursion of Kroumirs on March 30–31, 1881, provided the final straw. The Bey was formally invited to cooperate with France to restore order. When he refused, the government informed Parliament of its intention to restore order, not merely along the Algerian frontier, but in Tunisia itself. Three days later, on April 7, the government requested an emergency fund of six million francs, which was readily granted even though the precise nature of the expedition was not spelled out. If the government had really been involved in a conspiracy, as would later be charged, one would have expected to see the government's announcement followed up at once by action. It required nearly three weeks to scrape together an expeditionary corps before the invasion could be mounted.

The Bey could put up little effective resistance, and at his palace of Bardo near Tunis he had no alternative but to sign a treaty on May 12, 1881, which made Tunisia a French protectorate. No outward changes were made in Tunisian institutions, but a French Resident Minister became the legal intermediary between the two governments, and France guaranteed the security of the Bey. The treaty was overwhelmingly ratified by the French Parliament, though the Rightists in the Chamber abstained and Clemenceau cast the sole vote against it. But because Ferry was still uneasy about public opinion, especially with parliamentary elections coming up later in the summer, he withdrew all but 15,000 troops at once from Tunisia as proof of the success of the expedition. It was a mistake. In June, the season of Ramadan, an insurrection burst out in the name of a holy war against Christians, and the garrison had to be raised to 50,000 men. As the pacification was not completed until October, it gave the parliamentary Opposition an opportunity to snipe.

The government was charged with having been the dupe of Bismarck. And Rochefort, who claimed that he had smelled some dirty financial business at once, published an article called "Cherchez le Khroumir," in which he sought to prove that the Kroumirs were nonexistent and that the invasion was a plot of bondholders designed to force the price of Tunisian bonds up. He also claimed that the plot included the Consul, T.-J.-D. Roustan, and Jules and Charles Ferry.[55] The elections, held on August 21 and September 4, were a victory for the Gambettists and for the extreme Left, a defeat for the Right. Even though the Ferry supporters neither lost nor gained, he at once saw that his government was doomed, and that one of the Gambettists, perhaps even Gambetta, would soon have to form a government.

Meanwhile, Rochefort published a second article entitled "The Secret of the Tunisian Affair." He accused Gambetta, Roustan, and Challemel-Lacour of having formed an association with the intent, first, of forcing down the price of the bonds in order to buy them up for a few cents, and then pushing the French government into assuming the responsibility for the payment of the bonds; he likened this conspiracy to the infamous Morny-Jecker deal and the subsequent intervention into Mexico in the time of Napoleon III.[56] Note that Rochefort had added Gambetta to his list of villains, for, as he said at a meeting of the Society for Freethinking, he had become convinced that the responsibility for the Tunisian War was Gambetta's, who sought to gain prestige thereby in his ambition to become President of the Republic.[57] Both Roustan and Challemel-

Lacour filed libel charges against Rochefort, and the cases were scheduled for December.

Before they came up, a debate over Tunisian policy began in the Chamber, made inevitable not merely by the charges of financial irregularities, but by the opportunity—after the elections—to overthrow Ferry. Clemenceau led the fight, claiming that this ostensibly patriotic affair had really been a cloak for those who had something to gain. He offered no proof of financial machinations, nor could he deny the justice of Ferry's retort that "there are times in delicate matters and particularly in foreign affairs when silence is patriotic." No serious politician, in fact, believed that Ferry was corrupt, but nevertheless he lost the debate and his government was turned out. On Gambetta's resolution, however, the Tunisian Protectorate was saved so as not to injure the national prestige: "The Chamber resolves to execute the Treaty of . . . May 12, 1881, . . . but this is not a vote of confidence in the Government; it is implicit approbation of its action." [58]

President Grévy could no longer postpone bringing Gambetta to power, and he announced a government on November 14, 1881. He at once obtained new credits for the management of Tunisian affairs, indicating that if Parliament felt that Ferry had perhaps exceeded his instructions it did not oppose the occupation of Tunisia. Gambetta, in turn, promoted Roustan in the foreign service and sent him back to Tunis as a gesture of faith in his integrity.

Rochefort went about collecting evidence to prove that the poor Bey of Tunisia had been completely under the thumb of Roustan before the intervention, and he had a list of twenty-nine witnesses to be called when the libel case opened on December 13, 1881. [59] To most everyone's surprise, Rochefort was acquitted on the fifteenth; for while he had an abundance of gossip, he had proved nothing about Roustan's supposed guilt. One of Rochefort's associates told an informer, "We really expected him to be condemned, as we knew . . . he had not one shred of proof in hand." [60] Evidently the court disapproved of the Tunisian venture and hoped by its decision to force a more thorough parliamentary investigation.

Challemel-Lacour's suit went to court several weeks later and was thrown out on a technicality. He opened a second action on January 25, 1882, and the court overruled the earlier decision, saying that the writ was proper and valid. The case did not come up until June 29, 1882, and this time Rochefort and his publisher, Delpierre, were found guilty. Delpierre was fined 500 francs. Rochefort was fined 1000 francs, was ordered to pay Challemel-Lacour 1000 francs damages, and had to pay the court costs.[61] These fines were perhaps not too burdensome for a man whose newspaper was then earning him 100,000 francs a year and who could afford nearly 10,000 francs that year for pictures alone.[62] On the other hand, one finds increasing indication, by 1882, that Rochefort was losing his reputation for wit. Not only were many radicals weary of him, but a reliable informer noted that he had run into a "vague hostility" toward Rochefort almost everywhere, even in the offices of *L'Intransigeant*.[63] Clearly, Rochefort's extremism in the Tunisian affair had done him no good, and the accession of Gambetta to power was the most obvious of all possible proofs that Rochefort had been soundly whipped in the matter.

As noted earlier, the Opportunists had been so occupied after 1871 with getting a Republic established and with foreign affairs that they had not accomplished much in the way of social or financial reform. Gambetta, however, had many reform projects in mind, and, with the Republic apparently on its feet, he put his cabinet to work on them at once. He wanted to lower compulsory military service from five to three years; he wanted to introduce a general income tax; he wanted an insurance plan to protect those injured on the job; he favored granting labor the right to form permanent associations; and he wanted to establish a government loan agency to aid farmers. But with Parliament divided into a flock of rival groups, he saw no way to promote his reforms through Parliament unless he could obtain a more homogeneous Chamber. He proposed, therefore, to amend the Constitutional electoral laws, after which he would dissolve Parliament and order new elections. He meant to replace the seventy-five Life Senators with seventy-five Senators elected by both houses for nine-year terms, and he wanted the *scrutin de liste* in balloting for the Chamber.

The *scrutin individuel,* the method by which each voter may vote for only one candidate on the ballot, had been generally used by monarchical regimes in the nineteenth century; whereas the *scrutin de liste,* the system by which the ballot contains a list of candidates who are voted for simultaneously, amounted to a party balloting. It favored the better organized parties and had been in the Republican tradition until 1875 when the conservatives had managed to eliminate it from the Constitution. If Gambetta could get his way, the weaker parties and splinter groups would surely lose out to the stronger parties, and the Chamber could then conduct itself more in the British fashion. Rochefort concluded that Gambetta was really maneuvering for dictatorial power. Ordinarily, as a Republican, Rochefort would have favored the *scrutin de liste,* but as the country was endangered by a "Gambettist *coup d'état,*" he claimed to have no alternative but to oppose the amendment.[64]

Rochefort's hatred of Gambetta was unquenchable. He would later write that "[Gambetta] had arrived at that point of swollen pride when men in power seek to have forgotten, and forget themselves, their origin. Son of a dealer in colonial merchandise, he hastened to liquidate his father's business. The idea of kicking a marquis in the belly causes this man, who reprimanded the majorities, to lose his composure. He likely counted among his ancestors some serfs who beat around the ponds to make those frogs shut up who were impertinent enough to trouble the sleep of the local lord." And he went on to denounce the *arrivisme* of Gambetta for daring to lunch with Edward Prince of Wales[65]—this from the marquis who, despite his disuse of title, had evidently not forgotten *his* origin.

Rochefort was not alone in opposing the constitutional amendment: opposition came from both those who feared Gambetta's social reforms and those who feared a dissolution. There was little opposition to the reform of the Senate, but Gambetta was beaten 268 to 218 on the *scrutin de liste* and had to give his resignation, January 26, 1882. And he fell from power permanently, the great man from whom so much had been expected, after only seventy-four days in office.[66] Such a parliamentary system was obviously doomed to ineffectiveness, and it would not be long before those who had done most to preserve its ineffectuality would emerge as its sharpest critics.

Two days after Gambetta's resignation, a joint-stock investment bank called the Union Générale closed its doors, a financial fiasco described for the first time in France by the word *krach*. Its significance far transcended the world of finance, however, for one can trace the rise of a militant anti-Semitism in France from the subsequent scandal, an anti-Semitism that Rochefort shared and that would come to a head in the Dreyfus Affair. The latest study of the *krach* concludes that the whole truth about it may never be known, so that at best we are confronted with a problem in "probabilities." [67]

Beginning about 1874, French agriculture had experienced a depression, a general lowering of prices owing to increased production in the western world. French industry, on the other hand, was relatively unaffected, thanks to increased orders to repair damages from the recent war and to a public works program sponsored by Freycinet. Under these artificial circumstances, activity increased on the stock exchange, and the market kept rising. In mid-1878, Eugène Bontoux founded his bank, the Union Générale, with a capital investment of 25 million francs. It seemed to be well-directed, and its initial wise investments indicated that the bank would be profitable for investors. New issues of shares were repeatedly put on the market, until by November 5, 1881, the bank had achieved a capitalization of 150 million francs and the shares had risen from 500 francs to 3,096 francs.

The Union Générale, however, had its dubious aspects. First, its prospectus hinted at both a banking and an anti-Semitic crusade. That is, Bontoux and his closest associate, Feder, meant to mobilize Catholic capital in their ambition to make the bank the leading joint-stock investment concern in France; and they were allied in their crusade with the Länderbank in Austria against the Rothschild colossus. Toward that end, the board of directors was staffed with aristocratic titles rather than men of financial experience. People of all walks of life did invest in the bank, attracted by the great names on the board, but the aristocracy were among the heaviest investors.

Second, the true value of the stocks was considerably less than the market price, for Bontoux used bank money to buy them, creating an artificial demand. This demand steadily forced up most stock prices, not merely those of the Union Générale.

The Rothschilds began their counterattack in 1881, occasionally throwing blocks of Union Générale stock on the market. And they had a useful ally in the Minister of Finance, Léon Say, a Republican who valued the open support the Rothschilds had given the Republic. Stock values reached their peak on January 10, 1882, by which time both Bontoux and Feder recognized that the game was up, as the bank's resources were exhausted. Both men sold their personal holdings without warning, Bontoux realizing nearly two million francs and Feder nearly three million. Then an unstoppable slide in stock values began, and the bank closed its doors on January 28.[68]

Meanwhile, Freycinet had formed his second government to replace Gambetta, and the Attorney-General took action as soon as the first victim registered a complaint. Bontoux and Feder, charged with swindling and abuse of public confidence, were arrested on January 30, then released on a bail of 100,000 francs. The judicial inquiry took five months, during which Bontoux posed as the victim of a Jewish conspiracy, of the Freemasons, and of a servile magistracy. Their trial took place in December of 1882, and both men were sentenced to five years in prison and were fined 3000 francs. They appealed the verdict at once, but the Court of Appeal upheld the principle of their conviction though reducing the prison sentences two years. Bontoux did not wait to be jailed, but fled abroad where he lived for five years.[69]

That Bontoux and his associates had been engaged in criminal practices seems at the time to have made less of an impression than the fact that the Rothschilds had successfully counterattacked. And ruined stockholders too often held Jewish finance responsible for the crash. Moreover, Jewish finance was seen as hand in glove with leading Republican politicians of the Opportunist stripe; and while Rochefort refrained from claiming that Gambetta had made a killing out of the crash, he noted that Gambetta "had a special knack for finding a niche for dishonest men." [70] A marked increase in anti-Semitism was one of the significant results of the crash. Equally important was the subsequent decline in investor confidence, an illness that seriously handicapped the growth of French business and industry for at least a decade and that contributed to conservative gains in the election of 1885.[71]

Subscriptions to *L'Intransigeant* indicate that Rochefort was extremely popular at the time of his return from exile in 1880, but that popularity dwindled as evidence of his unprincipled, self-seeking character piled up. And subscriptions to *L'Intransigeant* ebbed with his popularity. In 1882 a police informer named Howe, who had the ear of several employees on *L'Intransigeant,* repeatedly reported Rochefort's financial situation was increasingly precarious. He also noted that unfortunately Rochefort had no inclination to reduce his living expenses and was still betting heavily at the tracks, buying pictures, and indulging himself in a new young mistress named Lucie who was costing him heavily in several ways. This woman, described as a monument of stupidity, was aging him and preparing him for an impoverished old age. He seemed to be increasingly prideful and unwilling to recognize any talent other than his own, and his judgments had become so overwhelmingly negative that his associates were alarmed.[72] By mid-1883 Howe predicted that the business officers of *L'Intransigeant* might be driven to oust Rochefort as the only way to regain readers. They had lost those of the Left and were attracting too many notorious reactionaries, "people with titles and chateaux." [73]

But Rochefort survived at *L'Intransigeant,* in part at least because he had seized upon a new controversy to exploit in the manner of Tunisia, the French venture in Tonkin. French interest in Southeast Asia dated from the time of Louis XIV and was an aspect of that monarch's general policy of reducing Hapsburg power and promoting Catholicism. Accordingly, French missionaries from the outset reflected His Majesty's faith in the superiority of French culture, and their greatest successes from the start were in the Kingdom of Annam. If merchants tended to follow in the footsteps of missionaries in East Asia, French penetration was always peculiarly characterized by national pride, a pride in French civilization, in sharp contrast to the commercial zeal more characteristic of other European colonizing powers. The eclipse of France overseas in the eighteenth century proved to be a temporary setback, and the Catholic revival in the nineteenth century provided a new wave of missionaries. What is more, French governments after 1815 were not indifferent to ventures that might regain the prestige lost by defeat.[74]

One of the results of the Anglo-French War with China in 1860 was a decision to retain Saigon and Cochin China, territory occupied in 1858 as a protest against persecution of Christians by the Annamite government. The Emperor of Annam, who actually acknowledged the suzerainty of China, signed the Treaty of Saigon, June 5, 1862, which gave the French a firm territorial foothold in Indo-China. From that time on, the French navy promoted imperialism more effectively than the missionaries, and French merchants and explorers usually provided the incidents that made trouble with the government of Annam. Jean Dupuis, for example, began the exploration of the Red River in Tonkin (1873), and François Garnier seized Hanoi and the Red River delta. Annamite protests led to a further understanding with the French and a second treaty signed at Saigon in 1874. Hanoi was returned to the Emperor Tu Duc, but he now recognized unconditional French sovereignty in Cochin China. He also began to appeal to China for aid against French inroads.

Yet public interest in East Asia was slight. Gambetta was one of the few public figures to favor expansion of the Empire, and he died on December 31, 1882. Aside from the Navy, which wanted strong bases overseas, most of the enthusiasts were geographers and explorers, who regularly gathered at the Café de la Petite Vache in Paris. By 1883, the Geography Society of France openly promoted colonial expansion, just at a time when some members of the French foreign service were becoming convinced that France ought not to lag behind the other powers in the race for new territory, and at a time when increasing protectionism led businessmen to seek new markets. Even so, it is now evident that the initial moves in the 1880's came not from Paris, but from colonial officials, military and navy officers, and individual explorers, whose actions would be then ratified by Paris since the national honor was then involved.

The first governor of Cochin China, for example, took it upon himself in 1882 to send a force of four hundred men under Henri Rivière up the Red River against river pirates. Rivière took possession of Hanoi with the governor's sanction. Naturally this brought a vigorous protest from the Chinese and led the government of Premier Duclerc to instruct its minister in Peking to negotiate a settlement. This diplomat, named Bourrée, worked out an agreement by which both China and France pledged not to intervene in Tonkin. Meanwhile, the Duclerc government, concluding rather reluctantly that it must send reinforcements to Cochin China, sent an expeditionary force of 3000 to guarantee the national honor in case a satisfactory solution was not achieved with the Chinese. This brought Rochefort into the fray, for he sensed instantaneously that Premier Duclerc and other Opportunist politicians had reached secret agreements with the likes of Jean Dupuis, out of which they expected to realize vast profits from the development of gold mines in Asia.[75]

Thus, when the Duclerc government asked the Chamber for funds to provide an expeditionary force, Rochefort wrote: "After the first eleven million, the Duclercs and the Jauréguiberries [the admiral who was then Minister of the Marine] will easily demonstrate that it is absolutely necessary to grant them forty more, else leave this brilliant conquest unrealized. And, as in the case of Tunisia, when we are entrenched in Tonkin at the price of frightful sacrifices, we shall have to quadruple them in order to maintain ourselves there. At that point, we shall also realize that Tonkin is as unproductive as it is uninhabitable, that the colonists there are exposed to continual incursions by Tartars and Chinese, and that we shall have spent for a dubious fantasy ten times the money necessary to construct schoolhouses in every village and in every hamlet on French soil." [76]

Shortly after, Henri Rivière found his position in Hanoi untenable, began his retreat, and was ambushed and killed. To the end, Rochefort insisted that the promoters of the Tonkin intervention had invented the story that Rivière had been blockaded in Hanoi, for surely he could have evacuated the city as easily as he got in! [77]

Ferry, the man who had earlier sanctioned the invasion of Tunisia, resumed the premiership in the midst of the Tonkin crisis, on February 21, 1883. At that moment, the treaty with China negotiated by Bourrée had not been ratified, and the colonialists hoped to prevent its ratification, not because of the commercial interests in Tonkin, but because of their concern for French prestige. Until his second ministry, Ferry was not a colonialist. Yet in 1883 he developed a colonial program with a threefold purpose: to infuse the French with new vitality so that they might recover from their defeatist psychology; to civilize an inferior people and raise them to equality; and to provide new markets for French exports.[78] Consequently, Bourrée was recalled and his nonintervention treaty disavowed, an act that humiliated the diplomat and led him to spread vicious rumors about the government's interest in Tonkin upon his return to Paris. To replace the treaty of nonintervention with China, Ferry proposed to establish a protectorate over Tonkin, and only seventy-eight deputies opposed him on the issue.

When Emperor Tu Duc resisted Ferry's proposal, however, the French were forced to bombard the Annamite capital, Hué. Tu Duc then signed a treaty recognizing a French protectorate over both Tonkin and Annam, August 25, 1883. The French were gambling on the weakness of the Chinese Empire and expected no resistance from that quarter. But Ferry had no luck in these ventures. Chinese troops resisted French attempts to occupy Tonkin and left him open to charges—chiefly by the Left—that he was bogging down the French military in useless campaigns and not building the national strength to recover Alsace-Lorraine. Not until May 11, 1884, was a French naval captain able to negotiate a preliminary convention in Tien-Tsin with Li Hung-chang, the most powerful of North Chinese officials. Difficulties arose out of the wording of the convention, for the French had used no professional diplomat in the negotiations; and in June, a French column was ambushed by Chinese troops. Perhaps it was a legitimate misunderstanding, but Paris felt it was a deliberate trap, and Ferry demanded that the Chinese at once evacuate Tonkin and pay a 250 million franc indemnity.

Rochefort saw it otherwise: "Hardly a month ago I wrote essentially this: 'The pretended treaty of Tien-Tsin, signed by a mandarin named Li Hung-chang and a ship captain named Fournier, has just as much value as one which I might sign with a German whom I might meet on the boulevards and who pledged to restore Alsace and Lorraine to us.' " Whatever Ferry might say, Rochefort assured his readers, China had betrayed no one—because she had signed no convention. He finished by accusing, not China, but the French government of treason.[79]

Ferry was so infuriated by the turn of events that he let his anger get the better of his judgment. Without consent of Parliament, which was then on vacation, he ordered naval retaliation against Chinese ports and the arsenal at Fouchow. The Leftist attack upon Ferry, led by Clemenceau, grew shriller, and he was accused of being the dupe of Bismarck and of wanting to divert popular attention abroad in order to avoid promoting social reforms. The Right was ever willing to give Ferry trouble in repayment for his anticlericalism. Even so, he won a substantial vote of confidence in November of 1884. This victory encouraged him to increase military pressure upon the Chinese, and French troops crossed the southern Chinese frontier. To encourage the Chinese to come to terms, he then dropped his demand for an indemnity and seemed on the verge of obtaining peace.

But Ferry's luck ran out a third time. The Chinese military, which had not been informed of the imminent cessation of hostilities, passed to the offensive on March 22, 1885, forcing the French to retreat. The French press blew up in alarm, ignored the good state of the French forces and that an agreement with China had been reached, and predicted catastrophe. The parliamentary opposition jumped at the opportunity, and Ferry could not well defend himself because his agreement with the Chinese was not yet on paper. Clemenceau heaped abuse upon him and the moderate Alexandre Ribot asked for his resignation: "You must resign. You owe it to the Chamber whom you led without telling it where you were taking it. You owe it to the Republic on whom you have inflicted the first of her humiliations." [80] Ferry's ministry was thus overturned on March 30, 1885.[81] His real mistake had been to wage war without parliamentary consent, for the Chinese indeed recognized the French protectorate over Annam on June 9, 1885.

The real humiliation, thus, came not to the Republic, but to the Opportunists, whose prestige suffered despite the victory for their colonial policy. Ferry had come to be called *le Tonkinois*. Rochefort styled him "the last of the cowards," a description that Rochefort could not have believed, since as late as 1884 he had commented on Ferry's courage at the time of the Government of National Defense.[82]

By 1885, Rochefort was in serious danger of becoming both a man without a party and a man without an income. He had made good on his promise in 1880 not to reconcile himself to Opportunism and had hurled more than enough mud at its chief representatives, Gambetta and Ferry; and he never shrank from an opportunity to abuse anyone even remotely associated with the reduction of the Commune. Yet he did not enjoy the confidence of the Left, which had had its doubts about him ever since his performance at the Noir funeral in 1869 and his tightwire act of ambiguity in 1870–71; and he had fairly well exhausted the credit to be squeezed from his pose as a victim of a politically inspired court, especially in the light of mounting evidence that he himself was a monument of selfishness and vindictiveness.

Perhaps Rochefort could still excite those professional radicals whom Paris always housed and who could be rallied by any nitwit with a desire to regain Eden by no later than the following Friday, but the intellectual radicals found him tiresome. "Words get their meaning from those who pronounce them," wrote the Socialist Jules Guesde. "And when Rochefort, who jokes about 'the theories that I parade from meeting to meeting and which are impossible to refute because nobody understands them,' then becomes the master-in-socialism who needs 'ten minutes to solve the social question' and resolves it later in five words: 'bread for one cent'—I smile, and I am not alone." [83] Rochefort's response that Guesde was an imbecile fooled no one at *L'Intransigeant* into thinking that Rochefort had had the better of the exchange,[84] and the staff was made uneasy by the knowledge that ridicule cannot indefinitely overpower common sense.[85]

One staff member had quit in disgust at the time of Joseph Reinach's exposure of Rochefort. Another member, Alphonse Humbert, resigned in 1883, not because of any one incident, but after a series of minor matters dating from his first day on *L'Intransigeant*. His chief complaint was that Rochefort could not bear contradiction, that he demanded complete respect for his authority as editor-in-chief but could not be counted on to support his staff members loyally.[86] Subscriptions continued to fall off, until by the beginning of 1884 they were a bare 13,000.[87] By mid-year, Rochefort attempted to cut salaries on the paper in half but had to restore them several days later to avoid immediate collapse.[88] His bad humor increased along with the paper's debts, and he blamed everyone on the staff except himself.[89]

One must agree with some of the radical journalists of the day that Rochefort's scandalmongering after 1880 was only in part a matter of politics and of revenge. He sought notoriety in order to revive the sagging interest in his paper,[90] and he was utterly indifferent, as in the days of *La Lanterne,* to any consideration of good taste. After Olivier Pain was reported shot in the Sudan for anti-British activity, Rochefort worked hard to foment demonstrations at the British Embassy. "Generals who pay bashibazouks to shoot a defenseless Frenchman," he wrote, "are worthy of the old Queen who has taken one of her servants as a lover." [91]

Vociferous nationalism was the final element in Rochefort's profile. If he opposed the French ventures into Tunisia and Tonkin, it was not as a merchant of goodwill. He had resigned from the National Assembly in 1871 in an emotional protest against the cession of Alsace and Lorraine, and like many others of the Left he saw colonial adventures as deflecting French military energies from their proper target. When Italy responded to the French protectorate over Tunisia by allying herself to Germany and Austria, Rochefort became as outspokenly anti-Italian as he had earlier been enthusiastic for the country of Garibaldi. He described King Umberto of Italy as a vile German. Of course, he added, a government is not the same as a people, and Umberto had separated himself from the Italians in the way that the French were separated from their government under the Second Empire.[92] He received enough letters from Italy to suggest that not all the Italians felt themselves to be separated, and one Italian army officer, Lieutenant Gianni Bettini, came to Paris to demand recompense. Rochefort refused his challenge on the grounds that Umberto could fight his own duels, and he washed his hands of the rest by writing that "it is the privilege of well-known men to be the prey of cranks." [93] It was a point on which Umberto and he could have agreed.

CHAPTER VII

Boulanger

1885-1889

He presented himself as Caesar, lived as Catiline, and succumbed as Romeo!

SÉVERINE

PARLIAMENTARY elections were scheduled for the autumn of 1885, to be followed in December by a renewal of the presidency. In March of that year, the *scrutin de liste* had been revived, shortly before Jules Ferry gave way to the Brisson government; for Gambetta was now dead, and the danger of dissolution had gone with him. Thus, the Republicans could go to the polls that year with the electoral form to which they had been traditionally attached. On the other hand, the Republicans did not find it possible to make a common cause, so that in most departments there was both a Radical list and an Opportunist list, and occasionally a Socialist list. In contrast, the Monarchists and Bonapartists tried to make a common cause against the Republic and were often successful in presenting one list under the heading *Union conservatrice.*

194

Rochefort's decision to present himself for election was probably a device to recapture public attention. Evidently he hoped to secure a place on the Radical list in Paris that Clemenceau was recruiting, but he was denied a spot and finished up on a Socialist list called Guesdist-Blanquist.[1] (Jules Guesde was a Marxian socialist, the Blanquists essentially professional revolutionaries.) Though he said nothing about it in his memoirs, Rochefort was last on this list of thirty-eight candidates to be elected in the second balloting.[2] Rochefort represented the Blanquist element on the ticket, then led by Dr. Edouard Vaillant.

The Conservatives made great gains in the elections of 1885. Rochefort attributed these gains to public reaction against the Tonkinese expedition,[3] but the usual assumption today is that the crash of the Union Générale was the chief cause of the swing to the Right. In the first balloting, the Conservatives won 177 seats to only 129 for the Republicans. But while the Conservative vote was indeed higher than it had been in 1881, the fact that the total Republican vote in 1885 was 55 per cent of the total clearly showed that Republican divisions had cost them many seats. The Republicans were forced to coalesce for the runoff elections on October 18, when they won 243 seats to only 25 for the Conservatives. The Republicans, therefore, emerged from the elections with a solid majority in the Chamber, but the Conservatives held roughly one hundred more seats than they had in 1881. What is more, the power within the Republican majority had shifted to the Left, for in the combined Republican lists, radicals had often been favored over the moderates. The result was a built-in parliamentary instability, for the moderate Republicans in the center, henceforth known as the *Union des Gauches,* had only about 200 members, while the monarchical Right contained an equal number and the radical Left about 125.[4]

The National Assembly met on December 28, 1885, to name the President of the Republic. The Republican majority reelected Grévy rather than risk a fight over this grand old man of French republicanism. Premier Brisson, who had hoped to be elevated to

the presidency, was greatly disappointed, and recognizing the diffi-
culties he was about to experience with the new Chamber, he re-
signed. Freycinet then managed to form his third government on
January 7, 1886, and he took as his Minister of War a protégé of
Clemenceau, General Georges Boulanger, hoping thereby to rally
Radical support to his middle-of-the-road regime.

Rochefort's single reason for entering the Chamber was to
gain notoriety for himself by introducing a full amnesty bill. Not
only was Berezowski, a would-be assassin of Napoleon III, still in
jail, but a number of coal miners, detained after the strike at the
Anzin mines in 1884, were still imprisoned. In 1884 Rochefort
had raised money through *L'Intransigeant* for the striking miners
and had gone off to the Department of Nord to deliver the money
in person, accompanied by Maurice de Talleyrand-Périgord.[5] Now,
in 1886, Rochefort meant to deliver the miners from jail. His proposal to bring the amnesty measure up for debate, however, was
crushed 347 votes to 116, the government making it a vote of confidence. Rochefort thereupon repeated his performance of 1871
by resigning from the Chamber at once.[6] There could no longer be
any doubt that Rochefort was no politician. "I have promised to
give my constituents an amnesty," he wrote the presiding officer of
the Chamber. "I have not been allowed to give it to them. I am,
unhappily, too far along to lose four years of my life in battles in
which I see myself destined to be perpetually beaten."[7] Shortly
after, he gave a speech in which he claimed that recent cabinets had
neglected the social problem because they regarded the people as a
mass of animals. For the same reason, they had been sending many
young and brave soldiers to the slaughterhouse of Tonkin.[8]

These were not the only issues Rochefort brought up in the
aftermath of his resignation: He added anti-Semitism. If anti-
Semitism became more militant in France only after the crash of
the Union Générale, we must suspect that Rochefort was strongly,
if not openly, anti-Semitic long before that event. For even if there
were no evidence of that passion—which there is—it would be hard
to imagine that a man as filled with hatreds and suspicions as Roche-

fort would stop short of that classic opportunity for their expression. He was not an anti-Semite because of Jews, but an anti-Semite because of himself. As Jean-Paul Sartre said, "If the Jew did not exist, the anti-Semite would invent him." [9]

But we need not speculate about this matter. In his memoirs Rochefort described a dinner at which he and Victor Hugo, who had the ability to think in verse, talked about French finance and the Jewish peril, whereupon Hugo recited four rhymed lines about Achille Fould, the Jewish Minister of Finance under Napoleon III.[10] Scattered throughout Rochefort's memoirs are fond references to North African Arabs, and he described Adolphe Crémieux's decree of 1870, which granted French citizenship to the Jews of Algeria, as "monstrous" and providing for the ruin of that country forever. He thought that Gambetta, who was of Genoese origin, was really Jewish and had a deep prejudice favoring his former coreligionists.[11] Joseph Reinach, Gambetta's associate and Rochefort's exposer in 1880, was a Jew, a fact that struck Rochefort as significant. By the time Rochefort resigned from the Chamber in 1886, his prejudices were so well known that one editor could write: "I bet my collaborator, Louis Launay, even money that at the first political or electoral obstacle, M. Henri Rochefort, who, in the steeple-chase of October 18th, had difficulty following the pack and who has never forgiven the Jews for being persecuted by his ancestors the marshals of France, would call me a Jew. He calls me Hebrew. . . . I must say that Louis Launay paid off without waiting for the *I told you so.*" [12]

Rochefort's attention next fell on General Boulanger, the new Minister of War in the Freycinet cabinet. Boulanger was a handsome, dashing creature—just the man, in Clemenceau's view, to restore the prestige of the French army against the day when the colonial Opportunists could be driven from office to be replaced by those who thought in the direction of the Vosges. Although the Opportunists argued that the colonial ventures would revive the national strength and verve, the Radicals continually accused them of being the dupes of Bismarck. Boulanger's other recommendation to Clemenceau was his reputation for being Radical Republican, perhaps the only general of this political belief in the army, or so Clemenceau told Rochefort.[13] Boulanger thus presented an opportunity to republicanize the army as well as restore its prestige. These goals were to be achieved by Clemenceau through Boulanger, however, as Clemenceau did not think highly of Boulanger's abilities, in fact believed him to be mediocre in ability and called him *Boulboul* behind his back.[14]

The new Minister of War had served in Africa, Italy, and Cochin China under the Second Empire, had fought as a colonel in the defense of Paris, and had had the good fortune to be wounded there so that he escaped any association with the subjection of the Commune. Toward the end of 1871, however, the commission to revise army ranks felt that he had been promoted too swiftly and reduced him to the grade of lieutenant colonel. Furious, he resigned from the army; but the Minister of War, General de Cissey, persuaded him to stay on. His rancor nevertheless remained, and he wrote several weeks later that "after despondency has come a sort of cold fury against those who have done me so much ill and against those who have aided them. And so, I sense the real reason that has kept me in the army: I want to be able to gain vengeance, and, that day come, I shall be merciless, I beg you to believe it." [15] Fifteen years later he was Minister of War at the age of forty-nine.

His immediate reforms were trifles, but important trifles. After the Franco-Prussian War, France had abandoned her professional army for one based on universal service, and the new type of army required higher standards of hygiene and comfort, not to speak of more flexible discipline. At about the time Boulanger took over the administration of the army, reforms to that effect were just being instituted. It was his good luck to complete them and to get the credit, for there is no question that the morale of the army improved.[16] Upon assuming office, he also transferred a brigade of cavalry known to be especially monarchical in sentiment from Tours to Nantes—in other words, farther from Paris.

Because of the Conservative gains in the elections of 1885,

talk of a possible restoration revived. Some Republicans, including Boulanger, thought it was time to exclude members of former reigning families from France. But Freycinet thought that was unnecessarily extreme until, on May 15, 1886, the Comte de Paris gave a magnificent wedding reception for his daughter that was practically royal and seemed designed to belittle the humdrum formalities of the Republic. There were altogether too many members of the *haut monde,* the diplomatic corps, Parliament, and the army at the reception for the Republicans' taste, and they reacted by passing the exclusion law of June 23, 1886. Pretenders and their direct heirs were immediately banished. Other princes of the pretending families were denied entry into the army and other public services, though the rights of those already in service were preserved.[17]

Boulanger seized the occasion to prove his republican zeal. Without even consulting the Prime Minister, he struck from the ranks of the army the Orléans and Bonaparte princes: General of Division Duc d'Aumale, Colonel Duc de Chartres, Captain Duc d'Alençon, Reserve General Duc de Nemours, Brigadier Prince Murat and his son, a lieutenant. Boulanger had clearly exceeded the law, and the Duc d'Aumale wrote a public letter to the President of the Republic on July 11: "You are striking at the foundation of the army. . . . [As the] ranking officer on the General Staff, having fulfilled in peace and war the highest functions that a soldier can exercise, it is my duty to remind you that military grades are out of your reach, and I shall remain: Le général Henri d'Orléans, duc d'Aumale."[18] The government felt forced to back up Boulanger, and Aumale was expelled from France by decree on July 13. This apparent Republican victory was to be celebrated the following day.

A great military review was held at Longchamp, and Boulanger appeared on his black horse Tunis. He was acclaimed, while poor President Grévy was ignored, and the Republican politicians suddenly were aware that, though Napoleon III and Gambetta were dead, a new man had arrived who had captured the hearts of the people, a man on horseback. Boulangism was born.

The Royalists, of course, were irate, and one of them, Senator Baron de Lareinty, accused Boulanger of cowardice. This led to the anticipated duel, which was fought with pistols and resulted in no bloodshed. Boulanger's pistol, however, failed to fire, a revealing omen for those who looked for one.[19]

Far more serious was Boulanger's reaction to the Duc d'Aumale's next move. Toward the end of July, 1886, Aumale published a letter he had received from Boulanger on May 8, 1880, in which Boulanger thanked the Duke for having had him named a general, adding: "Blessed will be the day when I shall again be able to serve under the orders of Your Royal Highness." Boulanger at once protested its publication, after which Aumale's lawyer admitted that the text had been faulty and published the correct version: "I shall always be proud to have served under such a chief as you, and blessed will be the day that I am recalled under your orders." Boulanger again denied the authenticity of the letter, adding to the now established fact of his ingratitude a lack of devotion to truth.[20] There is no evidence that the general public much cared, but Boulanger's political associates began to see his character in a new light.

Boulanger was not only identified as a Republican, but with the radical wing of the party. This meant that as he became a popular, heroic figure, the anti-Opportunists rallied to him as the leader who might rid them of the hated parliamentarians and at the same time achieve the military revisions originally planned by Clemenceau. Rochefort, who had seen Boulanger only once before 1886, offered him his support against a probable Opportunist-Conservative coalition,[21] as did Paul Déroulède, head of the Patriots' League, who urged Boulanger to suppress the parliamentarians and establish authoritarian power.[22] Déroulède had been known since the 1870's as a nationalistic hothead bent on revenge against Germany, and he had been one of the founders of the Patriots' League in 1882.

It is important to emphasize that Boulangism was more than an expression of indignant nationalism. We have noted before that after 1871 the Opportunists had necessarily been primarily concerned with establishing a durable Republic against formidable odds in the aftermath of shattering defeat and civil war. As a result, they had neglected social and economic problems, and they had also shied away from a renewal of an unequal conflict with Germany. Accordingly, the Opportunists were seriously vulnerable to complaints and jeers, which Madame de Séverine well summed up in her *Notes:* "Boulangism means disgust, not with the Republic, God knows; but with *your* Republic; with the Republic as made by your friends; with this bastard regime, without heart or guts, which, in seventeen years, has done nothing for the poor, nothing for the people, nothing for those to whom it owes everything."[23]

The Freycinet government did not last out the year, but fell in December over economic and financial squabbles. The cabinet was reshuffled, with René Goblet taking the prime ministry; but most of the ministers, including Boulanger, stayed on. Boulanger's survival as Minister of War was bad news for Bismarck, who was already troubled by tense relations between Russia and Austria, and whose *Dreikaiserbund* was in 1886 again in difficulty over the Bulgarian question. Though Bismarck knew that Grévy and the majority of the French cabinet were for peace, Boulanger's presence in the Goblet government suggested that there was danger of war over Alsace-Lorraine. Certainly the Boulangist press anticipated war. Rochefort wrote that in the forthcoming conflict, Italy would be an ally of Germany, having been promised Nice, Savoy, Corsica, and Provence by Bismarck. He also claimed to know that the German government had alerted the Red Cross to prepare its field hospitals. Happily for France, he concluded, the Bazaines, the Trochus, and the Bourbakis were all gone; and since the Republican leadership in Parliament was not trusted by the people, he predicted that the Chamber would be dissolved by the people in the event of war. He did not specifically mention Boulanger as the alternative to the Chamber, but his readers could get the point.[24]

Considering the militant climate, Bismarck meant to get increased military funds from his parliament, and in his Reichstag speech of January 11, 1887, he tried to frighten the lukewarm deputies. "Under no circumstances will we attack France," he said. "On their side, the majority of the French do not wish to attack us. But in difficult moments, France has always been led by determined minorities. There exists in France men who seek a war against Germany and whose task is to promote the sacred fire of Revenge."[25] Boulanger's response was to call up reservists, an order that a horrified Grévy forced him to cancel. When Boulanger threatened to resign, Grévy agreed that the time had come for him to do so. But Boulanger stayed on.[26] Almost to prove Boulanger's extremism, the Reichstag rejected Bismarck's military budget and was dissolved for its resistance.

Rochefort kept up the drums, nevertheless, insisting that Bismarck sought to foment war, claiming that within a month there would be a deliberate border violation designed to draw French fire.[27] His claim is the more interesting, because it makes us wonder whether Rochefort knew that General Boulanger, without informing his colleagues in the cabinet, was using French border commissioners as part of his espionage system in Alsace-Lorraine. This could easily lead to border incidents, as indeed it did in April of that year.[28] Meanwhile, Bismarck secured a more pliant Reichstag which, in March, voted him the military funds he desired.

This border incident of late April, 1887, more generally known as the Schnaebele affair, is a splendid example of how easily the public can draw all the wrong conclusions from an incident involving foreign relations. Schnaebele was a frontier officer stationed at Pagny-sur-Moselle, a village southwest of Metz. German Intelligence had discovered that he was an intermediary for French spies working in Alsace and for Alsatian irredentists, and a trap was laid. On April 20, the French government received contradictory information: one report indicated that Schnaebele had crossed the frontier by invitation and had then been arrested; the other report indicated that German agents had seized Schnaebele on French territory and had whisked him across the border. Rochefort rather predictably believed the second report and likened the deed to Napoleon's illegal seizure of the Duc d'Enghien from Baden in 1804.[29]

On April 23, the French cabinet met to discuss the crisis, and

Goblet and Boulanger were all for sending the Germans an ultimatum. President Grévy suggested that it might be wise to wait for
an official German explanation, a suggestion that the Foreign Minister backed. After conducting an inquiry, the Germans admitted
that Schnaebele had crossed the frontier on invitation, which Bismarck chose to regard as a safe-conduct pass. Thus, Schnaebele
was released on the thirtieth, and the affair was finished except for
two conflicting repercussions: The French public chose to see it
as a great French victory in which their *brav' général* had forced
Bismarck to back down; while most French politicians finally had
their eyes opened—the Radicals excepted—as to the seriousness of
Boulanger's tactics and the feebleness of his judgment. What they
began to learn from the Duc d'Aumale's exposé was baldly revealed
as the truth about Schnaebele's inspiration was unveiled; for the
French government agreed with Bismarck that Boulanger had used
Schnaebele improperly. Boulanger would have to go, but because
of his booming popularity, the whole cabinet would have to go
with him.[30]

All that remained was to find some pretext to bring down the
Goblet government, and it was found in the complaint that the
government was not encouraging sufficient economies in the budget.
Goblet evidently never did realize that he was a victim of a trans-
action designed to oust Boulanger without making him a martyr.[31]
Rochefort, more practiced at sensing conspiracies, was sure that
one had taken place.[32] The government fell on May 18, after which
there ensued a two-week cabinet crisis over whether Boulanger
should be included in the new government. In that interim, a by-
election was held in the Seine (May 23, 1887), and Rochefort
asked his readers to write in Boulanger's name on the ballot to
make clear the public's wish to have him in the cabinet. Although
Mesureur, the actual Radical candidate for the seat, was elected,
39,000 ballots carried Boulanger's name. This was too much for
President Grévy, who proceeded to form an Opportunist cabinet
under Maurice Rouvier with support from the Right. This government was formed on May 30.[33]

On that day, the ex-Minister of War sent a message to the

troops: "You will be, under my successor's orders, what you have been under mine: devoted to your professional duties and faithful to the constitutional laws, the respect for which much dominate all other sentiments in your hearts. I shall be the first to give you the example of this double military and republican discipline." [34] Despite this statement of devotion, Boulanger at first refused to accept a regular military appointment appropriate to his rank, but the Rouvier government was determined not to have him in Paris for another Fourteenth of July celebration and forced the command of the XIII Corps at Clermont-Ferrand upon him. Ostensibly it was a promotion, since he had never before commanded even a division; but the Radicals saw the appointment as the deportation it really was. His train was to leave on the evening of July 8, 1887, from the Gare de Lyon, and Paul Déroulède and his Leaguers were out in force when Boulanger emerged from the Hôtel du Louvre to make his way to the train. Their violent demonstrations convinced Clemenceau that he had been promoting a dangerous man. Boulanger's rashness at the time of the Schnaebele affair had worried Clemenceau; the Gare de Lyon scene completed the rupture. He made it clear in parliamentary debate that Boulanger had lost his support. Déroulède and Rochefort were thus left as the leading Boulangists. [35]

Rochefort's analysis of the cabinet crisis that forced out Goblet and Boulanger bears examination. He wrote that during the cabinet crisis "German financial Jewry" were under orders from Bismarck. Since the French stock market was controlled by German Jews, they were ordered to manipulate the market, high or low depending upon whether Boulanger seemed to be out or in. Thus could Bismarck rid himself of his most dangerous enemy! As for the Frenchmen, Rochefort explained that President Grévy had long been jealous of Boulanger for dimming presidential popularity, while Baron Jacques de Reinach (both uncle and father-in-law of Joseph Reinach) had a grudge against Boulanger for preventing a fraud in coffee supplies Reinach had offered to the army. [36] Rochefort offered no evidence to back up these charges.

Whatever Boulanger's popularity, Rochefort does not seem to have enjoyed much, though he had certainly gained the public eye. In May, during the cabinet crisis, he published the fact that the French Federation of Socialist Workers had refused in 1884 any further patronage by *L'Intransigeant*. (They were moderate, "gas-and-water" socialists, sometimes known as Possibilists or Broussists.) Yet, Rochefort added, one of their number, Jules Joffrin, had come in person to the offices of *L'Intransigeant* to ask that he continue to receive the paper's backing.[37] An angry Joffrin then published an open letter to Rochefort in a number of journals. This letter was less than flattering, and, moreover, it recalled Rochefort's relations with the Left: "The public will judge between your statements and mine. Some samples: In January, 1870, you said . . . that Vermorel . . . was a police spy: You lied! In February, 1871, you refused to include on your journal's list Auguste Blanqui, saying that he acted basely with Barbès in May, 1839, and you added Taschereau's calumnies to yours: You lied! The 29th of October, 1870, you affirmed that Bazaine had not capitulated: You lied! In '81, you denied having written a letter to Gambetta: You lied! You say that in '84 I asked to be listed by your journal: You lie! . . . And finally, Monsieur, you affirmed at the time of your polemic with M. Jules Guesde, that you had in your desk the proof that my former comrade in proscription, Jules Vallès, worked for the municipal police: Again you lied!"[38]

Rochefort, who usually required far less provocation as an excuse for a duel, softly suggested that Joffrin come to his office to see the original correspondence.[39] Joffrin, sensing his advantage, explained further that he had gone to the offices of *L'Intransigeant* in 1884, but to protest his inclusion on its electoral list, which had put him in a false light.[40] Two days later, he struck again, calling Rochefort *"le bookmaker"* and reminding the Left of Rochefort's "cowardice" on January 10 at the burial of Victor Noir: *"Cette maladie d'entrailles."* [41]

Though *L'Intransigeant* reported that Rochefort was cheered at the military review on Bastille Day, 1887, along with shouts of

"Vive Boulanger!," several newspapers reported the contrary, noting cries of *"À bas Rochefort!"* One paper added that Rochefort was right to leave midway through the ceremony, as he had no place there.[42] Rochefort responded: "After abasement comes infamy. The cry *Vive Boulanger!,* presumably meaning *À bas Grevy!,* is now listed among the most seditious [of shouts]. The era of persecutions is upon us."[43]

Shortly after, Jules Ferry gave a speech in Épinal, July 24, 1887, in which he referred to Boulanger as a "night-club Saint-Arnaud." (Saint-Arnaud was Minister of War at the time of Louis Napoleon's *coup* of December 2, 1851.) From Clermont-Ferrand, Boulanger sent two seconds, General Faverot and the self-titled Comte Dillon, to Ferry to demand reparation through arms. Ferry refused the challenge because Boulanger's seconds imposed drastic terms that did not conform to the established code of dueling: an unlimited number of bullets to be fired until one participant should be hit; then a final exchange with one bullet at twenty paces. Ferry's seconds would only agree to the same terms used in the Lareinty-Boulanger duel, and that Boulanger's seconds rejected. Rochefort commented: "Since yesterday, Ferry has risen in rank: He was the last, he is now the first of the cowards."[44]

It is entirely conceivable that Boulangism would have faded away, due to the semiexile of the hero and Rochefort's unpopularity, had not the government itself become the focus of a new and humiliating scandal in the fall of 1887. The Wilson affair gave the Boulangists a new opportunity. Daniel Wilson, of Scottish origin, had been in French politics since 1869 and had early earned a reputation for dubious electoral maneuvers. In 1881 he married the daughter of President Grévy, whose personal hostility to Gambetta Wilson shared. Wilson had then taken up residence at the Élysée Palace, where the presidential façade served to protect the shady business deals in which he engaged. The discovery of one of his rackets, a traffic in decorations, grew out of a police investigation into another matter.

On the eve of army maneuvers, a newspaper had published

some information on the mobilization of the XVII Corps, information that was supposedly secret. In the consequent investigation, the police were led to the home of a woman from Limousin. Thinking that the investigating agent was a customer for a Legion of Honor medal, she discussed the price with him, and he led her on to see what governmental associates she had. The closest was General Caffarel, an officer on the General Staff. Both were arrested on September 29, 1887, and letters that compromised some rather lofty individuals were seized in both their homes: General Boulanger; General Comte d'Andlau, a Senator from Oise; Baron de Mackau, a leading Royalist in Parliament; General Thibaudin, a former Minister of War; and the Deputy Daniel Wilson.[45] A formal legal inquiry began on October 9.

Two of the letters concerned Boulanger, but there was nothing damning in them.[46] Boulanger rightly protested his innocence, but his telegram to the Minister of War, Ferron, was insolent in tone and forced the Minister to discipline him with thirty days of close confinement. Naturally the Boulangists were led to suspect that the Rouvier government expected to saddle Boulanger with the guilt for the scandal then being uncovered.

General L'Andlau, meanwhile, appeared at the legal inquiry to protest his innocence. Then he abruptly fled to Argentina, where he died in poverty seven years later. The trial began on November 7, and the Limousin woman was given a sentence of six months in jail, General Caffarel a fine of 3000 francs, and General d'Andlau, *in absentia,* five years in prison, 3000 francs fine, and the loss of civil rights for ten years. But what of Daniel Wilson, who legally could not be served a summons as long as he lived in the presidential palace? He had consented to move to a new private home just built by his father-in-law, who had known nothing of Wilson's traffic and was determined to protect him. This put the Rouvier government on the spot, for the Right seemed likely to withdraw its support, not wishing to be caught in an Opportunist mess, and the Left was delighted with its opportunity. To confuse the issues even more, some Opportunists were happy to see Grévy and Wilson embarrassed, for they had obstructed Gambetta's rise in former years. Unable to bring Wilson to trial immediately, the Rouvier government found itself overturned on November 19, 1887,[47] the motion, as usual, introduced by Clemenceau.

Grévy then began to recognize the seriousness of his personal situation, for he could find no one to replace Rouvier, and on November 27 he indicated that he would resign the presidency of the Republic. But when the Radicals realized that Jules Ferry might be the Opportunists' choice as Grévy's successor, they hesitated in their attack upon Grévy despite his anti-Boulangism.

Rochefort, meanwhile, had been having a field day:

> Grévy de Syracuse, born about 430 B.C., died in 368, has been called a tyrant by inclination, because, while claiming to limit himself strictly to his constitutional role, he nevertheless exercised absolute power. Diodorus of Sicily tells us that Grévy de Syracuse pushed economy to its most extreme limits. One day he had the massive gold cloak covering the statue of Jupiter removed and had it replaced by a plain woolen cloak, "infinitely preferable to the other one which was too cold in winter and too hot in summer." . . . The only thing comparable to his avarice was his cowardice. . . . Following a gathering which took place in the Winter Arena, the people flowed into the streets loudly crying "Long Live Boulanger." Hearing these shouts addressed to this general whom he always feared to see appear at the head of a hundred thousand men to overthrow him at the palace, he was taken with a convulsive shaking and called to his aid, not only Mollard and Wilson, but his entire civil and military household. . . . Finally . . . Grévy de Syracuse was reduced to retiring to the Jura . . . to make himself into a schoolmaster in the village of Mont-sous-Vaudrey. He explained to the children the beauties of opportunism and the advantages of the Tonkin expedition. . . . When he died, they found fifteen million in his mattress.[48]

Suddenly, to avoid Ferry, the Radicals held an emergency meeting on the night of November 28 at Durand's restaurant opposite the Madeleine to see if they could put together an acceptable government that would spare Grévy the necessity of resignation. Clemenceau was there, along with Rochefort, Eugène Mayer, Georges Laguerre, and other Radical notables. The majority felt that if a cabinet including Clemenceau, Boulanger, and Floquet could be assembled, President Grévy could be saved and "Ferry-Tonkin" blocked. Clemenceau, however, was wavering, for he feared Boulanger's ambitions, but this suggested coalition came to nothing when it was discovered that both Freycinet and Floquet were hoping to succeed Grévy, not to save him.[49]

The following night, November 29, the Boulanger clique gathered at the home of Georges Laguerre in the rue Saint-Honoré; this time Boulanger was present, as was the ex-Prefect of Police, Andrieux. Clemenceau was there but would no longer allow himself to be proposed as a member of the new cabinet; for he had decided that Grévy could not be saved and was seeking a compromise candidate. The Boulangists talked about dividing up the posts among themselves, but the evening ended without a final decision. During the evening, Boulanger withdrew for his first meeting with Baron de Mackau, the Royalist leader, out of which grew a plot for a *coup d'état* in favor of the Comte de Paris. The Leftists chattered on in the meantime, unaware that their hero had gone over to the unspeakable Right. Years later, Rochefort would make no mention of it in his memoirs.[50]

On December 2, 1887, Grévy at last gave way, opening the presidency for Clemenceau's compromise candidate, Sadi Carnot. Carnot had a great Republican name and was a brilliant engineer, but he had no particular political talents. His election on December 3 was further sign that Parliament did not mean to allow a man of outstanding political leadership to reach the summit. "Vote for the stupidest," Clemenceau is said to have advised in advancing Carnot, by which he meant the least experienced. Parliament had forced

Carnot's three predecessors from office; now, presumably, it had a figurehead in the office who could not matter.[51] But he was an upright man who represented the best in the Republican tradition, and the Republic was rather in need of a virtuous symbol in 1887. His first attempts to select a Prime Minister failed, until he fell upon Pierre Tirard, a rather inconspicuous member of former cabinets. Tirard formed a cabinet that was largely Opportunist, and his task was somewhat easier, since most of the Radical parliamentary chiefs, following Clemenceau, were no longer promoting Boulanger or his Leftist associates for cabinet posts.[52]

With the new government formed on December 12, 1887, it was possible to continue the investigation of Daniel Wilson. New incriminating documents were produced, and on February 23, 1888, he was sentenced to two years imprisonment, 3000 francs fine, and the loss of civil rights for five years, for his traffic in decorations. A higher court subsequently overruled the verdict. While not denying that his conduct had been abusive, the court ruled that he had not specifically broken any law. Even so, we are entitled to be astonished when we find that Wilson, despite his dishonorable behavior, was reelected to represent Indre-et-Loire and remained in politics until 1902.[53] As the saying went, how beautiful was the Republic under the Empire!

But let us return to Boulanger, whose biographer has so nicely characterized as a Cromwell for the Republicans, a Monk for the Royalists, a Saint-Arnaud for the Bonapartists, General Revenge for the patriots, and Caesar for his country.[54] Clemenceau and most of the Radicals had abandoned Boulanger when they realized that he was not merely anti-Opportunist, but opposed to parliamentarianism; and Boulanger had at once turned to the Royalists as men favoring stronger executive power. Their leader, Baron de Mackau, had come to believe that the throne would never be established except through a *coup d'état*. If the popular Boulanger was being abandoned by the Left, perhaps he could be used temporarily for a restoration of the Comte de Paris. Hence, Mackau, a former Bonapartist turned Orleanist, was willing to receive the recent expeller of the Orléans princes. A second meeting took place in Boulanger's apartment at the Hôtel du Louvre on December 26, 1887, in which the General repeated his willingness to proceed with a *coup* as soon as he could regain the Ministry of War.[55]

But the Bonapartists also hoped to profit from the Wilson scandal and Boulanger's rift with the Left. Their nominal leader, Prince Jerome-Napoleon, then living in Switzerland, had never enjoyed public confidence, even during the Second Empire, so that they saw Boulanger as a possible compromise leader to help them reestablish strong executive power and a plebiscitary Republic. Georges Thiébaud, a young journalist with a personal grudge against the Royalists, took it upon himself to arrange a meeting between Prince Jerome-Napoleon and Boulanger; and despite Boulanger's recent transactions with Baron de Mackau, Thiébaud and Boulanger slipped away from the secret agents watching him and called on Prince Jerome-Napoleon at the Villa de Prangins on the Swiss side of Lake Geneva. Evidently the Prince was friendly enough, but he was quite unimpressed by Boulanger. Out of this meeting on January 2, 1888, came no promises of support.[56]

The government, in the meantime, was perfectly aware through its police that Boulanger had come to Paris on several occasions even though he had been refused official permission to leave his command. They were also aware that he was corresponding with Thiébaud, Déroulède, and the dubious Comte Dillon. In by-elections scheduled for February and March, 1888, Boulanger's name was to be entered in several departments, despite his military position and through no obvious efforts on his part. "My formal wish being, thanks to the situation that I occupy," he wrote to the Minister of War, "to devote myself exclusively to my military duties, I have the honor to ask you, in order to put an end to the demonstrations which have just been manifested and which tend to recur on my behalf, either to be willing to publish this letter or to authorize me to write and publish one in which I should beg my friends not to mislead votes to me which I cannot accept."[57] Rochefort complained that this letter failed to calm governmental fears, which indeed was true.

Nor was the Leftist press any longer under illusions about Boulanger or, for that matter, about Rochefort.

"Well, dear readers," wrote an editor of *Le Prolétariat,* "what do you think now about M. Rochefort and his journal? That his subscriptions are rising? So I hear. On the horizon of the Republic rises the aura of military dictatorship. Everyone sees it. We are on the verge of Brumaire or December. Everyone senses it. The old Republicans . . . squeeze a knife handle or a pistol butt in their pockets. Already there is regicide in the air. M. Rochefort alone, guided by his single preoccupation, printing his paper, defends General Boulanger, the assassin of May, 1871, the quite small Napoleon of tomorrow. M. Rochefort is dishonoring himself." [58]

When Boulanger received between 4,000 and 16,000 write-in votes in five departments in the by-elections of late February, the Tirard government decided to move against him. The first step, on March 17, 1888, was to remove him from the command of the XIII Corps and to put him on detached service at half-pay, thus keeping him politically ineligible. The order, drawn up by the Minister of War, General Logerot, was countersigned by President Carnot.[59] As luck would have it, the Court of Appeal quashed the verdict against Daniel Wilson two days later, undeniably giving the appearance that the government protected slimy swindlers while abusing gallant generals. The Tirard government hardly deserved the title Opportunist!

A few days later, on March 25, the so-called Committee of National Protest entered Boulanger's name in the Aisne by-election, and for the first time he received enough votes to win. The government put him on the retired list the next day even though he had resigned the newly won seat in the Chamber. Their charge against him was that he had left his command at Clermont-Ferrand without authorization. Boulanger's conduct had been sufficiently improper to worry the government about his intentions. Had the government had any idea that he had already begun transactions with the Right, its action might have been more drastic. With his military career at an end, Boulanger now turned to active and open politics.[60]

Who were the Boulangists at that point? Most of the Radicals had abandoned the General, and his Royalist support was still kept secret. Only a small group of journalists and deputies were recognized as Boulangist: Rochefort primarily, along with his associate Eugène Mayer; Thiébaud and Alfred Naquet, the latter a peculiar Jewish chemist, a Radical well along the road to anarchism; and the deputies Laguerre, Laisant, and Laur. Comte Dillon was more or less the manager of the Committee of National Protest with the task of raising campaign money; and Arthur Meyer of *Le Gaulois* helped him get it from the very rich Duchesse d'Uzès, whose money was not so much for Boulanger as against the Republic. Baron Hirsch, the Austrian-Jewish banker, also contributed. One is struck, first of all, by the fact that the inner circle was dominated by anti-Semites and Jews; and, second, by Comte Dillon's task of combining the Extreme Left with the Extreme Right if Boulanger's cause were to be successfully promoted.[61] The party, if one can call it a party, was perilously close to being a coalition of all possible extremes, propelled by the twin monsters, Hatred and Envy.

Four days after Boulanger was abruptly retired from the army, the Tirard government unexpectedly fell after a fluke vote, which was not directly related to the Boulanger affair. It was followed by a government under Charles Floquet, a Radical Republican, on April 3, 1888. Several more by-elections were upcoming, one on April 8 in Dordogne, and one in Nord on the fifteenth. Boulanger, now an acknowledged candidate, won both seats easily and chose the seat of industrial Nord, which he was eligible to take only on June 4.[62] Camille Pelletan, writing in Clemenceau's own paper, *La Justice,* now began a series of articles in which he echoed the line laid down by *Le Prolétariat* in March: "The Rochefort of another day, the Rochefort of last year, . . . would have railed at this Boulangist parade. The Rochefort of today is in it. . . . [Yet], M. Boulanger receives Bonapartist votes. He has the support of M. Émile Ollivier and of M. de Maupas. . . . I ask you [M. Rochefort] if M. Boulanger does not seem to you more Bonapartist than decency will tolerate." [63]

Pelletan kept up the attack in subsequent issues, always asking how Rochefort the Republican could explain the Rightist alliance with Boulanger, be himself allied to Boulanger, and still call himself a Republican! The answer was first given, not by Rochefort, but by another journal: "Even before becoming a Boulangist, M. Rochefort has for a long time been regarded as a reactionary by the advanced elements of his party." [64] Pelletan then spelled his query out more specifically and did get a response from Rochefort. Claiming that Rochefort really had come to prefer the Empire to the Republic as then established, Pelletan asked: "Is not 'Rather the Empire' your motto?" [65] To which Rochefort answered, "We love the Republic too much to ever join [the Clemenceau-Ranc-Joffrin alliance]." [66]

The great day for Boulanger's entry into Parliament came on June 4, 1888. A large crowd gathered to watch his progress from the Hôtel du Louvre to the Palais-Bourbon. Handsomely attired, he drove out into the rue de Rivoli in an open carriage accompanied by several friends. Instead of taking the most direct route, his carriage made a wide sweep through the Place de la Concorde—to the right of the Obélisque—for the benefit of the throng. An estimated 10,000 people were in the Place to give him an ovation. And by one of those marvelous coincidences that are somehow more frequent in Paris than elsewhere, an advertising van heralding a coming circus got itself in front of Boulanger's carriage, so that his progress lacked some of the desired seriousness. [67]

Boulanger rented a charming villa for the summer in the Bois de Boulogne, which became a kind of party headquarters; and nearly every morning, Rochefort and Dillon drove from Neuilly to confer with the General. Their immediate goal was revision of the Constitution to reduce the powers of Parliament in favor of the President of the Republic. [68] Boulanger brought forth such a resolution shortly after taking his seat in the Chamber, widening the gulf between the Boulangists and the anti-Boulangists; for Clemenceau's response was to found the League of the Rights of Man, which was at once anti-Opportunist and anti-Boulangist. On July 12, Boulanger again went to the rostrum, this time to propose both revision of the Constitution and dissolution of Parliament preparatory to new elections.

In the course of this meeting insulting words were exchanged by Boulanger and the Prime Minister, Floquet.[69]

The expected duel followed, before which Boulanger resigned his seat. He was confident of victory over the septugenarian Prime Minister and hopeful that he could increase his authority by running for a new seat in an upcoming by-election in l'Ardèche. To everyone's surprise, the short, stout, aged Floquet gave Boulanger a bad sword cut on the throat, while Clemenceau howled with laughter. This engagement took place on July 14, and its result prevented the General from campaigning in l'Ardèche for the July 22 balloting.[70] He was beaten by a Republican and by all odds should have been finished.

Yet he recovered enough to campaign for three vacant seats in Nord, the Somme, and Charente-Inférieure, which came up for election on August 19; and from the Duchesse d'Uzès he had campaign funds of a size almost unknown in that day and age. There was a time when historians accounted for Boulanger's electoral successes as a measure of the nation's disgust with parliamentary corruption. It is now evident that where he campaigned in earnest and with great ostentation, and where money was spent in large quantities, he won. Where no particular preparations were made, he lost. In the election of August 19, everything possible was done, and he won all three seats.[71] The Republicans knew then that they were in trouble. One fact, however, seemed in their favor. Boulanger's electoral victories had all been provincial, and radical Paris had yet to declare herself. When a seat fell vacant in the Seine later in 1888, the Republicans felt sure that Paris would not desert them, just as the Boulangists could not forget the demonstrations of 1886 in the General's favor.

The battle was now finally joined, the Republicans aware that they were fighting to save the parliamentary Republic, the Boulangists rallying every element of the population that was at all anti-Opportunist, whether for political, social, economic, or religious reasons. Typical of the attacks upon the governing Republicans that autumn was that of Numa Gilly, mayor of Nîmes and a deputy. He called himself a Socialist, but was in fact an irresponsible windbag whose ambitions had led him to clamor aboard the Boulangist bandwagon. In a speech on September 3, he charged that the Budget Committee of Parliament was corrupt: "When one sees into what hands the fortune of France is placed, and who are the men making up this Budget Committee, one shudders at the unrestrained waste which presides over the distribution of the tax income which you have taken so much trouble to pay to the tax-collector. They prosecuted Wilson—pure comedy—in order to have it believed that they are more honest than he. But, out of thirty-three members on the Budget Committee, you have at least twenty Wilsons." [72]

Though Gilly offered no sustaining evidence, Rochefort instinctively believed his charges, even after Gilly subsequently published as proof a threadbare collection of hearsay entitled *Mes Dossiers*. The one interesting feature of that piece of literature was the author of its preface, Auguste Chirac, a notorious anti-Semite.[73]

The anti-Boulangists kept up a counterattack in their drive to win the vacant Parisian seat, especially trying to embarrass Rochefort. A committee was formed to raise funds for a monument to Victor Noir; and if *L'Intransigeant* refused the committee publicity, a public meeting was to be held for the announcement. A Leftist paper carried a story about the unsavory history of the Victor Noir memorial. Henri Rochefort, the article claimed, had recently admitted raising, in the spring of 1870, a total of 13,301 francs for the Noir funeral monument. Of this, 2,800 francs had been spent on actual funeral expenses and to send witnesses to Tours for the trial of Prince Pierre. The remaining 10,501 francs, thanks to the liquidation of *La Marseillaise,* had been given to Rochefort upon his emergence from prison that fall. Now that a monument committee had been formed, delicately calling itself the Antiplebiscitary League, why should not that money be turned over to the committee? Several other Leftist journals asked the same question.[74] After some weeks, Rochefort decided to give the money up, whereupon the journal initiating the controversy raised a further question: How about the 3 per cent for keeping the money for twenty years? In other words, another 6000 francs! [75]

La Bataille, one of the anti-Boulangist sheets expressly founded with the Paris election of January 27, 1889, in mind, also undertook to embarrass Rochefort. Its founder, Hippolyte Lissagaray, the Marxist historian of the Commune, reprinted testimony given in 1872 before the Commission of Inquiry on the Government of National Defense. The relevant testimony had to do with Rochefort's unsuccessful proposal, on November 1, 1870, to abandon Paris for a more secure city, leaving behind the Governor of Paris, "who will administer [Paris] with all the rigor that a state of siege requires. We shall go to another part of France, where we will be more respected." [76] This would indicate, thought Lissagaray, that Rochefort had always been with Boulanger, "shooter of Parisians." [77]

Rochefort predictably responded by challenging Lissagaray to a duel. This one was fought on Comte Dillon's property in Neuilly, and both Rochefort and Lissagaray were nicked in the brief encounter.[78] Undeterred, Lissagaray began a series of articles on Rochefort's career designed to make it clear that he was not trustworthy. These articles, which all appeared in the week before the election, began with Rochefort's "abandonment of the other radical leaders at the Noir demonstration," and went on to recall his "odious calumny of Vermorel"; his *"indelicatesse"* in revealing Bazaine's surrender of Metz; his pleading letters to Gambetta and Trochu, one of which he denied writing and the other of which was full of lies; his shabby treatment of his fellow escapees from Noumea; his beastly behavior at the time of Albert Joly's death, not to speak of his ingratitude to Gambetta. And finally, the articles pointed out that after his electoral humiliation of 1885, he had seized the first opportunity for revenge, Boulanger, after which his subscriptions had begun to rise. In sum, he was "a true Shylock without the excuse of being a Jew." [79]

The campaign for the Parisian seat was an exciting, fascinating one, with the Republicans confident that Paris, the fortress of the Left, would hardly vote for a candidate so clearly allied with the Right. What they had forgotten, and what Rochefort knew, was that there remained in Paris a residue of bitterness against the Op-

217

portunists for the repression of the Commune. Party dogmas counted for less in the election of January 27 than memories of the Bloody Week. The size of Boulanger's astounding victory, 245,000 to 162,000, over his Republican opponent, Edouard Jacques, suggests that he could have beaten even a more formidable Republican name. Not that Jacques was a nonentity, as he had presided over the Paris city council since 1872 and was president of the Departmental Council of the Seine, but he was not a major party figure.[80] The size of Boulanger's victory was evident by eleven o'clock that same evening, and masses of people jammed the boulevards expecting to see Boulanger ride off to the Élysée Palace to seize the government.

The Boulangists were meanwhile gathering for a victory dinner at the Café Durand. Between thirty and forty journalists and politicians came to acclaim the placid Boulanger and to be greeted by Rochefort, who was all nerves, talking incessantly and stopping only to laugh at his own phrases. When one of the journalists remarked about Boulanger's silence, Rochefort said, "The flag does not need to be articulate." [81] Perhaps not, but at least it has to be shown; and Boulanger could not be budged in the direction of the Élysée. Eyewitnesses differ as to which of the Boulangists present were ready to take to the streets, and different explanations for the General's passivity have been advanced. Did his military discipline make him shrink from an illegal action of such magnitude? Had he concluded that he would gain power legally within six months without a *coup?* [82] Remembering Napoleon III, did he fear the stigma of a *coup d'état?* [83]

Perhaps all those considerations were scrambled in a mind that no one has ever pretended was powerful. But let us consider a simpler fact: The Boulangists had no plan for a *coup d'état!* Despite their months of agitation, they were quite unready for action, a fact that Rochefort freely admitted that night to Frank Harris.[84] Later, Rochefort would claim that if Boulanger had made a move President Carnot would have fled like Louis XVIII.[85] But the success that Rochefort would later recall as a certainty did not seem at all certain at the time. The truth of the matter is that Boulanger was no Louis-

Napoleon, and Rochefort no Morny. This was not because the 1889 team was more scrupulous than the team of 1851, but because the Boulangists, in comparison, were cranky dilettanti whose histrionics were no substitute for political organization and planning. Rochefort, who had done more than his share to blow up the storm, was found wanting when the storm broke. The story is told that when it finally became obvious that Boulanger would not leave the cafe for the Élysée, Thiébaud took out his watch and said, "Five past twelve, gentlemen. Boulganism started to fall on the market five minutes ago." [86] When the General did not even appear at the Chamber next morning to take his seat, the parliamentary Republicans recaptured their courage.

Prime Minister Floquet prepared two measures, one of which was anti-Boulangist, the other directed generally against the Right. The first was a return to the *scrutin individuel* in place of the *scrutin de liste* to prevent the use of the General's name on many ballots to assist his supporters. The Republican coalition passed that bill on February 13, 1889. Floquet also proposed constitutional reform to make the Senate a body elected by universal suffrage, but the Opportunists left him on that issue, joining with the Right, and brought down his government on the fourteenth. The real issues were not those of constitutional reform: Floquet was thought too old to be an effective leader against Boulanger (though he had done well enough with his sword!), and an opportunity had simply presented itself for the Opportunists to regain power from the more radical Floquet.[87] Tirard then formed his second cabinet, which the Radicals supported out of fear of Boulanger.

In his memoirs, Rochefort portrayed his support of Boulanger as support for a providential man who came to give France a true Republic, and he found Boulanger the victim of the old Republicans who were wrong for not following him.[88] This explanation lacks authority for a variety of reasons. Chief of them is that we must suspect that Rochefort saw Boulanger as an instrument *against* the old Republicans; and, second, we have reason to suspect that he was willing to seize upon any issue to revive the sagging interest in

L'Intransigeant. Georges Sorel remarked that "if Rochefort, a thoroughly vulgar character, threw himself into the cause of nationalism, it was perhaps because of commercial spirit. . . . Rochefort thought about the sale of his fake news. He was a paper merchant." [89] Finally, if Rochefort was as devoted to the true Republic as he later professed, why his willingness to stick with Boulanger when the latter's republicanism could only be doubted?

Probably Rochefort was unaware of Boulanger's initial meetings with leaders of the Right in 1888. But Rochefort could no longer be accused of innocence when, on February 28, 1889, Boulanger and he accepted a dinner invitation, and he found at dinner the principal members of the Bonapartist Central Committee.[90] Several weeks later, Boulanger spoke at a banquet in Tours, claiming that while he did not mean to destroy the Republic, he meant to pass it through the crucible to rid it of imperfect elements that had brought only hate, mistrust, and abuse to France. The Republic, he said, must repudiate its Jacobinism, by which he probably meant anticlericalism.[91] Though he spoke as a Republican, the speech had a Bonapartist ring, not Royalist. If the former *lanternier* was made uncomfortable, he did not desert the cause.

The new Tirard government's counteroffensive against Boulangism was led by its new Minister of the Interior, Ernest Constans. Constans, an extremely ambitious and experienced politician, was regarded as a cynical self-seeker and apparently had thrown in his lot with the Republic only after having met Boulanger. His first prosecution was against the Patriots' League and its leading figures, Déroulède, Laguerre, and Naquet. The pretext grew out of a ridiculous incident involving a half-mad Russian adventurer who tried to cross the French colony of Obock with a missionary band bound on introducing the Orthodox faith into Ethiopia. When a French warship fired on them, the Patriots' League accused the government of an unpatriotic action in shedding friendly Russian blood. Constans chose to interpret the League's attitude as encouraging Russia to protest, thus presumably exposing France to a declaration of war. Since the government had not much of a case against the League, we can suspect that Constans really intended to intimidate the Boulangists, to baffle them with maneuvers and rumors. His second tactic was to establish legally the procedure of the High Court. The Constitution had only established the principle that the Senate should constitute the High Court, but had not formulated the actual procedure. Constans thus revealed his probable intention to prosecute Boulanger, not before an ordinary court of law, but before the Senate, a political court, where conviction would be reasonably certain.[92]

The trouble was that though the government had little *documentary* evidence of Boulanger's intentions, the safety of the regime depended upon exposing him; and under those circumstances, a court of law was hardly the desirable setting. Hence, Constans' final move was to let loose a flood of rumors of Boulanger's impending arrest—the Boulangists had no knowledge of what the government really knew—confident that Boulanger's weak character and *actual* guilt would cause him to flee. Constans knew his man. On March 29, the Senate passed the procedural law for the High Court, after which the cabinet voted Boulanger's prosecution, but kept its decision secret. The Attorney-General, Bouchez, resigned in protest against these devious maneuvers, but Constans saw to it that Boulanger was again warned of approaching danger. On April 1, Boulanger crossed the Belgian frontier on a train for Brussels, under the eyes of French police ordered to let him escape. Arrested, he could have become a martyr; in flight, he seemingly admitted his guilt.[93] Some of the Boulangists gave up on him then and there: "He slipped away like an enema," quipped Thiébaud. "He fled like a pimp," was Michelin's verdict.[94]

Boulanger had taken with him only his well-known mistress, Marguerite de Bonemains, and Rochefort believed that she had encouraged his flight because she was fearful he would end in prison. It remained for Rochefort and Comte Dillon to join them in Brussels, for they had also been warned, in Constans' devious way, of impending arrest. Rochefort was extremely pleased with his skill in evading the police whom he had seen watching him, and, happily for his self-esteem, it never dawned on him that he had been allowed to manufacture an elaborate flight.[95] To explain his continuing loyalty to Boulanger, in the face of other defections, Rochefort first tells us that Boulanger had accounted for his "dangerous visit" to Prince Napoleon at Prangins as having no political motive. He claimed that for one in the military profession, the Napoleonic name was a powerful, irresistible magnetism, and that he had gone simply as "the soldier who paid a visit to the nephew of the victor of Austerlitz." Finally, Rochefort explained that Boulanger had fled to Brussels because he realized that it was unlikely he could justify that visit before the High Court.[96] That much, at least, seems to have been probable, but what can be said for the Boulanger version of the Prangins visit or for anyone who would repeat it!

The Belgian exile did not last long. When Boulanger issued a statement to the effect that he had no objection to appearing before a regular French court, but that he rejected the jurisdiction of a Senate comprising men blinded by old grudges and the consciousness of their unpopularity, the Belgian government took offense.[97] After two warnings by Belgian authorities to stop Boulangist traffic between Paris and Brussels went unheeded, the refugees were given, on April 22, a forty-eight-hour notice to leave the country. They departed for England on the twenty-fourth.[98] Rochefort was to go six years without another Parisian lunch.

CHAPTER VIII

Exile Revisited

1889-1895

One must hit hard—with a club, like Rochefort, who has a hundred good ways of calling men thieves. He always strikes the same hammer blows—but always in a new attitude. . . . The era of pinpricks is past. The reader will be entertained only if we hurl immovable objects at each others' heads.

JULES RENARD [1]

THE Tirard government began its prosecution of the departed Boulangists by appointing Quesnay de Beaurepaire as Attorney-General; the former Attorney-General, Bouchez, had resigned rather than proceed with the incomplete evidence the government possessed. Quesnay de Beaurepaire was an unfortunate choice, since he had been a judge under the Second Empire—forced from the bench on September 4—and had returned as a zealous Opportunist in 1878. His devotion to justice was only too doubtful, though he was a useful companion for Ernest Constans. The second step was to ask the Chamber for authority to prosecute Boulanger, in other words, to remove his parliamentary immunity. This authority was readily granted on April 8. On the same day, the High Court was convoked for the twelfth. The Court appointed its board of inquiry, and that board deliberated until July, not giving its report until July 6.[2]

Quesnay de Beaurepaire was really unable to produce satisfactory evidence of either a plot or an attempt against the regime, for the simple reason that regardless of Boulanger's aspirations, he had never actually organized a *coup*. Moreover, the government was still unaware of Boulanger's discussions with Baron de Mackau and Prince Napoleon; though, as noted before, the police had reported his correspondence with men like Déroulède and Thiébaud and dinners with men quite obviously hostile to the Republic. The police also had a file of Boulanger's letters, along with the code to decipher those he wrote to his supporters. The prosecution made the obvious deductions from the evidence it had, and these deductions were apparently reinforced by the flight of the Boulangist leaders, which suggested they were guilty.[3] Lacking clear evidence the government was fortunate that the case did not have to be tried before a jury. Rochefort, Boulanger, and Dillon, of course, were equally insecure. If they had made no overt attempt to overthrow the regime, their excuse was really ineptitude rather than a scrupulous concern for legal procedures. Having not done what they wanted to do and meant to do, they could only fall back upon outraged breast-beating, which happened to be one of Rochefort's most highly developed professional skills.

"I address myself to the public and to its integrity," he wrote, "and I beg it to tell me what it thinks of a government which makes this declaration to a writer: 'You will be free to express your every thought in your journal; only, if it displeases us, we shall prosecute you, not for a press crime, but for an attempt against the security of the state.' The former sharpshooter for the Empress—I mean Q. de Glouvet de Beaurepaire and other waterclosets—has quite precisely revealed this nuance in his prosecutional gibberish."[4] It was the Rochefort of old! And he opened his next article with the name "Postérieur de Beaurepaire."[5] A few days later he mocked "the noble Beaurepaire" for presumably locking up the Rochefort cats as accomplices in Rochefort's attack upon Opportunism. Noting that cats are usually inoffensive and nonpolitical, Rochefort did "admit" that the largest of his three, named Moricaud, often sat on his shoulder while he wrote his articles.[6]

But satire failed to halt the government. On April 30, 1889, the High Court ordered the arrest of Boulanger, Rochefort, and Dillon for "attempts against the security of the state," in violation of Articles 87, 88, 89, and 90 of the Penal Code.[7] The board of inquiry then published a request that the defendants send attorneys to represent them, a request that Rochefort opposed on the grounds that it would be an admission on their part that the High Court was properly constituted and that they were subject to its decisions. "If," he then answered, "as a measure of our conciliatory spirit, it is absolutely necessary for us to engage a defender, we know of only one whom we would prefer to any other. . . . This defender is Cambronne. We should beg him to arrange us in a square; then, as his legal defense, to prepare especially, as his address to the High Court, the word which made him famous."[8] (General Cambronne covered Napoleon's retreat after Waterloo. There is a popular story, probably apocryphal, that when asked by the British to surrender, he shouted *"merde."* Hence, *le mot de Cambronne.*)

Rochefort's troubles were not limited to Paris. Nearly a month after arriving in London, he was driving in a carriage along Regent Street, when he was stopped by a man named Pilotell, who had been a police agent under the Commune in 1871 and had known of the Communal order to arrest Rochefort. Pilotell evidently struck Rochefort with a glove, whereupon Rochefort drew out a revolver and tried to fire. But he was so excited that he failed to remove the revolver from its case, and the London police interfered before any damage was done. At the police station, the revolver was found to be loaded, a fact that did not please the authorities. Rochefort got off lightly only because he was a foreigner; he had to pledge that he would not harm Pilotell and to post a hundred-pound bail as a guarantee against disturbing the peace.[9]

After the board of inquiry had made its report on July 6, 1889, the Attorney-General made public the indictment against Rochefort on the fifteenth. While the indictment was actually read by the Attorney-General, it has been generally accepted that he had the literary assistance of Joseph Reinach in its composition: "For a long time, he [Henri Rochefort] has made a profession of defamation and the appeal to violence. It is known what he did in 1871; but if that sentence has been expunged, the shame remains inexpungable. Boulanger's conspiracy could only have led to civil war, and Rochefort had a definite part in it. But what is inexplicable in this man, whose conduct during the invasion was known to everyone, is his odious affectation of patriotism. It is through the production of articles from *L'Intransigeant* that the Inquiry has best established his participation [in the conspiracy]. Beyond that, it is proper to add that he took a hundred thousand francs from the conspiratorial treasury for his newspaper; and that, from another witness, he confessed his role in these terms: 'Yes, Boulanger has great confidence in me; he does nothing without consulting me.'"

Separate indictments were also read for Boulanger and Dillon, followed by a summation that pertained to all three. They were accused of designing, between 1887 and 1889, a plot "either to destroy or to change the Government, or to incite the citizens or inhabitants to arm themselves against constitutional authority." Rochefort's specific role was described as having, "by culpable stratagems and tricks, provoked criminal attempt, or having given instructions for committing it; and having prepared or facilitated the action and, thus, rendering himself an accomplice of the said crime of attempt as specified above." [10] The complicity of the Right was also mentioned in the indictment, though the names of the Comte de Paris and Prince Napoleon were omitted. [11]

Rochefort's response was given in an interview to a correspondent for the *New York Herald,* but it was reproduced elsewhere. In the first place, he claimed, he had not become a friend of Boulanger until "they began to persecute him." Second, he was convinced that his "real crime" was his articles in *L'Intransigeant.* And, finally, he asserted that "all the main charges in the indictment are absurd." [12]

Nevertheless, the government followed up the indictment with a court order commanding Boulanger, Rochefort, and Dillon to appear for trial within ten days. If they did not, they would be declared rebels against the law, which meant suspension of their civil rights, denial of right to legal action, and confiscation of their property.[13]

Boulanger seems to have had a momentary desire to return to France to face the High Court; perhaps he was confident of public opinion, perhaps he was willing to gamble on the government's case not being well documented. But Rochefort was dead-set against it and predicted that Boulanger would be either poisoned or assassinated by government order if he set foot in France.[14] Moreover, Rochefort seemed confident that in the next parliamentary elections "our friends will be in a majority in the Chamber."[15] Therefore, why take any risk? Consequently, on August 14, 1889, Boulanger, Rochefort, and Dillon were all condemned in default to deportation to a fortified enclosure.[16]

Two days later the three condemned men published a manifesto in which they described their conviction as the product of a pact between the "majority of a dishonored Chamber and a Senate forever condemned by the country. The first said to the second: 'Get rid of men who threaten our reelection.' . . . But this orgy of arbitrary government, of calumny and prevarication is fortunately near an end. . . . We have confidence in the determination of the entire electorate . . . to destroy a filthy dictatorship and restore the honest Republic."[17] The manifesto was signed by all three men, but the literary style hardly hid its author.

Rochefort's verve during this period of flight and prosecution, however, almost did hide the fact of a serious family crisis, which must have touched Rochefort deeply. His elder son, Henri, committed suicide on April 28, 1889, approximately four days after Rochefort's arrival in London. One of the happier facets of Rochefort's character was his fondness for his children. But we also know that of the three, Henri had caused him the most concern, and not without reason, as Henri was the child who had most resembled the father in both appearance and temperament. Some years before, when Henri was fourteen, Rochefort had been criticized for being too lax with the boy, who was described as being lazy and not very bright, in contrast to Octave who was reared separately in the Adam household.[18] We may recall that in 1880, Rochefort was known to have been uneasy about Henri's reputation for wildness and about the unsavory revelations after the suicide of their Swiss maid. It was high time to pack him off to North Africa and military service. Even in Algeria, the troubles did not cease, for late in 1881 Henri tried to cane the editor of *Zéramna* in Philippeville for writing anti-*Intransigeant* articles; whereupon the editor replied with his own cane and gave better than he got.[19] Henri thus added the suspicion of brutality to his reputation for ineptitude.[20]

After his military service, Henri settled permanently in Algeria as a landowner, making only occasional visits to Paris, where he had in fact been at the time of his father's flight. At Rochefort's request, he then hastened his return to Algeria to avoid possible police retaliation, necessarily leaving behind a woman of recent acquaintance. What transpired in the next several weeks cannot be documented, but the police verdict to account for the suicide was disappointment in love rather than dismay at the turn of political events. The body was shipped to France on May 3 for burial on the eighth. Police agents in London were quite certain that Rochefort would not ask for a safe-conduct pass to attend the funeral,[21] even though it was known that the government was ready to grant a pass if he applied for one.[22] He did not. Thus, since Octave had by that time moved to Argentina, only Noémie Dufaux of the immediate Rochefort family was present. A number of Boulangist notables gathered for the occasion, but there was no political demonstration —nor any eulogies, in accordance with a family request. The funeral left more than a faint aura of mystery, naturally, about the strength of family ties.[23]

The general elections, which Rochefort had several times called the opportunity for a Boulangist comeback, were scheduled for September and October of 1889. But Ernest Constans, the Minister of the Interior, was determined to make that comeback as difficult to accomplish as possible. To supplement the earlier abandonment of the *scrutin de liste,* Constans got through a bill that made multiple candidacies illegal, with the result that Boulanger could present himself in only one electoral district, Clignancourt. Worse for his cause, many Rightists were disenchanted with him and stood clear by running as Royalists, Bonapartists, or simply as Conservatives.

In the first round of balloting, on September 22, Boulanger himself won a seat, for which, of course, he was ineligible as a result of his legal status. But Rochefort, running as a Boulangist candidate (Parti National) in the first district of the Twentieth Arrondissement, got only 3606 votes out of 10,443 voting.[24] This particular district then required a runoff election. In the second round of balloting, on October 6, the Boulangist defeat was confirmed. Rochefort was beaten 5843 to 4054, with nearly a fourth of the electorate abstaining. The party won only thirty-eight seats. Some notable figures, it is true, were elected: from Angoulême, Paul Déroulède of the Patriots' League; and from Nancy, Maurice Barrès, who was a Boulangist out of disgust for the regime, personal ambition, and pure dilettantism.[25] But the defeat of the notable Rochefort was an undeniable blow to the party and was not compensated for by Comte Dillon's victory in Morbihan.

The Right as a whole generally lost, too. They had won a total of 201 seats in 1885, but they were now reduced to 172. The "true" Republicans elected 366 members but received only about 53 per cent of the vote in gaining their great preponderance in seats. That relatively small percentage of the vote was only one indication of a general political climate that justified Republican uneasiness. That they had not essentially improved their electoral position over the elections of 1877 and 1885 meant that they were failing to convert dissidents to the Republic. Furthermore, the size of the parliamentary opposition meant that in order to survive the Republic required a coalition of Radicals and Opportunists, and such a coalition was something less than a bedrock foundation. That women did not yet have the vote was the one Republican bright spot, for the clerical tendencies of women and feminine enthusiasm for Boulanger would have given the Right a majority.[26] The Republic, in short, entered the 1890's on tiptoes.

Boulanger and Rochefort regarded the elections as a disaster, and the General joined his mistress, Mme. de Bonnemains, on Jersey, where he had been threatening to go after the first balloting had heralded failure.[27] His departure gave rise to rumors that a rift had opened between Boulanger and Rochefort, but the police were correctly informed that Rochefort continued to admire Boulanger.[28] By that time, of course, Rochefort knew of Boulanger's dealing with the Right; but the variety of explanations Rochefort gave to account for his continuing loyalty to the double-dealing General leaves us but one undocumented conclusion: that Rochefort was more or less willing to ally himself with anyone who would attack the Opportunists, and that his professed devotion to the Republic had come to be an automatic rather than a principled response. In an interview given to French journalists, Rochefort claimed that he had opposed the alliance with "certain Rightists." He concluded the interview by explaining that "he no longer believes in Boulangism or in anything else," except, that is, that he felt certain that war was imminent.[29] A casual remark, perhaps, but quite likely the truth.

His mention of war seems significant, too. In that and subsequent interviews, he made no attempt to hide his opinion that Boulangism was finished for the moment. In case of war, however, which he hoped would not come, he was convinced that the French government would probably flee and would be only too glad to let General Boulanger take charge.[30] We can only wonder what price Rochefort was willing to let France pay for the privilege of seeing the Opportunists in flight.

We need not wonder at all, however, about whether Rochefort developed a sense of guilt about his political past. His articles sent to *L'Intransigeant* from Britain were excessively repetitious, beating the same old horses and reflecting a simple faith in his own righteousness. May 6, 1890: "A great number of our compatriots are victims of a strange mental illness. They believe that there is justice in France." July 9, 1890: "Really, the only punishable fault of the

Nihilists, so viciously sentenced last Saturday, is to have believed that the France of today is the old France, a refuge for the proscribed and friendly to the persecuted." July 10, 1890: "As the government, which is imposed upon us, is careful to hide all that could interest us, we allow ourselves to teach the French what everyone in England knows, namely, that war is imminent."

Soon after, the awful truth about Boulanger and Boulangism came out in print. Beginning in August of 1890, *Le Figaro* ran a series of articles entitled *Les Coulisses du Boulangisme,* which revealed all too clearly Boulanger's association with the Right and his utter unreliability. Even the revelation was somewhat despicable, for the articles were signed by the pseudonym "Mermeix," whose identity was not long kept secret. He was D. C. Terrail, chief editor of *La Cocarde,* who had been elected deputy in October of 1889 as a Boulangist candidate to represent the Seventh Arrondissement— elected with the aid of Royalist money. He denounced the very deals to which he owed his own parliamentary position and justified the condemnation of Boulanger. Indeed, the information he revealed was of book length and provided grounds for prosecuting Rightist leaders like Baron de Mackau, a prosecution that the already shaky government preferred not to pursue. A significant part of Terrail's information came from the Duchesse d'Uzès, whose money had made Boulanger's electoral campaigns possible.[31]

A rash of duels grew out of the ensuing recriminations. Rochefort provoked two of these. The first was with the Bonapartist Thiébaud on September 5, 1890, after a rather embarrassing scramble to find a field of honor near the Belgian-Dutch frontier (duels were illegal in Belgium);[32] the second, with Raoul Canivet of *Le Paris,* was averted by the interference of Belgian authorities. Canivet noted that it was evident from the recent revelations about Boulangism that Rochefort had had a part in the royalist plot. Rochefort responded by saying that Canivet had stolen money from the Association of Republican Journalists three years before and therefore could not be relied upon. Canivet sought Rochefort in Belgium and on September 17 found him in the Ostend Casino, where he slapped

Rochefort with a glove. The Belgian authorities then cited each man for provoking a duel, and the matter was referred to the Tribunal Correctionel de Bruges. At the February 19 hearing, both men were fined ten francs and made to share the court costs.[33] Meanwhile, the Association of Republican Journalists investigated Rochefort's charges and, on October 3, 1890, it expressed its complete confidence in Canivet.[34]

Before his conflict with Canivet, Rochefort gave another interview, in which he was asked to comment on *Les Coulisses du Boulangisme*. Here was another opportunity for him to skate on the pond of equivocation. No, he had not known in advance of Boulanger's visit to Prince Napoleon; and had he, he would have opposed it. That idea, he remarked, came from those who were the first to abandon Boulanger—Thiébaud notably. But then, why should the Opportunists be so upset about the visit? Had not Prince Napoleon usually been called a Republican? As for dealing with the Royalists, Rochefort continued, that was a good thing, for it was intended to avoid the horrors of a civil war and to assure Carnot's election to the presidency. No, in sum, the revelations in *Les Coulisses du Boulangisme* had done nothing to alter his support for Boulangism.[35]

Certain aspects of Rochefort's support, nevertheless, seemed to require clarification. In the indictment of Rochefort, it had been stated that Rochefort had received one hundred thousand francs "from the conspiratorial treasury"; and several articles in the press claimed that what money he received came from the Duchesse d'Uzès, whom we already know as the principal contributor to Boulangism. Police informers also believed that *L'Intransigeant* had received financial gifts from a Royalist source.[36] On September 12, 1890, Rochefort wrote to the Duchess d'Uzès: "I read in the *Siècle* . . . that I received from General Boulanger two hundred thousand francs that you gave him for me. That makes twice that this idiotic calumny has reached my ears. I have not had the honor of meeting you, but if you knew me, you would know that I receive no money from anyone. Neither *L'Intransigeant* nor I touched one penny, not even in reimbursement for the considerable expenses encountered for the General's elections and for the revisionist propaganda, not even the price of a railway ticket or cab fare. I know that . . . you have said things about me which the director of *L'Intransigeant,* M. Vaughan, has asked you, Madame, to be good enough to explain." [37]

The Duchesse d'Uzès responded at once: "I read the letter that you sent to me in the newspapers; [the original] did not reach me. I do not hesitate, however, to repeat what I said to M. Vaughan, director of *L'Intransigeant* as well as former director of the *Petit Lyonnais,* when he came to show me some documents establishing that *L'Intransigeant* had received no sum during the campaign. This exhibition was perfectly needless. I NEVER GAVE ANYTHING TO L'INTRANSIGEANT, NOR FOR L'INTRANSIGEANT. Thus, you received nothing, as M. Arthur Meyer freely declared in *Le Figaro* of Monday, September 8th." [38] At this late date, we can do no more than air the controversy and let the reader draw his own conclusions.

During these months of revelation and recrimination, General Boulanger and Mme. de Bonnemains had resided on Jersey. By 1890 she became ill and steadily declined. In May of 1891, the couple moved to Brussels; but the move did not arrest the fatal illness, and she died there on July 19. Boulanger languished for two and a half months, then went to the Ixelles cemetery and blew out his brains over the grave of his beloved. His last testament, written on September 29, 1891, on the eve of the suicide, made it apparent that he was killing himself, not because he lacked faith in his party's political future, but because he had failed to recover from the loss of his dear friend. A copy of his statement was sent to Rochefort, who received it on the thirtieth. "All my life I have done my duty, nothing but my duty," Boulanger wrote, adding that he had done nothing for which to reproach himself. He asked that his testament be published.[39]

"Hannibal has killed himself," responded Rochefort, "beaten at last by a Scipio. Boulanger succumbed to blows given by German Jews and thieves and highwaymen. . . . This man . . . who was the master of the Republic and whose scruples alone prevented him from seizing it when it was offered to him, will have his legend and will be recorded in history, despite the mud and the excrement which the kept men of the vile press have vomited on him one last time." [40] Rochefort then went to Brussels for the funeral, recording that "all Brussels" turned out to pay homage to the great Republican and to give Rochefort an ovation as he left the cemetery.[41] A large crowd was indeed on hand, but how many there were the merely curious we cannot say. And we find no other mention of an ovation for Rochefort. A year later, he returned to Brussels on the anniversary of the funeral, though there was no public ceremony on that occasion.[42]

With Boulanger gone, there was immediate speculation about a possible amnesty for the other conspirators, and one can find a number of rumors reported in the Paris press by 1892. But Rochefort was doing little to endear himself to the government, and the police had information from staff writers on *L'Intransigeant* to the effect that he was full of an "insane hatred" for Constans, the Minister of the Interior, and that he also feared that Constans would order him assassinated if he were to return to Paris. *L'Intransigeant* itself was having trouble with Rochefort, because his articles had become too extreme to be published and required drastic expurgation.[43] Under the circumstances, it is hardly surprising that the government failed to throw open welcoming arms.

We must now backtrack somewhat to review the history of the Panama Canal scandal, as the Panama mess was contemporary with the Boulanger crisis. And since, as we shall see, the Panama Company was ultimately driven to bribe politicians and newspapers in a desperate attempt to avoid ruin, the corruption opened a new avenue for those already disenchanted with the Republic as then constituted. "This magnificent scandal," as its most recent historian has labeled it, may be thought of as a sequel to the crash of the Union Générale. Both were financial fiascos, both did damage to the Opportunists, and both encouraged the rise of anti-Semitism, setting the stage for a grander crisis, the Dreyfus affair. In each instance, a reasonably sound business prospect was compromised by dubious financing.

Interest in a Panama canal was revived in the 1870's by geographical societies after the opening of the Suez Canal. In 1876,
a new association was established, calling itself the Société Civile
Internationale du Canal Interocéanique, which sent out a small
expedition under a navy lieutenant, Lucien N. B. Wyse, to make
surveys for a canal. It was Wyse who negotiated the concession
from the Colombian government in 1878 under which the work was
ultimately pursued. At that point, the distinguished Ferdinand de
Lesseps, builder of the Suez Canal, entered the picture. When a
committee representing the International Congress of Geographical
Societies reported that a Panama canal would cost roughly 1200
million francs, and that the traffic would be insufficient to pay back
the capital investment, de Lesseps contradicted the committee report and used his prestige to get the Congress to sponsor the project
on May 29, 1879.

De Lesseps then organized the Panama Canal Company,
buying out the Wyse concession for 10,000,000 francs, half of it
in cash and half in stock of the new company. He also paid Co-
lombia the 750,000 francs, as required in the concession contract.
When the initial stock sales in 1879 failed, de Lesseps was led to
announce that the project would not require 1200 million francs,
but only 658 million. A second issue in 1881 then succeeded, and
the company was launched with a capital of 900 million francs. The
project was to require eight years. Yet by mid-1885 only a small
fraction of the digging had been accomplished, at a cost of 495
million.

At that point, the company proposed to raise more capital by
issuing shares that would be won in a national lottery, a method
that required parliamentary sanction. When it was discovered that
the entire Brisson government was opposed to the idea, the company
organized a pressure campaign directed by a banker named Martin,
who enlisted the support of several newspapers, not the least of
which was *L'Intransigeant*.[44] Let us hasten to add that obviously
the canal project was not a wild and hopeless dream, nor was
Ferdinand de Lesseps a crook. But he was aged and stubborn, he
had great faith in his project, and he was essentially indifferent to

costs and matters of money.[45] The pressure campaign was only the beginning of the suspicious use of company funds; but if the ensuing corruption looked like decay, it could also be argued that the scandal reflected the new industrial development, which was a sign of vitality.[46]

The government responded to company pressure by sending an investigator named Rousseau to Panama to report on the situation. His report, which was kept secret, expressed serious doubt that the operation could be completed by those then in charge. But a parliamentary committee that also investigated the operation proved to be more susceptible to company pressure and, in 1886, it recommended that the company be allowed to issue more stock. It was then estimated that the canal would be completed by 1889.

To achieve this parliamentary success, the company used the services of several more promoters: Baron Jacques de Reinach, a devious adventurer named Arton (or Aaron), and an accomplished embezzler named Dr. Cornelius Herz. All three were Jews.[47] How much company money they spent on "promotion" cannot be known exactly, but the best study to date estimates that nearly twenty-two million francs were spent on promotion, half going to newspapers and the remainder to the promoters as commissions.[48] The first major figure to be bought was Charles Baïhaut, the Minister of Public Works, who asked a million for his intervention on the company's behalf but settled for 375,000 francs. Baïhaut then drew up a law to make the lottery legal, which was presented for parliamentary debate on June 16, 1886. Despite the parliamentary committee's favorable report, the general response was unfavorable; and Freycinet, then Premier, forced the withdrawal of the bill the next day.[49]

The company thus had to face the likelihood of no governmental support, and de Lesseps was authorized to float a new bond issue of 600 million francs. Some money was raised, but not nearly enough. The promoters then went into high gear, spending lavishly on newspapers of all political stripes and upon deputies. The Rouvier and Tirard governments were unswayed; but on March 2, 1888, a Radical deputy named Alfred Michel brought to the floor of the Chamber a new proposal to allow the company to hold its lottery. A new parliamentary committee was appointed to investigate the question, and the committee reported favorably only after one member, Sans-Leroy, was bribed handsomely to secure a six to five vote. The law then passed both Houses, with both the cabinet and many members abstaining. This enabled the company to proceed with its new subscription in June of 1888, and seven million francs were spent on publicity to guarantee success.[50]

The funds spent on promotion, legal and otherwise, were nothing compared to the expense of getting stock issued and marketed. If roughly twenty-two million was spent on promotion, it is estimated that another hundred million was spent in getting the stock issued and marketed—more than 9 per cent of all the money raised. That money went into commissions; it did not include any interest on the money borrowed. As the normal commission was then between 1½ per cent and 2 per cent, the really scandalous thing about the Panama affair was the amount paid out in commissions, which averaged about 5.67 per cent. But it was not illegal![51]

Just as the company had hope of salvaging itself with the lottery, Dr. Cornelius Herz went off to Frankfurt, from where he asked Jacques de Reinach to pay the commission owed to him or else face exposure. Reinach panicked and asked de Lesseps for ten million francs to pay off Herz. De Lesseps refused, whereupon those politicians who knew what was going on warned Premier Freycinet of the situation. Freycinet understood the danger at once. If some of the bribes had gone to Boulangist newspapers, most of them had gone to anti-Boulangist papers and politicians. (We must remember that the Boulanger threat was still very much alive in 1888.) Though untarnished himself, Freycinet realized the necessity of keeping Herz quiet; and he met with de Lesseps privately, after which de Lesseps sent Reinach another five million for Herz.

Unfortunately, however, the lottery proved to be a failure, and the Panama Company closed its doors on December 11, 1888. Three days later, a court declared the company bankrupt and named a temporary administrator. A second court action on February 4, 1889, dissolved the company, and a former minister, J. M. Brunet, was named the liquidator. He appointed a board of five to assist him, and they went to Panama to investigate. Returning in March of 1890, they reported that there was no hope of salvaging the project. Worse, the financial picture was shocking. In seven years, 1,434,552,281 francs of French investments had gone into the company, of which only 579 million had been spent on actual construction. At least another 900 million would be needed to finish construction. What had been spent on construction had been badly spent, for the contractors had realized outlandish profits. The remainder had been spent on administration, promotion, and bribes.[52]

Many of the stockholders had been people of modest means, and they formed an association that repeatedly petitioned Parliament for redress. And it would have been expecting too much to suppose that the remnants of the Boulangist party would forget that Panama money had gone to the very newspapers and politicians that had triumphed in 1889. Boulangist newspapers had profited too—Laguerre's paper, *La Presse,* received 85,000 francs from Arton;[53] and Rochefort had written several enthusiastic articles on Panama in 1886,[54] for which he was alleged to have received 156,000 francs.[55] But with Jacques de Reinach, uncle and father-in-law of Joseph Reinach, as the chief distributor of Panama funds, it was inevitable that most of the bribes had gone to the anti-Boulangist interests. The Republican majority naturally tried to resist the outcry for legal investigation, but when all possible postponements were exhausted, the Attorney-General appointed a court investigator on June 11, 1891. The investigation lasted a year, and the report recommended prosecution of the President and Board of Directors of the Panama Company—Ferdinand de Lesseps, Charles de Lesseps, Marius Fontane, and Baron Cottu—for embezzlement and abuse of confidence, as well as of Gustave Eiffel, an engineer who had asked an exorbitant fee for his part in the construction.[56]

Of the opposition papers that set up a howl, none was more vociferous than Édouard Drumont's *La Libre Parole,* which was organized in 1892 as an anti-Semitic organ. Already known for his book *La France Juive, Essai d'histoire contemporaine* (1886), Drumont seems largely to have hated Jews as capitalists. Arton and Jacques de Reinach were his first targets, and Reinach tried to save himself by offering the names of Opportunist deputies to whom he had given bribes. Drumont published these names in November of 1892. But Reinach was also still in difficulty with Cornelius Herz, who, secure in London, was demanding more money. Then, on November 18, 1892, the Attorney-General, Quesnay de Beaurepaire, wrote the inevitable news to Joseph Reinach:

"My dear Friend, I am writing with a great tightening of my heart to warn you of the sad news which is coming your way, either today or tomorrow morning from another source. The citations in the Panama Affair have been issued at this moment, and they include a name quite close to you. The person in question ought to have forewarned you, since, on November 4th, the official investigator found him guilty. Believe that I am broken-hearted about this, and that duty, accomplished under my direction and in my jurisdiction, never cost me so dear." Joseph Reinach at once informed his uncle of the letter, whereupon Jacques de Reinach went to his suburban home, where he was found dead the next day. As the Attorney-General permitted a hasty burial without an autopsy, we can only assume that it was suicide—and record that there were rumors to the contrary.[57]

The dam was about to break, and Premier Loubet feared that the scandal could revive the anti-parliamentary wave of Boulangism and destroy the regime. The citations were indeed issued on November 19, and two days later the Boulangist deputy, Jules Delahaye, interpellated the government in a wild speech during which he accused one hundred fifty members of Parliament of involvement in the Panama affair—but named no names. Asked for names, he would do no more than demand the formation of a board of inquiry. Accordingly, a board was named, including twenty-three Republicans, nine Conservatives, and one Boulangist. When Delahaye was questioned by the board one week after his speech of accusation, he admitted that he had only what he called "moral proof" and named only Arton and Herz, claiming that the material proof would be found in the Reinach papers. And where were they? In the haste to get Reinach buried, no one had sealed his residence. Whatever incriminating papers there might have been were certainly no longer there. The board then demanded to see all the evidence unearthed by the Attorney-General's office in its investigation of the case; but Prime Minister Loubet refused, arguing that this would violate the principle of separation of powers. The Chamber, fearing popular opinion if it let the matter so rest, overthrew the ministry.

In the interim before the Ribot government took office on December 5, 1892, material evidence of political corruption was discovered in a bank: twenty-six checks had been drawn by Jacques de Reinach for a total of 3,390,475 francs, the two largest payable to Cornelius Herz, two others payable to Senator Albert Grévy and Senator Louis Renault. The remaining twenty-two were evidently endorsed by front men; but police investigation soon discovered the true beneficiaries. The new government was thus able to bring charges against five deputies and five Senators.[58] One had been a prime minister, five were former cabinet ministers, and three had held high administrative posts in addition to being members of Parliament. All but one belonged to the Republican majority. And all had parliamentary immunity. On December 20, the Attorney-General asked Parliament to lift their immunity, and the request was granted. But during that session, Déroulède asked what measures were to be taken against Cornelius Herz. His question was aimed straight at Clemenceau; for it was widely known that at one time Herz had been a silent partner in Clemenceau's La Justice.[59]

Déroulède went on to charge that Clemenceau had been in Herz's pay. Even though Clemenceau had long since bought out Herz, and even though Déroulède had not one shred of proof, such a charge under those circumstances was bound to be believed. The Boulangists, thus, had their revenge against Clemenceau, who was generally believed to be finished politically.[60] Two days later, a member of the board of inquiry returned from London where he had interviewed Cornelius Herz and brought back a photograph of a note presumably dictated by Reinach. Here Reinach had mentioned a sum of 1,340,000 francs to be divided among one hundred four deputies, but again unnamed. No further charges, therefore, were brought in 1892.

The Panama Company officials' case opened first, on January 9, 1893. Ferdinand de Lesseps, then eighty-eight, did not appear because of his age, and Baron Cottu had fled the country. The defense skillfully attempted to show that the company had been on a great crusade for civilization and that, on its mission, it had been subjected to the crass demands of businessmen and politicians, "as a caravan leader pays tribute to Sahara pirates." [61] The former minister Baïhaut was identified as one of the Saharans in the course of Charles de Lesseps' testimony and was arrested. Former Prime Minister Floquet was also accused of receiving a large sum by Charles de Lesseps, who then made public that the company had been pressured by Freycinet and Clemenceau to meet Reinach's demands for more money to pay off Herz. Ribot at once shuffled his cabinet to drop Freycinet, Floquet was forced to resign the presidency of the Chamber, and the Boulangist charges against Clemenceau seemed confirmed. [62]

A judgment was given in the case on February 13, 1893. Both Ferdinand and Charles de Lesseps were condemned to five years in prison and a three thousand francs fine; Eiffel was given two years and a twenty thousand francs fine. Several months later, the Court of Cassation reversed the decision on a technicality involving the statute of limitations, and Quesnay de Beaurepaire was severely reprimanded by the board of inquiry for this matter of incorrect procedure. But there was nothing to be done. Herz, meanwhile, had been arrested on January 20 in London at French request; but the demand for his extradition was denied on medical grounds. [63] Rochefort, who had been in communication with Herz in England, claimed that Herz was feigning illness. Perhaps this was so, since he soon sailed for the United States. [64]

Rochefort was interviewed in London on the Panama scandal,

and he claimed to know that the Orleanists possessed important documents relative to the case, which they were presumably withholding until the next elections. Thus, he feared that the Royalists rather than the Boulangists might be the party to profit from the scandal. He thought that the government was in an impossible jam. If it got Sans-Leroy acquitted, for example, that would be scandalous; but to allow him to be condemned would lead the "ex-deputy-extortionist" to denounce other deputies who had "sold their votes as he had." Asked if the Socialists might not be the party to profit from the scandal, Rochefort correctly noted that the Socialists were too deeply divided to stand together as a party.[65]

The Boulangists were exultant however, about one matter: Clemenceau, the man whose defection had cost the Boulangists their Radical support and brought a fatal confusion to the ranks, was now himself fatally compromised. No proof had been offered, true, and the case needed to be made stronger. Thus Rochefort wrote about the money Clemenceau had received from Herz: "I am neither accuser nor judge—only a simple phonograph. I have related the statement made to me by Cornelius Herz . . . that he gave Clemenceau between 3½ and 4 million francs." [66] *La Justice,* Clemenceau's paper, offered to open its books to an investigating committee as the only way to answer Rochefort's charge. And there was a good deal of journalistic speculation in Paris, during the first week of February, 1893, as to the best way to obtain direct testimony from Rochefort for the Herz case. Should he be given a safe-conduct pass? Should an English magistrate be empowered to question him? Or should a Parliamentary commission be sent to London to interview him?

Rochefort's response to these suggestions merits some consideration. He told an English reporter, "I do not want to accept a temporary amnesty from those of whom I am so suspicious, but I should be willing to receive persons judged appropriate to take my testimony. On the other hand, no one in Paris wants to hear what I have to say." He concluded with a fresh charge—that Herz amounted to a German spy because he had opposed Boulanger, "the only man the Germans have feared since the war." [67] Rochefort was probably right to suppose that no one in the government was interested in what he had to say; but we are entitled to suspect that he had no documentary evidence against Clemenceau and preferred to limit his attack to innuendo.

The trial for the political corruption cases opened on March 8, 1893, after the completion of the embezzlement case. Most of the implicated Parliamentarians escaped trial on grounds of insufficient evidence against them; and Arton had fled. Only three members of Parliament, the company officials, and Charles Baïhaut stood trial. The judgment was read on March 20: Charles de Lesseps was sentenced to one year in prison, Baïhaut was given five years in prison and a fine of 750,000 francs. The Parliamentarians were acquitted—they had demonstrated that the sums they took were legitimate honoraria—and retook their seats. The Ribot government did not survive the stain of the affair, for many of the younger and more virtuous Republicans felt that the older party leaders had not opened the Panama case promptly enough. The government was overturned on a minor issue on March 30. A new Republican era had already been forecast with the election of the forty-six-year-old Jean Casimir-Périer to the presidency of the Chamber to succeed the compromised Floquet.[68]

The elections of 1893, scheduled for August and September, would presumably show the effects of the Panama scandal. Perhaps only a few politicians had been enriched by improper means, but it was only too easy to regard the whole lot as corrupt and to turn to new men. The hopes of all those who opposed the parliamentary Republic were heightened, the various monarchists and socialists, and those who favored a plebiscitary regime. Yet the young Republicans were giving their party a new face, and a new attitude of the Papacy had begun to dissolve the traditional Catholic hostility to the French Republic. These factors confused the electoral picture for 1893. Nor could anyone know the effects of the anti-Semitic campaign conducted by the likes of Drumont. The religious re-orientation was perhaps the most unfathomable aspect of the situation, although, given the dismal prospects for the Republicans after the Panama unpleasantness, the Pope's encyclical of February 16, 1892, was a blessing for them.

Leo XIII, in the encyclical *Au milieu des sollicitudes,* advised French Catholics to accept the Republic sincerely and to work for revision of the anticlerical legislation within the framework of the Constitution. No doubt, the traditional preference of French Catholics for monarchy could not have been scuttled overnight by word from Rome; but it was an opening gun in undermining Catholic support for monarchy. This unexpected aid from Rome forced some anticlerical Republicans to insist that lay supremacy in such enterprises as education would be maintained no matter how many Catholics rallied to the Republic.[69]

The former Boulangists, or Parti National, were not united for the elections of 1893. Rochefort was the recognized leader of the more radical-revolutionary wing, which essentially followed an advanced socialist party line and plugged for revision of the Senate. He was reputed to be ready to spend considerable sums on the campaign.[70] The other wing, led by Paul Déroulède, was described as plebiscitary, for it favored strong executive power, with the President to be elected by universal suffrage. If the two wings fought a common enemy and remained reasonably friendly, they fought him for different reasons.[71] As for the question of an amnesty, Rochefort remained consistent in not wanting to accept any grace from men who had participated in his banishment; but he was also confident that those men would be beaten in the coming elections and that the victors would abolish the Senate and annul the verdict of the High Court.[72]

The first test of public opinion in 1893 should have frightened him. He decided to stand for office in the Paris municipal elections of April 16, roughly four months before his party entered the national elections, running in the St. Victor district of the Fifth Arrondissement. The Radical candidate, Lanton, was easily elected with 2766 votes and no runoff was necessary. A second candidate named Rossignol, who ran as a Clerical, received 1144 votes. And Rochefort, listed as a Revisionist, came in with a dazzling 339.[73] His showing, in short, was far poorer than in his last electoral attempt in 1889.

As for the national elections, the new young Republicans were led by Prime Minister Charles Dupuy, and they showed themselves grateful for the new attitude of the Papacy by welcoming the *ralliés* to the Republic. If this may have won over some conservative voters, the fact that the young Republicans refused to promise any revision of the lay laws would have caused the genuinely religious to hesitate. The more radical Republicans, fearing a possible moderate Republican-Clerical alliance in the making, ran separate candidates, in contrast to 1889. They favored a progressive tax on income and capital and saw their future as a coalition with the socialist parties.

The electoral results were surprising. The combined Monarchist-Revisionist Right won only seventy-six seats and the Right *rallié* won twenty-seven. This compared to the total conservative seats of 210 in 1889. The governmental Republicans won 279 seats, the Radical Republicans 143 seats, and the various socialists groups 41 seats. Obviously, then, the new Chamber would be more radical than before; but the most significant result was that the combined Republican parties achieved 82 per cent of the total vote, compared to 53 per cent in 1889. Floquet and Clemenceau were beaten, it is true, but so were three of the most vociferous enemies of parliamentarianism: Déroulède, Delahaye, and Millevoye. Many of the older Republicans were returned despite the upsurge of new Republican faces.[74] But how do we account for such a stunning Republican victory when its likelihood seemed so dim? Possibly the deaths of General Boulanger and Prince Napoleon removed the only serious candidates for the plebiscitary enthusiasts, and monarchy had steadily been losing its appeal as a result of the pretenders' ineffectual wrangling. Possibly, too, the survival of the Republic for over thirty years, longer than any other regime in the nineteenth century had endured, had given the Republic a lease on life by accustoming the French to living under that political form.

Toward the end of 1893 there began a series of anarchist outrages, which produced some major political repercussions. The first serious bomb-throwing took place in the Chamber of Deputies on December 9, 1893, causing little damage but much alarm. The Dupuy government had been turned out only a few days before through a combination of Conservative, Radical, and Socialist votes, to be replaced by another moderate government, that of Casimir-Périer. Four anti-anarchist bills were brought before the Chamber by his new government the day after the bomb-throwing and were passed without debate. Auguste Vaillant, the bomb-thrower, was quickly tried, condemned to death, and executed on February 7, 1894.

One of the new anti-anarchist bills, however, soon began to alarm the Socialists and Radicals. It was a measure that provided a sentence of forced labor for those who formed associations with a view to attacking persons or property. Could not such a law be arbitrarily invoked against Socialists as well as anarchists? As their alarm grew, so did the number of bombings. On February 13, an explosion in a cafe near the Gare Saint-Lazare killed one person and wounded twenty. A week later, another person was killed by a bomb in the rue Saint-Jacques. These threats to public order had the immediate political effect of drawing together the moderate Republicans and the Catholic *ralliés,* thus deepening Radical and Socialist suspicions that the majority Republicans were compromising traditional Republican anticlericalism.[75]

The problem for the anti-government forces was to exploit the situation without openly defending the anarchists. Rochefort's solution was revealed in a letter sent to a staff member of *L'Intransigeant.* It was intercepted and copied by the police. "Increasingly advise your collaborators to stick their necks out as little as possible when dealing with the anarchists. Let them prosecute the management, let them prosecute me, that's all right with me. But it would be most unfortunate to see one of our editors pulled into [court]. . . . This would be disastrous for the paper. . . . I would be delighted if someone could find a good issue based on a police mistake. . . . You could hit that hard. Don't miss the opportunity."[76] Shortly after,

Rochefort gave a demonstration of his recommended techniques in a letter intended to be read for him at the May 1 banquet of the Friends of the People organization: "Our government, where Leo XIII is king, is more interested in arresting honest women than in feeding them. It is true that its genuflections before the Pope's mule will do it no more good than its arbitrary arrests. . . . The police are always supported on religion. Well, we want neither the one nor the other!" [77]

The developing rift in Republican ranks enabled the Opposition to bring down the Casimir-Périer government after only a half year in office; but when the Radicals refused to form a government, it was necessary to bring back Dupuy on May 30, 1894. Casimir-Périer returned to the presidency of the Chamber. In the meantime, another bomb had been thrown, into a restaurant on April 5, wounding a number of innocent people. But on June 24, the outrages reached their climax in Lyons, when President Sadi Carnot was struck down by an assassin as he approached the Grand Theater for a gala performance. The assassin, a twenty-one-year-old Lombard named Santo Caserio, shouted "Vive l'anarchie!" after he struck with his knife. This was vengeance for the President's failure to pardon previously condemned anarchists.

New presidential elections were held at Versailles three days later, and the candidate of the Republican majority, Casimir-Périer, was elected on the first ballot. Rochefort was furious at the turn of events. Having aided and abetted extremism, he now saw the presidency vested in even more conservative hands, and his hopes for an imminent amnesty were cut short.[78] His response was to order the director of *L'Intransigeant* to step up the campaign against the President.[79] But the government also stepped up its campaign against extremism with a hotly debated press law passed on July 28, 1894. One of the earlier anti-anarchist measures had provided for the prosecution of editors who seemed either to encourage or apologize for acts of violence. The new law stipulated that such cases would be heard before correctional courts where there would be no jury.[80]

Like many other journalists, Rochefort believed these laws to be a renewal of censorship. Thus, he wrote a violent article entitled "Vomitory" in which he railed against the new system: "In truth, the magistracy treats [journalists] as Caserio treated President Carnot. It is summary assassination and death without right of response." And he went on to compare the courts to the Revolutionary Tribunal of 1793 as an instrument of arbitrary judgment.[81] When the courts proved not to be as arbitrary in fact as Rochefort predicted, he concluded that his article had had a tempering influence. But he was condemned *in absentia* to three months in prison for contempt of the magistracy.[82]

Casimir-Périer probably suffered unfairly from press abuse due to the fact that the press laws were instituted so soon after he was elected to the presidency. Because he came from the upper bourgeoisie with its conservative traditions, he was easily suspected of being reactionary—despite his record of having opposed President MacMahon in the 1870's. In the autumn of 1894, he did order the prosecution of an anarchist journalist named Gérault-Richard for an insulting article entitled "Down with Casimir." In the Boulanger era, Gérault-Richard had been a collaborator of Lissagaray on *La Bataille,* a journal that had repeatedly attacked both the General and Rochefort. Thus, at Gérault-Richard's trial, Jean Jaurès appeared in his defense, recalling his loyalty to the Republic and calling Boulangism an incarnation of Caesarism. This made Rochefort furious at Jaurès, whom he understood to have condemned all Boulangists equally.[83]

Gérault-Richard was sentenced to a year in prison. Despite this, the voters of the Thirteenth Arrondissement selected him as their deputy two months later in a by-election on December 23, 1894. His candidacy was generally considered pointedly insulting to Casimir-Périer; and having to chose between the two men, Rochefort decided to attack the President in the campaign. As he put it in *L'Intransigeant,* "When he has received four or five good lessons of the sort that we are advising the voters of the Thirteenth, the Tamerlane of the Élysée will perhaps understand that in France no one governs long at gunpoint."[84] Casimir-Périer felt Gérault-

Richard's election was intolerable, and he also felt he was being ignored by Premier Dupuy. The total picture seemed to suggest that he resign from the presidency. An appropriate occasion was presented to him upon the fall of the Dupuy government on January 15, 1895. Casimir-Périer resigned the following day, to be followed two days later by Félix Faure, who was known to favor a general amnesty. And as the motion that brought down Dupuy had come from the Left, Faure invited the more radical Ribot to form a new regime. He succeeded on January 27. Rochefort was at last confident that he would soon be returning home.[85]

If the amnesty law of February 2, 1895, was not all-encompassing, it was broad enough to bring Rochefort back from exile; and he sailed from England that same day on the *Foam* bound for Calais. There was a welcoming crowd at Calais, which included his son Octave, and there were further demonstrations on the way to Paris, especially in Amiens, and finally in the Gare du Nord.[86] Those who cheered him, however, were not greeting him as a Boulangist; they were largely working people who still believed him to be an unrepentant socialist. Yet in the coming Dreyfus affair, he would demonstrate that he had remained in the nationalist camp.[87] The police reported no alarming incidents upon his return, and, if anything, he avoided public meetings and banquets. *L'Intransigeant* published that his health was poor as a result of the London climate, and he soon departed for the Riviera for several weeks of recovery.[88] Other evidence suggests that while he was not in the best of health he was also uncertain of the government's attitude toward him and thought it best to be obscure for a time.[89] Most of the socialist leaders by then knew that he was not one of them, though the Broussistes and the Allemanistes feared that he would at least temporarily throw his support to the Guesdistes in his campaign to appear to be on the Left.[90]

By the 1890's, indeed, party leaders of all shades no longer took Rochefort's political pronouncements at face value. He was a curiosity whom they sought to explain, whose bellowing charges they might anticipate if only to sidestep them, and about whom they tried to be tolerant in the sense that one tolerates a child in unequal competition with adults. One could not talk to Rochefort as to other people, one former Boulangist editor explained. Just when you thought you had cornered him with some bit of inescapable logic, he would evade you with a remark at once natural and amusing—and you would be disarmed. But, the same editor complained, "Does Rochefort never stop to think about the consequences of his whims? Of the injustices that he commits? He who has said that he should be called Joseph because he has so often been sold by his brothers, does he never think of those former brothers-in-arms, faithful in the dark hours, whom he beats unmercifully one fine day? . . . He simply believes everything [bad] that is told to him and encompasses everyone in a grand conspiracy."[91]

Since Paris had never given either Victor Hugo or Louis Pasteur such acclaim as it gave Rochefort upon his return from exile, "why Rochefort?," asked another journalist. "Is Rochefort, thus, someone? No, he is something: a plaything . . . for several hundred thousand little children who are generally called *citizens*." Possessing neither political ideas nor skills, he simply attacked people in polemics that were almost entirely negative. Some of Rochefort's *mots* had been excellent, this journalist admitted, and he concluded his description by classifying Rochefort as "a past master of cock-and-bull." [92]

CHAPTER IX

The Anti-Dreyfusard
1894-1913

I am always instinctively suspicious of people who love to dwell either on their loyalty or on their patriotism.

ROCHEFORT [1]

OF ALL the great affairs of the Third Republic into which Rochefort threw himself with such verve, the case of Alfred Dreyfus is the most familiar to the general reader. The case broke in 1894 while Rochefort was still in exile and heavily engaged in undermining President Casimir-Périer, and Captain Dreyfus was brought to trial for espionage on December 19. On January 5, he was formally degraded at the École Militaire and then shipped off to Devil's Island. The public was largely convinced that the verdict if anything had been too soft. Death would have been a more suitable penalty. The Dreyfus case, in other words, did not immediately become an *affaire*—not until a few men began to suspect the validity of the evidence used to convict Dreyfus and to wonder about the irregularities at his court-martial. At that point, whether or not to reopen the case quickly blew up into a major national crisis. This crisis did not only grow out of the matter of seeing justice done; it encompassed many unresolved political and personal conflicts having little to do with the person of Captain Dreyfus. As a result, it has often been hard to find the real reasons why any given individual, by 1896 or 1897, had decided to be Dreyfusard or anti-Dreyfusard. Before retelling the story with a view to placing Rochefort in the *affaire,* let us disgress briefly in order to relate several other incidents in Rochefort's life after his return from exile.

March 18 was the anniversary of that dreadful insurrection known as the Commune. To mark it in 1895, Rochefort claimed that despite the reactionaries' objections the people had adopted that date as a national holiday. "With the bad faith which has made it famous, the Clerical, Opportunist, and Versaillese press criticize us for that Republican and Socialist revolution, accomplished— they repeat periodically—under Prussian bayonets. Well, it is precisely because the peace was signed and we found it dishonoring to the country that the Parisian population protested, arms in hand, against the treason which cast us bleeding and ruined under the German heel."[2] Note that while he had most recently been identified as a Nationalist of the Boulanger stripe, he was now openly identifying himself also as a Communard. Two years later, he reiterated that identification: "The more one gains experience in politics, the more one can see that France has had only one honest government: that of the Commune."[3] Now, not all Nationalists were Rightists in the 1890's, but most Rightists were Nationalists. The Communards were unquestionably Leftist. It is difficult to escape the conclusion that Rochefort, the master equivocator, was practicing his old art of being on both sides at once; and we can understand the writer who would soon note that "though an ironist by profession, I suddenly become serious in order to spit in the face of our old national trimmer, M. Henri Rochefort."[4]

If politicians could no longer take him at face value, why should they continue to deal with him at all? He had readers for one thing, and there was always the possibility of using him. For example, a nihilist group in Geneva, infiltrated by a French police informer, held that Rochefort knew absolutely nothing about socialism, politics, or economics. They believed he was totally unreliable personally, incapable of friendship or gratitude, and utterly devoid of insight into those around him. They accused him of being unable to tolerate real talent in the same office and to be concerned solely for money and self-advancement; and they classified him, finally, as an accomplished male whore. *But,* they also saw him to be "a demolition hammer" and were willing to use him.[5]

Anyone reading Rochefort's memoirs, published in 1896, could have easily found that he prided himself on his association with nihilists in Geneva during his exile there, and he would have been distressed to learn of their views of him. Yet, as if to confirm them, he who had written so appreciatively of the assassination of Czar Alexander II in 1881 attended a gala at the Opera in 1896 in honor of the memory of Alexander III and participated in the ceremony to lay the first stone of the new bridge to bear the Czar's name. This was Rochefort the Nationalist, of course, enthusiastic about the new alliance with Russia; but many members of his Intransigeant League were miffed,[6] and one editor commented: "M. Rochefort is getting old; but that is his least defect; he is losing his memory and cannot even remember what he has written [about the Romanovs in the past.]"[7] Several months later, he was removed as honorary president of the Intransigeant League for *moderation,*[8] a quality that had perhaps never before been attributed to him.

The appearance of his memoirs was unfortunately timed, for it coincided with his obvious political decline. Jean Allemane, the ex-Communard, was only too close to the truth when he wrote about those memoirs: "In his capacity as spoiled 'Dear Master,' M. Henri Rochefort seriously believes himself to have become the pivot around which all people and all things must revolve."[9] He was becoming, in fact, the recipient of few kind words: "The carnival season is not too far hence. It is again time, thus, to speak of Rochefort. . . . He is a past master . . . of vaudeville. In politics . . . he has never enunciated a doctrine: as a deputy, he only made interruptions. . . . He sometimes calls himself a socialist. . . . In truth he has never read the first word of Karl Marx. . . . He also calls himself a revolutionary. His part in revolutions consists of writing articles in his office designed to produce street demonstrations. . . . He spends his time insulting those in power, whoever they may be. . . . He has what one properly calls *l'esprit frondeur*, . . . and the astonishing thing is that such an individual, lacking intelligence, morality, and dignity of any sort, has for forty years been able to frolic with impunity in this country, midst amused silence from some and noisy approbation from others, playing the dual role of lover of justice and national insulter." [10]

Rochefort's private life also received some unflattering attention beginning in 1896. Madame Rochefort applied for a divorce that year on the grounds of having been separated from him for eighteen years.[11] He had long had a reputation for treating women shabbily, and the divorce revived interest in his marital record and opened him up to at least one blackmail attempt. Out of his past emerged a relative of his first wife, who took her story to a rival newspaper, *La Libre Parole,* the anti-Semitic and Nationalist sheet that featured Drumont, Mme. de Séverine, and Thiébaud, all ex-Boulangists of plebiscitary persuasion. The troublemaker was Mme. Charles Renauld, who claimed she had asked Rochefort to help her husband secure a more satisfactory job and that when Rochefort had made no response, she had to take her plight to the Municipal Council where she obtained relief. The police knew that she was an experienced extortionist and not in the least poverty-stricken;[12] but Mme. de Séverine grasped at the opportunity and accused Rochefort of denying his sister-in-law by marriage.[13] Rochefort answered that no such person existed.[14]

The divorce from his second wife [15] opened the way for him to marry Marguerite Vervoort, a mistress who had lived with him in Britain and who had hitherto been described as his niece. We may only infer from the fact that she had evidently left him briefly the previous year that he had decided it was time to regularize their domestic situation.[16] He was then sixty-six and she twenty-eight. The civil ceremony took place at the *mairie* of the Sixteenth Arrondissement, and it proved to be a mistake. He did not expect her to be virtuous, having known about her in the past, but as the years went on he fretted that her little affairs might make him appear ridiculous, a concern that may strike us as somewhat belated.[17] In time, they seem to have separated, though informally.

When Rochefort fled France in 1889, he signed over by contract the administrative and commercial direction of *L'Intransigeant* to Ernest Vaughn. Because his management was evidently excellent, Rochefort returned from exile in 1895 as well-to-do, a far cry from his financial state ten years before. For a time he showed himself very pleased with Vaughn's direction. Within a year, however, they were in deep conflict, evidently because Vaughn felt that he was entitled, considering the unexpected profits, to a greater compensation for the previous seven years than his contract had provided. Rochefort insisted on sticking to the letter of the agreement. The Court of Appeal appointed two lawyers to arbitrate the matter, and they gave their decision on December 9, 1896.

Some revealing figures were exposed in the hearing: for the seven-year period in dispute, Vaughn had sent Rochefort 700,000 francs as editor-publisher, in addition to one million francs as a stockholder; this averaged out to 242,000 francs a year. Vaughn had, in other words, done very well by Rochefort and seemed justified in his charges that Rochefort was ungrateful and unfair. As one editor put it, evidently the war against capitalism was not meant to enrich all of those who took part in it. "Rochefort's socialism does not extend that far. The arbitrators—in a bourgeois court—have found that a man who makes 1,700,000 in seven years can properly pay those whom he employs. Thus the rights of labor have been recalled for this socialist intransigent."[18] Another paper observed, "And there are still some naive enough to believe that this egotistical and greedy millionaire is a friend of workers!"[19]

The arbitrators found that Vaughn was entitled to a bonus appropriate to his long and valuable service and ordered Rochefort to pay him 20,000 francs.[20] Their association, of course, did not survive the dispute, and Vaughn left *L'Intransigeant* at the beginning of 1897. The split proved to be far more significant than could have been predicted from the financial squabble. As the demands to reexamine the Dreyfus case increased in 1897, Vaughn decided to found a paper of his own, *L'Aurore,* and most of his writers were Dreyfusards, Clemenceau and Anatole France among them.[21]

In retrospect, the original Dreyfus case contained every conceivable element likely to arouse passion rather than cold reason; but in the beginning it seemed to be nothing more than an ordinary instance of treason, efficiently tracked down by the French counterintelligence service and promptly punished by the military. French counterintelligence, headed by Colonel Jean-Conrad Sandherr, had known for some time that the German military attaché in Paris, Colonel von Schwartzkoppen, bought French military secrets from traitors. Thanks to a maid in the German Embassy who was given to examining paper in wastebaskets, French counterintelligence was given a brief memorandum on military information which its writer, whoever he was, proposed to sell to Schwartzkoppen. Major Joseph Henry of the counterintelligence staff took this memorandum to the French General Staff, which examined the information the traitor proposed to sell and came to the unhappy conclusion that only a General Staff officer in touch with several departments of the General Staff could have such information. This in turn suggested that he would be an officer in training, and that he was probably a gunner rather than an infantryman or cavalryman. This deduction reduced the number of suspects sharply, indeed, pointed primarily to Captain Alfred Dreyfus; and handwriting tests of the suspects confirmed the suspicion that Dreyfus was the man.

No doubt Sandherr was pleased by his discovery, for he was an anti-Semite, and Dreyfus was an Alsatian Jew. The first Jew to enter the General Staff, he was an able but conceited and unpopular individual. But this does not permit us to accept the later charge that Dreyfus was initially thought to be guilty *because* he was a Jew. When it later became recognized that he had not been guilty as charged, it was only too easy to suppose that the error had been deliberate and to forget that any organization will be inclined to conceal its errors when it recognizes them. In this case, the temptation would have been unusually great, considering that for reasons of national security the agency committing the blunder could ill afford a reputation for inefficiency. In short, we must assume that Colonel Sandherr necessarily wanted to find the guilty man, his evidence led him to Dreyfus, and the army professionals, if stung by the knowledge that an officer could be a traitor, could take some consolation in the fact that the traitor had turned out not to be "a real Frenchman." [22] When further evidence kept turning up suggesting that the traitor was still at large, the organizational instinct was to deny that an error had been made and to resist criticism with counterabuse.

Without much doubt, too, the first people to suspect that the case against Dreyfus was unfortunately weak were those who had arrested him and lodged him in the Cherche-Midi prison. Other handwriting experts were brought in, for instance, and they disagreed with each other. This should have suggested caution to the military, but the case had meanwhile assumed new proportions. On November 27, General Auguste Mercier, the Minister of War, had given an interview to *Le Figaro* that implicated the German government in the Dreyfus case. The remarks were injudicious, especially since a French general should have realized that the German military probably carried on its activities in ways that were unknown to the civilian departments of the German government. Thus, Mercier unwittingly gave the case new dimensions that proved to be a blessing for the Nationalist press alone.

The German Embassy correctly protested its ignorance of Captain Dreyfus and his alleged treason, a protest that the extremist press, represented by Rochefort, Drumont, and Barrès, naturally would not buy. When, because of the shaky nature of the case against Dreyfus, the French military decided that his trial should be heard in closed sessions, the extremist press saw at once that a spineless French government had given the order to protect

the German government from embarrassment. This set the stage for
Rochefort's attitude throughout the Dreyfus affair. In his mind, to
be a patriot was to continue opposing the very politicians he had
been attacking for over twenty years, and this route had the additional advantage of confirming his anti-Semitism. If such a posture
put him in alliance with the Army and the Church, institutions he
had also bitterly fought, that would have to be overlooked in the
interest of recovering Alsace and Lorraine.

Dreyfus' court-martial began on December 19, 1894, and he
was defended by the Maître Demange, a Catholic lawyer. Demange
protested the closed sessions, but to no avail; and it soon became
apparent to him why the prosecution had preferred the closed sessions. Its case was so leaky that Major Henry of the counterintelligence service was brought in to testify that an "honorable person,"
necessarily unnamed, had first revealed Dreyfus' treason—in other
words, that the case did not have to rest on the quicksand of handwriting expertise. As a last gesture, the prosecution introduced an
exhibit of four documents purported to demonstrate Dreyfus' guilt.
The most critical of these was signed "Alexandrine" and was alleged
to be a letter from the Italian military attaché in Paris, Panizzardi,
to Schwartzkoppen, a letter in which Panizzardi presumably discussed Dreyfus' willingness to sell the defense plans for Nice to
Italy. The defense was denied the right to examine this document,
and it is hardly surprising that Demange was furious about the procedures being used.[23]

The judges voted unanimously for conviction and awarded
Dreyfus the most serious penalties possible under the law: imprisonment for life and military degradation. On the day of that degradation, January 5, 1895, the German Ambassador presented a new
note to the French government: "His Majesty the Emperor, with
complete confidence in the honor of the President and Government
of the Republic, requests your Excellency [the Foreign Minister
Hanotaux] to tell M. Casimir-Périer that should it be proved that
the German Embassy has never been implicated in the Dreyfus case,

258

His Majesty hopes that the Government of the Republic will not hesitate to make the declaration. Without a formal declaration, the legends that the press continues to foster concerning the German Embassy may persist and compromise the Emperor's representative." It was signed by Hohenlohe, the German Chancellor.

Like most other outside observers, Casimir-Périer probably believed in the guilt of Dreyfus, but he was worldly enough to realize also that the German Embassy was probably unaware of Schwartz-koppen's secret machinations for the military. Thus he called in the German Ambassador, and it was agreed that a new bulletin should be put out by the French government absolving all foreign embassies in Paris of complicity in the case.[24] This diplomatic and proper solution could only heighten extremist complaints that the French government was subservient to Berlin.

Rochefort was even convinced that Dreyfus' very sentence was a concession to Germany: for Rochefort had also suffered deportation, and in his extraordinary way of reasoning, he saw himself being equated to "the abominable Jew." To him this was a deliberate German trick to discredit a French patriot. His open letter to Dreyfus bears consideration:

> Monsieur and dear Colleague, You cannot imagine to what degree, in learning of your condemnation to perpetual deportation to a fortified place, I felt myself flattered to be the equal finally of a captain attached to the General Staff. . . . In fact, the High Court, in its wisdom and its great integrity, . . . has decided that to call Constans "swindler" and to sell out France to Germany—along with the means to wreck our armies, devastate our homes, and to squeeze us out of the few millions which remain—merit exactly the same sentence. It is true that if, instead of being an officer, you had been only a common soldier and had called the colonel presiding over the court-martial a "cow," Casimir-Périer would have had you shot like a dog. For the word "cow," when applied to a superior, constitutes a crime against the common law,

while furnishing the enemy with the information necessary to kill three hundred thousand of us in an eminently political act.

But since, on the scale of penalties, we find ourselves on the same rung, permit an old habitual offender like me to give you some advice, the fruit of long experience. I have not often enough betrayed my country to permit me, in case that an amnesty should eventually be voted, to ask you to be good enough to name me as the one to reenter our good city of Paris on your arm. I know only too well what distance separates me, a vulgar *pékin* without any protection—not even that of Germany—from a military man who wears epaulets and in whom the highest European persons like William II, Rothschild, and the Grand Rabbi, your relative and namesake, are so warmly interested. . . . In appreciating my intent, you will pardon me for taking the liberty of writing to you . . . and the perhaps indiscreete familiarity which I have used in putting myself, so to speak, under your protection. Jews today are all-powerful, and it is not every day that one has the honor to be put on the same footing with a French officer who has such fine relations in Germany.[25]

From the start of the case, however, several people believed in the innocence of Dreyfus, especially his brother Mathieu, who knew that this kind of activity was entirely foreign to Dreyfus' character. His lawyer, too, thought that the meager evidence presented by the prosecution meant only one thing. It took a full two years, however, to recruit more powerful friends, men who would be called Dreyfusards by mid-1897. The first convert was Colonel Georges Picquart, who took over the direction of the counterintelligence service on July 2, 1895, upon Sandherr's retirement. Picquart, another Alsatian anti-Semite, was thought to be a safe man by the General Staff, but he was a Catholic and had a sense of fair play unknown to his superiors. We may imagine his perplexity when he discovered that the sale of military secrets was evidently continuing. He set himself to investigate.

In March of 1896, another interesting item was turned up in a wastebasket of the German Embassy, a little note written on thin blue paper to Major Esterhazy of the French army, signed simply with a *C*. For some reason, it had never been stamped or posted. "Monsieur," it ran, "Before all, I await a more detailed explanation than you gave me the other day on the question in suspense. Will you therefore be good enough to let me have it in writing to enable me to decide whether I can continue my relations with the firm of R—— or not." [26] Picquart consequently got a sample of Esterhazy's handwriting and came to the appalling realization that the handwriting attributed to Dreyfus had obviously been that of Esterhazy. His shock grew even greater when, in reporting his discovery to the army chiefs, he found that they preferred to keep the case closed. But he did not lose his head. He photographed the evidence in the Dreyfus file, wrote down some notes on the case, and consulted a lawyer, Louis Leblois.

A second key figure in the revisionist movement was Bernard Lazare, a Jewish journalist who had befriended Mathieu Dreyfus. In the spring of 1896, Lazare wrote a brochure entitled "The Truth About the Dreyfus Affair," which he did not publish until November of that year—and then only in Brussels. By then, Picquart had passed on his information to the General Staff, which recognized that interest in the case was becoming uncomfortably intense. Unfortunately for Picquart, four days after Lazare's brochure appeared, *Le Matin* published a copy of the original memorandum presumably written by Dreyfus. Major Henry convinced the General Staff that Picquart had furnished the copy to the newspaper to bolster his own proposal for reopening the case; and shortly thereafter Picquart was transferred from the counterintelligence service to duty in southern Tunisia.

It later came to light that one of the handwriting experts called in two years before had made a copy of the memorandum and was ultimately unable to resist the opportunity to sell his fascinating item to the press.[27] Major Henry, in the meantime, probably to counteract what in his mind were Picquart's misguided efforts, began to pad the

Dreyfus file with a few fraudulent documents of his own manufacture, entirely unaware of Picquart's photography before his reassignment. It is probable, but unproved, that Henry received the idea for his reprehensible task from those above him. He was a man of simple origin, devoted to the army, and one who accepted orders without question or second thought.

Thanks to the lawyer Louis Leblois, Picquart's suspicions were conveyed to Senator Scheurer-Kestner, then Vice-President of the Senate, but Scheurer-Kestner was not actually told that Picquart had convincing evidence to back up his suspicions. This put the Senator, who had serious doubts of his own, in a relatively weak position when it came to converting others; but he did write a convincing letter to the Radical Senator Arthur Ranc to ask for a reopening of the Dreyfus case, and the letter was published in *Le Temps*. The Dreyfus family also increased its pressure for a rehearing and wrote to President Faure. And on November 15, 1897, Mathieu Dreyfus wrote a letter to the Minister of War, General Billot, that Esterhazy was the guilty man and that he should be investigated.

By that time, the army felt itself sufficiently strengthened by the new "evidence" in the Dreyfus file to strike back at its critics. Indeed, some of the officers, unaware that Henry had manufactured that evidence, were probably convinced that Esterhazy was the victim of a conspiracy by Picquart and Leblois. Others thought that the conspiracy against Esterhazy had been engineered by a Jewish syndicate, which had painstakingly been collecting samples of French officers' handwriting in an effort to find one similar to Dreyfus'. This notion, plus news of the new evidence against Dreyfus, was fed to Rochefort by Major Pauffin de Saint-Morel.[28] Rochefort, swallowing the bait whole, was the first to publish information about the new evidence, going on to attack the so-called Jewish syndicate. In an article called "The Salvaging of the Race," Rochefort claimed that all Israel had felt the terrible blow of Captain Dreyfus's treason, and that the army would henceforth be virtually closed to the Jewish race. In the Panama scandal, he asked, "whom did we find as the chief agents of theft and corruption? Two Semites called Jacques de

Reinach and Cornelius Herz." As for Dreyfus, he ought to be regarded as lower than Bazaine, for, according to Rochefort, Bazaine capitulated because of a dynastic interest, while Dreyfus sold the blood of French soldiers to Germany as a butcher sells meat.[29]

By then, Rochefort saw that the issues and the protagonists in the Dreyfus case required the revival of Boulangism. He talked rather freely about handling the Dreyfus business by organizing a large patriotic movement led by a general. He even called this movement "a new Boulangism," and thought that either General Mercier or General Boisdeffre, the latter the Chief-of-Staff and a current favorite of Rochefort, could lead the movement. Ernest Vaughn, who had left *L'Intransigeant* the year before, was heard to remark, "Rochefort needs a general to cover his retreat." [30]

Confident that Esterhazy would be cleared by a court-martial of the charges made against him by Mathieu Dreyfus, the army ordered his trial on December 4, 1897. The trial was not convened until January 10, and in the meantime Rochefort focused his fire more directly on his old enemy Joseph Reinach, by then one of the better-known Dreyfusards. In several issues of *L'Intransigeant,*[31] he not only insulted Reinach, but charged that Reinach had forged documents to obstruct justice in the approaching court-martial. Reinach answered by opening a libel suit against Rochefort.[32] Let us follow the incident through before returning to the Esterhazy trial.

The libel case was heard on February 9, 1898. Rochefort was condemned to five days in jail, fined 1000 francs, and ordered to insert the judgment in *L'Intransigeant*. His business manager, Delpierre, was also fined 1000 francs; and together they had to pay Reinach 2000 francs damages.[33] "Reinach continues to enjoy complete immunity," Rochefort told his readers. "Also untouched are Mathieu Dreyfus and Colonel Picquart. Instead, the only ones struck by military and civil justice are two men [presumably Rochefort and Esterhazy] whose crime is to have encouraged by their acts and their writing the great national movement which is arrayed against the cosmopolite scum." [34] Rochefort did not appeal his sentence, hoping that his arrival at Sainte-Pélagie prison on February 20 could become the occasion of an anti-Semitic demonstration. The police reported that a crowd of nearly 6000 did gather for his entry but that he left prison on the twenty-fifth without incident.

The Esterhazy court-martial was held on January 10, 1898, and he was acquitted with an almost indecent swiftness. Picquart was thereupon arrested for having communicated military documents to Louis Leblois and was discharged from the army. The Esterhazy acquittal, however, was too much for the famous journalist and novelist, Émile Zola, who wrote an open letter to President Faure charging the army chiefs with deliberately withholding information favorable to Dreyfus and willfully protecting Esterhazy. His letter was published in Vaughn's *L'Aurore,* and the title, "J'accuse!.," was suggested by Georges Clemenceau. The army at once counterattacked by charging Zola with libel, but on only one point, his charge that Esterhazy had been acquitted on order. Zola could not prove this charge, and he fled to England rather than submit to the inevitable prison sentence.

Matters were not going as well for the army as these court cases might suggest; for the revisionists were neither silenced nor intimidated, and the French government continued to obtain new evidence that pointed to the ultimate necessity of reopening the Dreyfus case. Anti-Dreyfusard groups were formed designed to include ex-Boulangists, Nationalists, and Conservatives in general. Déroulède, for instance, revived his Patriots' League, while Jules Lemaître organized a new association called the League of the French Fatherland. But the Dreyfusards countered with the League of the Rights of Man dedicated to defending the principles of 1789, which they said were being threatened by the military. Its founders wanted to exonerate Dreyfus, but their chief intention was to rally all those who regarded "arbitrary action or intolerance" as a threat to civilization and progress.[35] The Dreyfus case, in short, had gone beyond a simple matter of justice for a condemned man and was seen essentially as a new attack upon the Republic—Boulangism in a new guise.

Today, it is easier to see that the Republic was evidently less threatened in 1898 than seemed the case in the heat of passions.[36] None of the army chiefs had any personal following, nor were any of them celebrated for great achievement or heroism. The parliamentary elections, scheduled for May of 1898, also failed to reveal any distinct shift to the Right and ought to have given the Dreyfusards confidence that the republican form was in no peril.[37] One could not, on the other hand, erase the memories and the emotions of the previous thirty years, and, given the bigotry and the vehemence of the anti-Semitic Nationalists of that day, one can hardly fail to appreciate the consternation of the Dreyfusards. If they had somewhat forgotten the case of Alfred Dreyfus the man, they had joined his cause with that of mankind. As for the other side, not all of them were bigots to be sure. Revenge against Germany was a more powerful motive by far than was anti-Semitism in recruiting support for the army. Right or wrong, the army had to be preserved for the day of reckoning; and for those who believed this, reopening the Dreyfus case could only prejudice the honor and prestige of the army.

In the parliamentary elections of May 8 and 22, *L'Intransigeant* supported candidates in each of the twenty Parisian arrondissements.[38] Rochefort's list of favored candidates included some Socialists, some Clericals, and what one unimpressed journal called "some débris from the Patriots' League."[39] What they had in common was opposition to reopening the Dreyfus case. Only nine of his twenty-eight candidates won election; but considering their various party affiliations, it is impossible at this late date to account for the victories and the defeats. What we do know for sure is that the Parisian Socialists in general thought it was high time to dissociate themselves publicly from Rochefort. The Socialists, as we know, were divided into factions, but the defeat of two of their leaders in the May elections, Jaurès and Guesde, helped them to see the need of closer cooperation and, in particular, to expose the bogus Socialists like Rochefort.

On June 1, 1898, Rochefort was condemned by the Socialists of Paris for activities injurious to the proletariat and roughly classified as a renegade.[40] This action was applauded by a number of

Leftist journals. "M. Rochefort's mission was to make us laugh," noted *L'Aurore,* "and in that he succeeded. . . . But some time ago M. Rochefort changed his style. . . . I regret that he got mixed up in politics. This was the opinion expressed twenty years ago by one of our [present] colleagues: 'M. Rochefort is an over-grown child. . . . He is very brave, very loyal, . . . but he is also very nervous, and his most devoted friends do not hide the fact that he is weathercock. He has a writer's temperament, nothing more. What has happened must necessarily have happened, given the contradictions in his behavior and the easiness of his friendships. The astonishing thing is that it did not happen sooner.' These words, of twenty years ago, . . . were written by Émile Zola." This was a sad end for Rochefort, the writer concluded, but not unmerited: "A career and an end like Beaumarchais'." [41]

"The work of Rochefort," noted another journalist in marking Rochefort's expulsion, "is a work of anger: His polemics are documented only in mud and filth. He has picked up every rumor . . . every legend . . . all the lies. . . . The end of this pamphleteer of talent, who was pitiless, seems pitiful. His enemies are resolved not to spare him, as he himself never spared others." [42] About twenty-one anti-Semitic deputies decided to call on Rochefort as a group to thank him for his recent electoral support,[43] and in the context of Socialist objections to him, their visit was rather damning. Rochefort still sought to be numbered among the Socialists despite their rejection of him; and a few days later, he organized what he called a Democratic Banquet for members of the French Socialist-Republican Party. The police were out in force, anticipating trouble from the other Socialist groups, who were beginning to call him Boubourochefort.[44] The leading rabble-rousers were present: "the Reverend Father Drumont," as *L'Aurore* called him, Déroulède, Laguerre, Clovis Hugues, and Rochefort's brother-in-law, the deputy André Vervoort. It was really a "down with the Jews" get-together, but it was also a public demonstration of the fact that they still considered themselves to be Socialists.[45] Rochefort gave the main speech; its tiresome theme was that the government was leading France down the path of military debacle. We may suppose that it was well received by that audience—as reported.[46]

The Left kept up its attack on Rochefort during the summer of 1898, increasingly rallying to Jean Jaurès who had been defeated in the May elections. To illustrate the sort of abuse Jaurès had taken from Rochefort during that campaign, one newspaper printed side by side a campaign statement by Jaurès and its Rochefort translation: [47]

JAURÈS	ROCHEFORT
My mother and my wife are Christian and practicing. I have not the right, I have never had the idea, of obstructing their liberty or blocking their desires. In our society, so sadly discordant and disturbed, how many families can represent one single faith to a child! Where there is no unity of belief, the education of children is a very delicate problem. With a diversity of conviction, but an equality of rights, an absolute, clear-cut system becomes impossible. In this case, the essential thing for us (and I have always been alert to it) is not to give our children for one moment to parochial instruction.	M. Jaurès declares that if he has had his child baptized with a special water that an absurd legend proclaims was made holy by the foot bath that the Nazarene took, it is in order that the young Jaurès girl, when she grows up, will be free to choose her own way and to lead her life according to the lights of her reason!

And another Drefusard journal reminded its readers that long before Rochefort had been excommunicated by the Socialists as a group, he had been many times slapped and kicked by his isolated victims, beginning with Pyat and Flourens in October of 1870.[48]

Rochefort endeavored to focus his attack upon Jaurès the Dreyfusard, not Jaurès the Socialist. Here is a typical attack: "M. Jaurès, who shed a sexton's skin to take on Cabrion's, and who, from Marseille where he recruits for Dreyfus, has had us sent some papers signed with words borrowed from an incomprehensible dialect—which is really the zenith of the Dreyfusard mind—M. Jaurès openly advertizes himself today as a recruiting sergeant in the service of the Treason Syndicate." [49] These attacks, in fact, were failing.

Police-informer reports of that summer regularly noted that the subscriptions to *L'Intransigeant* were beginning to drop.

Far worse for the anti-Dreyfusards, however, were new disclosures that blew their legal position right out of the water. The Italian Ambassador to Paris quietly informed the French government that the document supposedly written by the Italian military attaché was evidently a forgery and should be examined. The Cabinet had the document studied by an expert who found that the Panizzardi letter was actually a composite of two letters, after which the villains of the piece fell into the web of their own making. Esterhazy was ordered to restand court-martial, and Henry, realizing the game was up, confessed to the forgeries. Placed in fortress-arrest at Mont-Valérien, Major Henry slashed his throat with his razor on August 31, 1898. The reopening of the Dreyfus case was now a certainty,[50] and Esterhazy thus fled, first to Belgium and then to Britain. Even so, the government had difficulty in obtaining a new Minister of War who would take the necessary initiative.

Much of the Right was paralyzed by Henry's disclosures and suicide, but not so the hard core of extremists for whom the matter of justice in the Dreyfus case had never been a real issue. Their continuing opposition to reopening the case in the fall of 1898, and the new excuses they hatched for blindly supporting the army in general and Major Henry in particular, gave birth to a new movement, the Action Française. True, it was not formally organized until 1908, but it had its intellectual foundation in Henry's suicide —or sacrifice, as its followers were wont to see it. Thus did the Dreyfus affair extend its tentacles well beyond Dreyfus' ultimate vindication, leading to the France of Vichy. Though Rochefort was not one of the founding fathers of the Action Française, his contributions to the climate that produced the movement were of the first rank.

On the day after Henry's suicide, Rochefort was in print on the topic; and nowhere in his article was there the slightest hint that he suspected why the dead Major had been obliged to become a forger.

"Henry's crime is at once odious and stupid. Odious, because to the very real misdeeds of a condemned man [Dreyfus], imaginary ones have been added. Stupid, because the Dreyfus dossier contained a hundred-fifty proofs of his guilt, all undeniably convincing; and to add to them a false document was to cast doubt on the true ones." [51] Two days later, Rochefort was at work contrasting the suicide—the act of an honorable man ashamed of his deed—with the continuing existence of Dreyfus, Picquart, and Leblois, men who presumably felt no dishonor. [52]

These themes were recast somewhat within the week by Charles Maurras, then a little-known writer for the *Gazette de France,* the Legitimist journal. He gave the issues a better argument than most of the other anti-Dreyfusards could have mustered. From his pen, Major Henry emerged as hero whose blood was the first to be spilled in the *affaire*—the gallant soldier whose forgery was only meant to harm the enemies of France. Maurras' case for martyrdom side-stepped the problem of Dreyfus' guilt or innocence—the main issue in other words—to claim that what was at stake was a strong army supported by a united people. [53] His was a new form of an old argument: that reason of state must take precedence over the rights of an individual.

Charles Maurras, while evidently a Nationalist ally of Rochefort after 1898, was quite a different man and attracted to his movement men of considerable literary quality—Maurice Barrès and Léon Daudet, for example. Moreover, the Action Française was a Royalist movement, while Rochefort continued to profess Socialist-Republicanism—whatever he was in fact. Nationalism in Rochefort seems largely to have derived from the particular details of his career and the quirks of his personality. In the gentlemen of the Action Française, it was more broadly based and more complex; it was a political movement designed to save French civilization from what they saw to be the gathering vulgarization born of the democratic principles of the French Revolution. They were, in short, tradition-alists, leading them to champion both classicism and royalism. [54]

Rochefort, neither classicist nor royalist, with them only as an intransigent, was embarked upon the last great equivocation of his career.

His daily attacks upon Dreyfus in the autumn of 1898 were of such violence and vulgarity that the reader today, turning to those issues of *L'Intransigeant,* wonders if they could have made anything but a sour impression. When the Court of Cassation granted Madame Dreyfus the right to see her husband's dossier under the new circumstances, Rochefort wrote: "Dreyfus himself is only a tiny wrongdoer, a four-penny scoundrel, if one compares him to those supreme court lapdogs who have just granted Mme. Dreyfus access to her infamous husband's dossier. The vile creature was guilty of the lowest treason. It is high treason that [the judges] have just publicly committed by giving to the traitor's wife documents which contained all our secrets about military espionage. . . . The truth is that the cabinet has organized a plot against France, and that, for positions, for degrees in the Legion of Honor, for money, the Court of Cassation has cooperated. . . . It is the most cynical declaration of war ever made upon public opinion." [55] Meanwhile, *Le Radical* noted that "for hygienic safety, shut up the nose and ears when approached by Rochefort the stercorous"; [56] and *L'Aurore:* "It is useless to waste time in calling the ex-man-of-wit's attention to the fact that allowing Mme. Dreyfus's lawyer access to this dossier marks a return to sane traditions of justice, law, and morality." [57]

New municipal elections in Paris in the fall of 1898 also revealed that the public was shifting to the Dreyfusard cause. Every last one of the candidates supported by *L'Intransigeant* was beaten, most of them so far behind in their races that they were out of sight. It was expected that the anti-Dreyfusard candidate in the intellectual and artistic Sixth Arrondissement would be badly beaten (he got 88 of the 2601 votes cast), but when the anti-Dreyfusard candidate for the Clignancourt district (the district Boulanger had carried in 1889) got only 711 of 12,369 votes cast, the rejection of Rochefort and neo-Boulangism was spelled out for all. [58]

Yet Rochefort kept up his Jew-baiting. Toward the end of

1898, he received an invitation from Max Régis, a former mayor of Algiers, to come to North Africa to study the Jewish problem there. This was a nice euphemism considering that Régis was a notorious anti-Semite. Rochefort left Paris on January 4, meeting Régis in Monte Carlo, where they were joined by Édouard Drumont, another expert on North African problems. On February 3, Rochefort moved on to Marseille to take ship for Algiers and discovered that it was to be the *Isaac-Péreire,* named for the Jewish financier. This necessitated finding another ship, apparently the *General Chanzy.* He returned to Marseille about ten days later after a most uncomfortable reception in Algiers, for the French officials treated him not as a tourist, but as an obnoxious revolutionary.[59] *L'Intransigeant* reported that at least he had returned to Marseille in triumph, but other observers claimed that he was booed and pelted with objects other than flowers and required heavy police protection.[60]

On February 16, 1899, President Faure died, removing an enemy of revision and giving the Dreyfusards hope that they might break the judicial logjam by electing one of their own camp as President. Their choice was the rather colorless but moderate Émile Loubet, then presiding over the Senate. His candidacy succeeded two days later on the first ballot, spurring some of the Nationalists into action. Déroulède favored a *coup d'état* at the time of Faure's funeral, scheduled for February 23. His Patriots' Leaguers were to be the core of the uprising, but he negotiated for support from Royalists, Bonapartists, and leading anti-Semites. The police knew that Déroulède was up to no good and that he had met with Millevoye, Thiébaud, Max Régis, and others on the twentieth. Thus, they denied his request for a place in the funeral procession. Nevertheless, as the procession left Notre Dame, several hundred agitators rushed among the escorting troops, hoping to rally them for an attack upon the Élysée Palace. The attempt failed ridiculously, and Déroulède was arrested.[61] Rochefort had not been present, perhaps because, at sixty-eight, street demonstrations were no longer suitable amusement.

The government now began its ponderous movements toward

vindicating Captain Dreyfus. The first step was to ask the Court of Cassation to review the verdict of his court-martial of 1894; and as part of that review, Esterhazy was interviewed from the safety of London. Having no longer anything to lose, he confessed that he had been the author of the memorandum attributed to Dreyfus. The court then quashed the original verdict and ordered a new court-martial for Dreyfus—this time to be held at Rennes, far from the passions of Paris. But he who had not seen that Major Henry's suicide altered the Dreyfus case was equally unready to accept the obvious about Esterhazy. On the day after the Court of Cassation ordered the retrial, Rochefort had this to say: "Esterhazy's confession, the great *coup* held for the closing of the Supreme Court theater, in fact amounts to the most simpleminded of last-moment maneuvers. If, as he testified, . . . he had been futilely offered a large sum to get him to acknowledge himself to be the author of the memorandum, has he now decided to accept it, since the day before yesterday he revealed that the Treason Syndicate had offered him a high price. And, if they could pay him to tell this truth, could they not equally pay him to invent a lie?" [62]

Rochefort was not alone in his indignation. Even though a great majority of the Parisians had by that time returned to support the Republic and the government's policies, much of the *jeunesse dorée* remained vociferously anti-Dreyfusard. When Presideni Loubet appeared at Longchamp on June 11, he was freely insulted by them; and, inadequately protected, he was even struck by the cane of Baron de Christiani. The public quickly showed its disapproval of such insane behavior, and one of the immediate results was a presidential decision to strengthen the cabinet for a showdown on the Dreyfus issue. Loubet's idea was to bring into the government as many political parties as possible in order to confront the Nationalist diehards with an insuperable barrier. The result was the René Waldeck-Rousseau government of June 22, 1899. Its membership ranged from General Gallifet at the Ministry of War, a Rightist remembered for his anti-Communard services, to the Socialist Millerand at the Ministry of Commerce. Waldeck-Rousseau, a moderate

Catholic and Republican, let it be known at the outset that the Church would be the first to suffer for its anti-Dreyfus stand and that he intended to strike at the religious orders. This was the government in power, then, when Dreyfus was brought back to France to face his second court-martial on August 7, 1899.

This time, the prosecution was reduced to the most absurd maneuvers to prove that the original memorandum had been written by Dreyfus. The former Minister of War, General Mercier, was the chief witness for the prosecution. He sought to explain that the original copy of that memorandum was not used in the initial trial, because it bore marginal notes by William II of Germany. To prevent its use, Germany had threatened war, forcing the French government to use at the trial a copy of the memorandum, which had been traced by Esterhazy on thin paper. Casimir-Périer, who had been President at the time, denied in his testimony that there had been any threat of war; and the prosecution's case should have been laughed out of court without further ado. Yet that shameless court once again found Dreyfus guilty, though this time dividing on the verdict five to two. In a final piece of hypocrisy, the court did —because of "extenuating circumstances"—reduce his sentence from life imprisonment to ten years.

This outrageous performance infuriated the Prime Minister, who had to realize that there was probably no hope of obtaining justice from a military court. The only course left open, therefore, was to get Dreyfus pardoned. This meant, however, accepting the verdict of the court-martial and that the crowd who engineered Dreyfus' convictions would be untouched for their criminal performance. Would Dreyfus accept a pardon in order to bring an end to the affair? Some like Clemenceau and Zola argued that he must not accept it, that the legal battle might go on. Others, including his family, believed that he had suffered enough. And that proved to be his own view. On September 19, 1899, President Loubet signed the pardon, which had been prepared by General Gallifet, and Alfred Dreyfus became a free man.[63] Only after some years did the Republicans feel sufficiently strong to undertake the legal rehabilitation of

Dreyfus. In 1906, the Court of Cassation quashed the verdict of 1894. Dreyfus was thereupon restored to the army and promoted to the rank of major. Picquart was promoted to be a general and was later a Minister of War.

There was no changing Rochefort's mind about the matter; he remained an unrepentant anti-Dreyfusard to the end. But he was nearing seventy, and his career as an effective polemicist had come to an end. Though he continued to call himself a Socialist, he was generally regarded as a Rightist as a result of his efforts for Boulanger and against Dreyfus. And Rightist he had indeed become, though no conservative. Early in 1900, his paper carried an advertisement for a political meeting in Bordeaux at which he would preside: "After the unexpected pardon of Dreyfus, the scandals of the High Court, the indignities and calumnies of the cabinet, we have thought that the hour has come to tell the people that the national conscience still has its defenders and its apostles, and that the French soul still has enough vigor to resist the shame from above and the blows given it by the countryless [Jews]." [64] And when a suitable anti-Dreyfusard anniversary would come along, such as the anniversary of Dreyfus' degradation, one could expect that it would be publicly observed and that Rochefort would be among the celebrants in company with his new comrades-in-arms, the gentlemen of the Action Française. [65]

Not that the ranks of the Right were firm after 1900. They contained both Republicans and Royalists. To mention overthrowing the Republic would alienate Republican voters, and the Royalists could not even agree on the nature of the monarchy should there be a restoration. And what was the chance for a restoration? Because the monarchical deputies in the Chamber were pathetically few in number, a legal change of state was out of the question. If they were to succeed in a *coup d'état,* how long could it last in the face of widespread popular support for the Republic? The Rightist leaders recognized that a *coup* was impractical and no one but Rochefort talked in revolutionary terms. "And, as no one could conceive of Rochefort supporting a majority, it is evident that he would separate himself from a coalition in the wake of its electoral victory." [66] There would be, in sum, no *coups d'état* nor any unity on the Right.

Even the Rightist press was in difficulty after 1900. The public bought extremist sheets like Rochefort's *L'Intransigeant* and Drumont's *La Libre Parole* in times of scandal. When hot issues simmered down, readers turned to more discreete and reliable papers for their daily news.[67] *L'Action Française,* first published as a daily in 1908, suffered the same financial embarrassment already being experienced by the popular Nationalist press. Rochefort, meanwhile, had left *L'Intransigeant* in October of 1907, after a long series of disagreements with his colleagues; [68] and hoping to eliminate competition and to develop a financially satisfactory readership, the founders of *L'Action Française* offered Rochefort collaboration. He rejected it, saying, "You are mad, you will not last three months, and then what would I do?" [69] One notices at once that he did not reject their offer because *L'Action Française* was a Catholic-Royalist paper, a response that would have seemed more appropriate. Why, indeed, had the founders of *L'Action Française* hoped to snare him in the first place? Because Rochefort could be a man of great personal charm and, despite their political differences, Rochefort was liked by Léon Daudet. Knowing that Rochefort was not encumbered with any philosophical doctrine, Daudet might well have presumed that Rochefort was at last ready to make common cause with fellow-Nationalists whose aristocratic tastes and prejudices he had so long evinced *malgré lui*. For all the revolutionary utterances, Rochefort was, as Daudet knew, a *frondeur*.[70]

When one has waded through "the adventures" of Rochefort's career, to become sated with his petulance, his acidity, and those eternal crusades in which principle was so much more apparent than real, it is perhaps only irritating to be reminded that Paris forgave him everything because of his wit. "Paris is ready to laugh at everything," Daudet noted, "for fear of being obliged to cry about everything; she is given to pity, to anger, and above all to wit; she does not respect, or hardly respects, established authorities." [71] The Rochefort wit was so often crude, so often envenomed when used for political or personal purpose, that it is only just to recall that he was known for his charming conversation in the *salon* and for an occasional article where his wit was delicious rather than malicious.

Here, for instance, is a letter, written in his seventieth year to Mme. Tavernier, apparently a mistress of whom he was very fond: "Excellent friend, if by chance you should meet Madame Tavernier whom I have not seen for fifteen years and who perhaps has changed her address, you would be ever-so-kind to let her know that she is expected for lunch on Saturday, rue Pergolèse. Jules Lemaître, of whom I believe her to be very fond, will be on hand." [72] Not merely his immediate friends but his readers had reason to know that he could be most amusing and mild when the topic was not political. The following is a major portion of a letter he wrote from London to the editors of *L'Intransigeant* on December 1, 1893, after having seen a performance at Covent Garden:

> It is a habit of the English public to follow the text of the opera which it is attending, whose action it understands only imperfectly since the artists . . . sing only in Italian or in French. Thus, on entering the lobby of the theater, one is approached by several hawkers who offer the libretto. On that particular evening, they were playing *Aïda;* but the sellers, having doubtless exhausted their stock of texts for that production, surreptitiously passed out libretti for *Haydée,* the comic opera by Auber, to the arriving audience.
>
> I had rebuffed with some indignation this attempt at fraud, and I supposed the other spectators had done the same. Thus, I was literally stupefied in noticing . . . a woman on my left—a woman in glasses—oh! in London, the women wearing glasses— . . . absorbed in the couplets and the recitatives of Scribe [the librettist for Auber] without perceiving that they had no relation to what was transpiring on stage.
>
> But my astonishment changed to horror when I saw before, behind, and around me that most of the spectators in the orchestra were holding the same libretto, by which they were following the singing with a superb seriousness,

and who took Aïda for Haydée and Rhadames for Lorédan without the slightest hesitation.

And, to make things unbelievably complicated, something to which your London correspondent, M. Johnson, can attest as he also attended the performance, all the unfortunate victims of this deliberate hoax turned their pages at the same place at the same time! In each row of seats, one saw pages flipped over simultaneously, and all eyes fell upon the succeeding pages with a redoubling of attention.

No doubt, those mystified creatures were watching each other, and as soon as one made a movement, the others hastened to imitate. But nothing was funnier than this simultaneous riffling of paper in the midst of catastrophic situations which resembled in no way those which an entire audience seemed to enjoy so avidly.

The most difficult obstacle to be overcome was the dénouement, *Haydée* having only three acts, while *Aïda* has four of them and seven scenes. All seemed as well as could be. My neighbor and her neighbors got up first to leave at the end of the third act, supposing that the production was ended. Then, as the musicians remained at their desks, everyone sat down again, and the third act of *Haydée* was used over again for the fourth act of *Aïda*.

I do not know if you can sufficiently realize how much I was entertained by the confusion which lasted until the lowering of the last curtain; but I declare that never has a lyric drama made me laugh so." [73]

In his old age, Rochefort doted on his grandchildren as he always had on his children. Henri, of course, had committed suicide when still a bachelor; and Octave emigrated as a young man to Argentina. A graduate engineer from the École Central, Octave had some mining experience in Algeria before becoming a teacher of geometry and statistics in Buenos Aires. In the 1890's, he returned temporarily to France to build a typewriter factory in Passy and was, thus, on hand when his father returned from exile in 1895. But Octave soon returned to Argentina and never saw his father again.

Noémie Dufaux, however, had three children by her Genevan husband; and though they continued to live in Switzerland, Rochefort saw them frequently. The three were named Lili, Henri, and Armand; and when they were in Paris, Rochefort would take them to the Jardin des Plantes, where he could at once please them and indulge his own liking for animals and birds.[74]

For a man who had been described as frail and nervous even in his prime, and whose stomach would fail him in moments of crisis, Rochefort proved to be remarkably durable. And we should not make the mistake of concluding that he never took seriously or personally those emotional causes into which he flung himself so frequently and passionately. Despite the personality defects that made him a political extremist and one who was almost always *against* rather than *for,* and however often he may have initially embarked upon a crusade to shore up sagging subscriptions, once engaged he seems to have been the most zealous believer in the campaign and utterly devoted to the notion of his own righteousness and disinterestedness. For example, not only do his articles in *L'Intransigeant* demonstrate his studied indifference to the new evidence that made necessary a revision of the Dreyfus case, but what little of his private correspondence remains clearly shows that he believed that Dreyfus was guilty. "You see how awful this Chamber is," he wrote to Mme. Tavernier on March 26, 1901. "Providing that one pays it, nothing bothers it. It delivers us to the Foreigner with an extraordinary calm." A few months later he wrote her that "save for the debauchery of the Center, the ministry would have been turned out the other day. But there is treason everywhere, and we will end up by proving that Dreyfus is the most honest one we have left in France." [75]

Ten years before he died, his friends already despaired for his life, since he seemed so continually stricken with ailments serious for a man of seventy-two. "He is overly impressionable," wrote a close friend in 1903, "and the slightest obstacle or the least change in the weather affects his organism and gives him terrible heart pains. He needs to be surrounded by friends, to be able to forget his suffering and to help him forget the difficulties the awful politics, which beset our beautiful France, give him." [76] Perhaps Rochefort drew strength from such cheerful friends as this who saw the world as he saw it. As the same friend wrote a few days later, "Rochefort has nothing wrong in the stomach, nothing but nervous contractions of the pylorus: He needs rest, a regimen, hydrotherapy, and freedom of the stomach, the best and surest of all the freedoms, since they take all the others from us one after the other, so that perhaps we shall only be able to keep that one!" [77]

When Rochefort left *L'Intransigeant* in 1907, after twenty-seven years, he joined the staff of *La Patrie,* where he was a name more than an effective collaborator. He remained there for his final six years, convinced, as he told Frank Harris, that his old teeth could still bite.[78] He died on July 1, 1913, of uremic poisoning in Aix-les-Bains, where he had been for several weeks. The body was shipped to Paris on the third for a funeral on the sixth at the Montmartre cemetery.[79] The seven eulogies delivered all tended to concentrate on Rochefort's patriotism; and the only members of his family present were Noémie Dufaux and her children. Maurice Barrès attended, as did Alexandre Zévaès, who would later publish a life of Rochefort.[80]

There was another mourner: If one visits the animal cemetery in Asnières, one can find the grave of his favorite black Persian. Its tombstone reads: "Kroumir, Henri Rochefort's cat, died of grief ten days after his master, July 10, 1913." [81]

But surely Rochefort would have wanted us to end on a more jocular note. Besides cats, he was fond of birds and owned a South American parrot that he had taught to say "Vive la République." One day when the bird had become unusually bored at being left alone all day, it broke its chain and used its long beak to break vases and to slash upholstery. When Rochefort walked into the demolished room, the irate creature screamed at him "Vive la République." May we not wonder if that bird was a superb satirist?

NOTES

CHAPTER I

1. *Le Rappel,* October 25, 1896.
2. *Les Aventures,* I, 3–8; and Noële Roubaud, *Henri Rochefort Intime* (Paris, 1954), pp. 9–11.
3. *Les Aventures,* I, 23–33; and Alexandre Zévaès, *Henri Rochefort, le pamphlétaire* (Paris, 1929), pp. 9–10.
4. *Les Aventures,* I, 52.
5. B.N. Dept. of Manuscripts (Collection Rothschild autographes du XIX° Siècle), *Ode à Béranger* (1847), my translation.
6. *Les Aventures,* I, 57.
7. A.N. 48 AP 1.
8. *Les Aventures,* I, 104.
9. *Ibid.,* 128.
10. Pierre de la Gorce, *Histoire du Second Empire,* V (Paris, 1894–1905), 396.
11. *Les Aventures,* I, 164.
12. Zévaès, *op. cit.,* p. 17, my translation.
13. *Les Aventures,* I, 157.
14. Enid Starkie, *Baudelaire* (New York, 1958), p. 121.
15. Zévaès, *op. cit.,* pp. 280–82, gives a complete bibliography of Rochefort's works.
16. A.N. 48 AP 1, copy of Noémie's birth certificate.
17. Ernest Blum, *Biographie complète de Henri Rochefort par un ami de dix ans* (Brussels, 1868), pp. 47–48.
18. *Les Aventures,* I, 190.
19. Irene Collins, *The Government and the Newspaper Press in France, 1814–1881* (London, 1959), pp. 114–15.
20. André Bellessort, *La Société fran-çaise sous Napoléon III* (Paris, n.d.), p. 254.
21. Collins, *op. cit.,* pp. 116–28.
22. *Les Aventures,* I, 201–02.
23. *Le Charivari,* October 4, 1861.
24. *Les Aventures,* I, 202–04. In the *Memoirs* of Comte Horace de Viel Castel, I (London, 1888), pp. 209–11, there is further evidence of "vandalism" at the Louvre.
25. Alphonse Daudet, *Quarante ans de Paris* (Geneva, 1952), pp. 114–16; and *Les Aventures,* I, p. 195.
26. *Les Aventures,* I, 227–28.
27. *Ibid.,* 231.
28. *Ibid.,* 232–33.
29. de la Gorce, *op. cit.,* V, 398.
30. Zévaès, *op. cit.,* p. 31.
31. *Les Aventures,* I, 237.
32. *Ibid.,* 238–40.
33. Comte Maurice Fleury and Louis Sonolet, *La Société du Second Empire,* III (Paris, 1911), p. 182.
34. Frank Jellinek, *The Paris Commune of 1871* (London, 1937), p. 63.
35. Roger L. Williams, *Gaslight and Shadow* (New York, 1957), p. 63.
36. *Les Aventures,* I, 246–48.
37. *Ibid.,* 248–51.
38. Edmond and Jules de Goncourt, *Journal,* V (Paris, 1891–1907), p. 195.
39. Bellessort, *op. cit.,* p. 294.
40. Theodore Zeldin, *Émile Ollivier and the Liberal Empire of Napoleon III* (Oxford, 1963), is the most recent good study of Ollivier's controversial career.
41. Marcel Proust, *Jean Santeuil* (New York, 1961), p. 486.

42. *Les Aventures,* I, 256.
43. Zévaès, *op. cit.,* p. 34.
44. *Les Aventures,* I, 304.
45. *Ibid.,* 314–19.

CHAPTER II

1. Irene Collins, *The Government and the Newspaper Press in France, 1814–1881* (London, 1959), pp. 148–49.
2. *Les Aventures,* I, 322.
3. André Siegfried, *De la IIIe à la IVe République* (Paris, 1958), p. 202.
4. Pierre de la Gorce, *Histoire du Second Empire,* V (Paris, 1894–1905), p. 400.
5. André Billy, *Les écrivains de combat* (Nevers, 1931), p. 112.
6. *La Lanterne,* #1, May 31, 1868, pp. 20–21.
7. *Ibid.,* #9, July 25, 1868, p. 52.
8. *Ibid.,* #2, June 6, 1868, p. 77.
9. *Ibid.,* #1, May 31, 1868, p. 47.
10. *Ibid.,* #4, June 20, 1868, pp. 181–82.
11. Gustave Flaubert, *Correspondance* (Sept. 9, 1868), V (Paris, 1926–33), p. 404.
12. Edmond and Jules de Goncourt, *Journal,* VI (Paris, 1891–1907), p. 13.
13. *La Lanterne,* #5, June 27, 1868, pp. 289–90.
14. *Ibid.,* #2, June 6, 1868, pp. 65–66.
15. *Les Aventures,* I, 343.
16. Paul Guériot, *Napoléon III,* (Paris, 1933–34), II, 132.
17. *La Lanterne,* #2, June 6, 1868, pp. 89–93.
18. *Ibid.,* #3, June 13, 1868, p. 147.
19. Roger L. Williams, *Gaslight and Shadow* (New York, 1957), p. 50.
20. *La Lanterne,* #3, June 13, 1868, pp. 167–71.
21. Police Carton B a/1246.
22. Adrien Dansette, *Louis-Napoléon à la conquête du pouvoir* (Paris, 1961), pp. 21–32.
23. *La Lanterne,* #6, July 4, 1868, pp. 301–02.
24. *Ibid.,* #5, June 27, 1868, pp. 239–40.
25. *Ibid.,* #7, July 11, 1868, p. 385.
26. *Les Aventures,* I, 360–61.
27. *La Lanterne,* #8, July 18, 1868, pp. 469–71.
28. *Ibid.,* #9, July 25, 1868, pp. 1–2.
29. Émile Ollivier, *Journal 1846–1869,* II (Paris, 1961), 333.
30. *La Lanterne,* #10, August 1, 1868, p. 24.
31. *Les Aventures,* I, 372–73.
32. *Ibid.,* II, 3–6.
33. Flaubert, *op. cit.,* V, 401.
34. Theodore Zeldin, *Émile Ollivier and the Liberal Empire of Napoleon III,* p. 107.
35. *La Lanterne,* #13, August 22, 1868, p. 8.
36. *Ibid.,* pp. 25–26.
37. *Les Aventures,* II, 23–29.
38. *Ibid.,* pp. 70–74.
39. *La Lanterne,* #20, October 10, 1868, p. 57.
40. *Ibid.,* #12, August 15, 1868, p. 15.
41. *Ibid.,* #16, September 12, 1868, p. 47.
42. *Ibid.,* #20, October 10, 1868, p. 20.
43. *Ibid.,* #19, October 3, 1868, p. 35.
44. *Ibid.,* #29, December 12, 1868, p. 23.
45. *Ibid.,* #23, October 31, 1868, pp. 41–42.
46. Guy Chapman, *The Third Republic of France: The First Phase 1872–1894* (London, 1962), p. 264; and André Maurois, *Olympio ou la vie de Victor Hugo* (Paris, 1954), p. 487.
47. *Les Aventures,* II, 85–87.
48. George Sand, *Correspondance* (1812–1876), (Paris, 1884), V, 315.
49. *Les Aventures,* II, 88.

50. *La Lanterne,* #29, December 12, 1868, pp. 58–62.
51. Roger L. Williams, *op. cit.,* p. 276.
52. Ludovic Halévy, *Carnets,* II (Paris, 1935), p. 69.
53. *Les Aventures,* II, 89–96.
54. Flaubert, *op. cit.,* V, 56.
55. *Ibid.,* VI, 93.
56. Sand, *op. cit.,* V, 326–27.
57. Police Carton B a/1246, letter dated September 25, 1869 (among letters seized by police in December of 1873 at the Delimal home).
58. *Les Aventures,* II, 99–101.
59. Police Carton B a/1246.
60. *Le Figaro,* November 13, 1869.
61. *Le Gaulois,* November 20, 1869.
62. *Les Aventures,* II, 110.
63. Ollivier, *op. cit.,* II, 399–400.
64. Reported by Eugène Morand in *Le Figaro,* December 2, 1869.
65. *Les Aventures,* II, 120; and Edmond Bazire, *Rochefort* (Paris, 1883), p. 18.
66. J. Monteilhet, *Les Institutions Militaires de la France, 1814–1932* (Paris, 1932), pp. 44–49.
67. *Les Aventures,* II, 121.
68. Jules Gesztesi, *Pauline de Metternich* (Paris, 1947), p. 283.
69. de la Gorce, *op. cit.,* VI, 9–10.
70. Eugénie de Grèce, *Pierre-Napoléon Bonaparte 1815–1881* (Paris, 1963), pp. 292–99.
71. de la Gorce, *op. cit.,* VI, 11.
72. de Grèce, *op. cit.,* p. 317.
73. *La Marseillaise,* January 9, 1870.
74. *Les Aventures,* II, 130.
75. de la Gorce, *op. cit.,* VI, 12; and de Grèce, *op. cit.,* p. 319.
76. *Les Aventures,* II, 132.
77. de Grèce, *op. cit.,* pp. 320–32.
78. Ollivier, *op. cit.,* II, 418.
79. *La Marseillaise,* January 11, 1870.
80. *Les Aventures,* II, 131.
81. *Ibid.,* p. 141.
82. de la Gorce, *op. cit.,* VI, 16–17.
83. *Les Aventures,* II, 142.
84. Ollivier, *op. cit.,* II, 419.

85. *Les Aventures,* II, 143–44; and de Grèce, *op. cit.,* pp. 340–42.
86. Police Carton B a/1246, secret report to Prefect of Police from Genoa, October 16, 1872; and *Les Aventures,* II, 145.
87. Léon A. Daudet, *Flammes: Polémique et polémistes* (Paris, 1930), pp. 142–48.
88. Police Carton B a/1246.
89. *Le Rappel,* February 6, 1870.
90. Jules Rouquette, *Rochefort* (Paris, 1871), p. 11.
91. *Les Aventures,* II, 143.
92. Report signed by Nogent-St. Laurens, Police Dossier E a/14.
93. *Les Aventures,* II, 150.
94. Ollivier, *op. cit.,* II, 419.
95. de la Gorce, *op. cit.,* VI, 25–26.
96. *Le Figaro,* February 8, 1870; *Paris-Journal,* February 10, 1870; *Les Aventures,* II, 152–62; Gustave Flourens, *Paris Livré* (Paris, 1871), p. 7.
97. de Grèce, *op. cit.,* pp. 334–75.
98. *Les Aventures,* II, 172–73.
99. Rochefort to Piétri, February 13, 1870, Police Carton B a/1246; published same date in *Le Siècle.*
100. *La Marseillaise,* March 12, 1870.
101. *Les Aventures,* II, 165.
102. *La Marseillaise,* March 17, 1870.
103. Sand, *op. cit.,* VI, 26–27.
104. *Les Aventures,* II, 189–90.
105. *La Cloche,* August 3, 1870.

CHAPTER III

Part 1

1. Rochefort's *Carnet,* Police Dossier E a/14.
2. Jacques Chastenet, *Histoire de la Troisième République,* I (Paris, 1952–1963), p. 13.
3. *Enquête parlementaire sur le Gouvernement de la Défense Nationale* (Paris and Versailles, 1872–1875), Report of Comte Napoléon Daru, #1416B, p. 63.

4. *Ibid.*, Dépositions des Témoins, Jules Favre, I, 332.
5. *Ibid.*, Dépositions des Témoins, Jules Ferry, I, 383.
6. Jules Simon, *Souvenirs du 4 septembre*, p. 253.
7. *Défense Nationale*, Daru Report, #1416B, p. 50.
8. *Ibid.*, Dépositions des Témoins, Louis Jules Trochu, I, 280.
9. *Ibid.*, Dépositions des Témoins, Adolphe Crémieux, I, 580.
10. Edmond and Jules de Goncourt, *Journal*, IV, 20.
11. Étienne Arago, *L'Hôtel de Ville de Paris au 4 septembre et pendant le siège* (Paris, n.d.), p. 25; *Défense Nationale, Dépositions des Témoins*, Charles Floquet, II, 280; and *Les Aventures*, II, 200–01.
12. *Défense Nationale*, Daru Report, #1416B, p. 70.
13. Juliette Adam, *Le Siège de Paris, Journal d'une Parisienne* (Paris, 1873), p. 73.
14. *Les Aventures*, II, 205–11.
15. *Ibid.*, 222–24.
16. Michael Howard, *The Franco-Prussian War* (New York, 1962), p. 227.
17. *Défense Nationale*, Report of Eugène Chaper, #1453, pp. 12–13; and Daru Report, #1416B, pp. 132–37.
18. Chastenet, *op. cit.*, I, 24.
19. *Défense Nationale*, Chaper Report, #1453, pp. 10–23.
20. *Les Aventures*, II, 225; *Défense Nationale*, Daru Report, #1416B, p. 166.
21. John Plamenatz, *The Revolutionary Movement in France, 1815–1871* (London, 1952), p. 133; and *Défense Nationale*, Daru Report, #1416B, pp. 86–87.
22. *Défense Nationale*, Daru Report, #1416B, p. 147.
23. Chastenet, *op. cit.*, I, 25.
24. Maxime Du Camp, *Souvenirs d'un demi-siècle* (Paris, 1949), II, 139.
25. *Défense Nationale*, Dépositions des Témoins, Louis Jules Trochu, I, 281.
26. *Ibid.*, Daru Report, #1416B, p. 143.
27. Chastenet, *op. cit.*, I, 27.
28. Howard, *op. cit.*, p. 232.
29. *Défense Nationale*, Daru Report, #1416B, p. 154.
30. *Ibid.*, Dépéches Officielles, II, 260.
31. *Les Aventures*, II, 229–30, 255–56, 280.
32. See' two works on this subject: Melvin Kranzberg, *The Siege of Paris, 1870–1871: A Political and Social History* (New York, 1950); and Robert Baldick, *The Siege of Paris* (New York, 1964).
33. Edmond Bazire, *Rochefort*, p. 71; and Du Camp, *op. cit.*, II, 140.
34. Goncourt, *op. cit.*, IV, 69–70.
35. *Défense Nationale*, Daru Report, #1416B, pp. 102–104.
36. *Ibid.*, pp. 87–88, 125.
37. *Ibid.*, Chaper Report, #1453, p. 8.
38. *Ibid.*, p. 31; and *Ibid.*, Daru Report, #1416B, p. 126.
39. *Les Aventures*, II, 227–28; and *Défense Nationale*, Chaper Report, #1453, pp. 37–38.
40. *Défense Nationale*, Daru Report, #1416B, p. 91.
41. *Ibid.*, pp. 127–28.
42. *Ibid.*, Chaper Report, #1453, p. 40; and *Les Aventures*, II, 237.
43. *Les Aventures*, II, 221.
44. *Défense Nationale*, Dépositions des Témoins, Louis Jules Trochu, I, 300.
45. *Les Aventures*, II, 240.
46. Adam, *op. cit.*, p. 89.
47. *Ibid.*, p. 111.
48. *Ibid.*, p. 124.
49. *Défense Nationale*, Chaper Report, #1453, p. 44.
50. Adam, *op. cit.*, p. 107.

51. François J. Charles-Roux, *Alexandre II, Gortchakoff et Napoléon III* (Paris, 1913), p. 508.

52. *Ibid.*, pp. 515–21.

53. *Les Aventures,* II, 242; and Arago, *op. cit.*, p. 239.

54. Simon, *op. cit.*, pp. 318–19; and *Défense Nationale,* Dépositions des Témoins, Louis Jules Trochu, I, 289.

55. *Défense Nationale,* Daru Report, #1416B, pp. 172–74.

56. *Ibid.*, p. 173.

57. Arago, *op. cit.*, p. 241.

58. Simon, *op. cit.*, p. 324; *Défense Nationale,* Chaper Report, #1453, p. 53; and Daru Report, #1416B, pp. 179–81.

59. *Défense Nationale,* Daru Report, #1416B, p. 188.

60. *Ibid.*, p. 189; *Les Aventures,* II, 245; *Enquête parlementaire sur l'Insurrection du 18 mars,* Deposition of Colonel Ibos, II, 424; Simon, *op. cit.*, p. 330.

61. *Défense Nationale,* Daru Report, #1416B, pp. 195–96.

62. *Ibid.*, p. 200.

63. *Ibid.*, pp. 205–13; and Simon, *op. cit.*, pp. 337–48.

64. *Insurrection,* Deposition of Louis Jules Trochu, II, 37; and *Défense Nationale,* Dépositions des Témoins, Louis Jules Trochu, I, 298–99.

65. *Défense Nationale,* Dépositions des Témoins, P. F. Dorian, I, 527–30.

66. *Les Aventures,* II, 111–12.

67. *Ibid.*, II, 243–44.

68. Adam, *op. cit.*, p. 151.

69. *Défense Nationale,* Dépositions des Témoins, P. F. Dorian, I, 527.

70. *Ibid.*, Chaper Report, #1453, p. 56; Daru Report, #1416B, p. 238; and Dépositions des Témoins, M. Dréo, II, 62.

71. Simon, *op. cit.*, p. 357; and *Les Aventures,* II, 246.

72. Adam, *op. cit.*, p. 198.

73. *La Lanterne,* #7, July 11, 1868, p. 385.

74. Ernest Cresson, *Cent Jours du siège à la Préfecture de Police, 2 novembre 1870–11 février 1871* (Paris, 1901), pp. 12–13.

75. *Défense Nationale,* Daru Report, #1416B, pp. 239–47.

76. *Ibid.*, pp. 257–58; and Simon, *op. cit.*, p. 270.

77. *Défense Nationale,* Daru Report, #1416B, p. 262.

78. Charles-Roux, *op. cit.*, pp. 520–21.

79. André Castelot, *Le Grand Siècle de Paris* (Paris, 1955), p. 336.

80. *Les Nouvelles,* December 4, 1870.

81. Goncourt, *op. cit.*, IV, 159.

82. *Défense Nationale,* Daru Report, #1416B, pp. 280–83.

83. Goncourt, *op. cit.*, IV, 133.

84. *Défense Nationale,* Daru Report, #1416B, pp. 337–38.

85. *Ibid.*, pp. 312–18; and Simon, *op. cit.*, p. 428.

86. *Défense Nationale,* Daru Report, #1416B, pp. 319–22; and Simon, *op. cit.*, pp. 429–31.

87. *Défense Nationale,* Daru Report, #1416B, pp. 347–56.

88. *Le Combat,* January 25, 1871.

89. *Les Aventures,* II, 317.

90. Simon, *op. cit.*, pp. 441–54; and *Défense Nationale,* Daru Report, #1416B, pp. 361–84.

91. *Défense Nationale,* Daru Report, #1416B, p. 541.

92. *Ibid.*, p. 387.

93. *Ibid.*, pp. 417–19.

94. *Défense Nationale,* Dépéches Officielles (Dispatch from Lisbonne, Prefect of Hérault, February 3, 1871, 12:36 P.M., #7230), I, 337.

Part 2

1. Maurice Reclus, *L'Avènement de la IIIᵉ République, 1871–1875* (Paris, 1930), pp. 10–17; and *Enquête parlementaire sur le Gouvernement de la Défense Nationale,*

Report of Comte Napoléon Daru, #1416B, p. 373.

2. Raymond Manevy, *La Presse de la IIIe République* (Paris, 1955), p. 49.

3. *Les Aventures*, II, 318.

4. Rochefort's *Carnet*, Police Dossier E a/14.

5. The complete list is given in Alexandre Zévaès, *Henri Rochefort, le pamphlétaire* (Paris, 1929), p. 112.

6. *Le Mot d'Ordre*, February 4, 1871; *Les Aventures*, II, 321; and Ernest Cresson, *Cent Jours du siège à la Préfecture de Police, 2 novembre 1870–11 février 1871* (Paris, 1901), pp. 324–28.

7. *Les Aventures*, II, 326–38.

8. John Plamenatz, *The Revolutionary Movement in France, 1815–1871* (London, 1952), p. 138; Jean T. Joughin, *The Paris Commune in French Politics, 1871–1880*, I (Baltimore, Md., 1955), pp. 23–24; and Reclus, *op cit.*, pp. 18–24.

9. Reclus, *op. cit.*, pp. 25–26.

10. *Les Aventures*, II, 340.

11. Émile Zola, *La République en marche, Chroniques parlementaires 13 février à 16 septembre 1871*, I (Paris, 1956), pp. 20–22.

12. *Ibid.*, I, 23–25; and Jacques Chastenet, *Histoire de la Troisième République*, I (Paris, 1952–1963), p. 57.

13. Reclus, *op. cit.*, p. 30; and Chastenet, *op. cit.*, I, 58.

14. Juliette Adam, *La Siège de Paris, Journal d'une Parisienne* (Paris, 1873), p. 349.

15. *Le Mot d'Ordre*, February 13, 1871.

16. Michel Mohrt, *Les Intellectuels devant la Défaite, 1870* (Paris, 1942), pp. 19–53; Léon Blum, *L'Oeuvre de Léon Blum (1891–1905)* (Paris, 1954), p. 212; Reclus, *op. cit.*, pp. 137–38; and Chastenet, *op. cit.*, I, 282.

17. "Mea Culpa," *Le Mot d'Ordre*, February 14, 1871.

18. Zola, *op. cit.*, I, 18.

19. *Ibid.*, I, 26–27.

20. Reclus, *op. cit.*, pp. 32–35.

21. Zola, *op. cit.*, I, 62.

22. *Les Aventures*, II, 344.

23. Reclus, *op. cit.*, p. 37.

24. Frank H. Brabant, *The Beginning of the Third Republic in France: A History of the National Assembly, February-September 1871* (London, 1940), p. 129, from the *Annales de l'Assemblée Nationale*, I, 109–25.

25. *Le Mot d'Ordre*, March 7, 1871.

26. *Les Aventures*, II, 353–55; and Manevy, *op. cit.*, pp. 52–53.

27. Wilfred de Fonvielle, *Les Dernières causeries de H. Rochefort, annotées, commentées et refutées par Wilfred de Fonvielle* (Brussels, 1871), pp. 13–14.

28. Plamenatz, *op. cit.*, p. 139; and Zola, *op. cit.*, I, 83.

29. Zola, *op. cit.*, I, 77–101.

30. Reclus, *op. cit.*, p. 42; and Plamenatz, *op. cit.*, pp. 139–40.

31. Chastenet, *op. cit.*, I, 67; and Reclus, *op. cit.*, pp. 44–45.

32. Aimé Dupuy, *1870–1871, La guerre, la commune et la presse* (Paris, 1959), p. 98.

33. Joughin, *op. cit.*, I, 26; and Manevy, *op. cit.*, pp. 43–45.

34. Plamenatz, *op. cit.*, pp. 141–43; and Reclus, *op. cit.*, pp. 46–49.

35. Zola, *op. cit.*, I, 117.

36. *Ibid.*, I, 119–24.

37. *Ibid.*, I, 125–28, 154.

38. Joughin, *op. cit.*, I, 30–32; and Plamenatz, *op. cit.*, pp. 145–46.

39. Joughin, *op. cit.*, I, 35–40.

40. Arthur Adamov, *La Commune de Paris, 18 mars–28 mai 1871, Anthologie* (Paris, 1959), pp. 27–28; and Plamenatz, *op. cit.*, p. 147.

41. de Fonvielle, *op. cit.*, p. 41.

42. *Le Mot d'Ordre*, April 2, 1871.

43. Denis W. Brogan, *France Under the Republic: the Development of Modern France (1870–1939)* (New York and London, 1940), p. 63.

44. *Le Mot d'Ordre*, April 2, 1871.
45. *Les Aventures*, II, 371.
46. Adamov, *op. cit.*, p. 237.
47. J. Hampden Jackson, *Clemenceau and the Third Republic* (London, 1946), pp. 33–35.
48. *Le Mot d'Ordre*, April 3, 1871.
49. Joughin, *op. cit.*, I, 34–35.
50. *Les Aventures*, III, 4.
51. *Le Mot d'Ordre*, May 20, 1871.
52. Quoted in Jackson, *op. cit.*, p. 32.
53. Jean Destrem, *Rochefort et la Commune* (Paris, 1871), pp. 5–15.
54. *Le Mot d'Ordre*, April 3, 1871.
55. *Ibid.*, April 4, 1871.
56. *Ibid.*, April 5, 1871.
57. *Ibid.*, April 6, 1871; and *Les Aventures*, II, 373.
58. *Le Mot d'Ordre*, April 6, 1871.
59. *Les Aventures*, III, 7.
60. *Le Mot d'Ordre*, April 6, 1871.
61. *Ibid.*, April 9, 1871.
62. *Les Aventures*, III, 23.
63. *Le Mot d'Ordre*, April 9, 1871.
64. *Le Vengeur*, April 10, 1871.
65. *Le Mot d'Ordre*, April 14, 1871; and *Les Aventures*, III, 25.
66. *Le Mot d'Ordre*, April 8, 1871.
67. *Ibid.*, April 8, 1871.
68. de Fonvielle, *op. cit.*, p. 117.
69. *Le Mot d'Ordre*, April 14, 1871.
70. *Ibid.*, April 16, 1871.
71. *Ibid.*, April 17, 1871.
72. de Fonvielle, *op. cit.*, pp. 89–90; see also Jules Clère, *Les Hommes de la Commune* (Paris, 1871), pp. 206–08.
73. *Les Aventures*, III, 74; and de Fonvielle, *op. cit.*, p. 90.
74. *Les Aventures*, III, 32.
75. *Le Mot d'Ordre*, April 25, 1871.
76. *Ibid.*
77. *Ibid.*, April 27, 1871.
78. Gustave Flaubert, *Correspondance*, IV (Paris, 1926–33), p. 57.
79. *Les Aventures*, III, 65–66.
80. *Le Mot d'Ordre*, May 3, 1871.
81. *Ibid.*, May 5, 1871.
82. *Ibid.*, May 11, 1871.
83. *Ibid.*, May 13, 1871.
84. *Les Aventures*, III, 81.
85. Chastenet, *op. cit.*, I, 97–98.
86. Gerstle Mack, *Gustave Courbet* (New York, 1951), pp. 261–69.
87. *Le Mot d'Ordre*, May 18, 1871.
88. *Ibid.*, May 20, 1871.
89. de Fonvielle, *op. cit.*, p. 169.
90. *Les Aventures*, III, 77.
91. *Ibid.*, III, 82.
92. Chastenet, *op. cit.*, I, 104.
93. Reclus, *op. cit.*, pp. 65–66.
94. Destrem, *op. cit.*, p. 13.
95. Police Dossier E a/14.

CHAPTER IV

1. Gustave Flaubert, *Correspondance*, VI (Paris, 1926–33), p. 246, letter to Princess Mathilde, June 21, 1871.
2. *Les Aventures*, III, 82–83.
3. Jules Clère, *Les Hommes de la Commune* (Paris, 1871), p. 110.
4. *Le Mot d'Ordre*, May 4, 1871.
5. *Paris-Journal*, August 8, 1874.
6. Police Carton B a/1246, report dated London, August 3, 1874.
7. *Les Aventures*, III, 84–91.
8. *Ibid.*, 98–100.
9. *Ibid.*, 108–10.
10. *Le Voltaire*, December 12, 1880.
11. Maurice Reclus, *L'Avènement de la IIIe République, 1871–1875* (Paris, 1930), pp. 75–83.
12. Jean T. Joughin, *The Paris Commune in French Politics, 1871–1880*, I (Baltimore, Md., 1955), pp. 68, 78–79.
13. *Enquête parlementaire sur l'Insurrection du 18 mars* (Versailles, 1872), Deposition of Louis Jules Trochu, II, 37.
14. *Ibid.*, Deposition of Edmond Adam, II, 159.
15. *Ibid.*, Deposition of Claude-Anthime Corbon, II, 603–609.
16. *Ibid.*, Deposition of Colonel Gaillard, II, 248–249.

17. *Les Aventures,* III, 111–14.
18. Frank H. Brabant, *The Beginning of the Third Republic in France: A History of the National Assembly, February-September 1871* (London, 1940), p. 453.
19. *Le National,* December 14, 1880; and *Les Aventures,* III, 122–23.
20. *Les Aventures, III,* 124–26.
21. *La République française,* December 16, 1880.
22. Brabant, *op. cit.,* p. 421.
23. *Ibid.,* p. 454.
24. *Les Aventures,* III, 120–21.
25. Henri Malo, *Thiers* (Paris, 1932), p. 516.
26. *Les Aventures,* III, 129–41.
27. A.N., BB. 24/830 Dossier 719–S.77.
28. Noële Roubaud, *Henri Rochefort Intime* (Paris, 1954), pp. 75–79.
29. Juliette Adam, *Le Siège de Paris, Journal d'une Parisienne* (Paris, 1873), p. 119.
30. *Ibid.,* p. 151.
31. *Ibid.,* p. 440.
32. Juliette Adam, *Mes illusions et nos souffrances pendant le Siège de Paris* (Paris, 1906), pp. 349–50.
33. Victor Hugo, *Choses Vues* (Paris, 1897), pp. 275–76.
34. A.N. 48 AP 1, Rochefort to Destrem, n.d.
35. Archives de la Charente Maritime (La Rochelle), *Registre d'écrou de Fort Boyard.*
36. *Les Aventures,* III, 144–49.
37. A.N. 48 AP 1, Gambetta's secretary to Destrem, November 22, 1871.
38. *Ibid.,* Rochefort to Destrem, May 8, 1872.
39. Police Carton B a/1246, April 10, 1872.
40. *Ibid.,* May 7 and 10, 1872.
41. A.N. 48 AP 1, Rochefort to Destrem, July 1, 1873.
42. Archives de la Charente Maritime (La Rochelle), *Registre d'écrou de Saint-Martin de Ré.*

43. *Les Aventures,* III, 179–84; and A.N. 48 AP 1, Rochefort to Destrem, August 24, 1872.
44. *Le Figaro,* November 8, 1872.
45. A.N. 48 AP 1, Rochefort to Destrem, October 10, 1872.
46. *Ibid.,* Rochefort to Destrem, n.d.
47. *Ibid.,* Rochefort to Destrem, October 30, 1872.
48. *Le Figaro,* November 7, 1872.
49. A.N. 48 AP 1, Rochefort to Destrem, October 10, 1872.
50. Police Carton B a/1246, report of police officer escorting Rochefort, November 6, 1872, to the Chief of Police of Versailles.
51. *Le Figaro,* November 7, 1872; *Le Pays,* November 8, 1872; *Paris-Journal,* November 8, 1872.
52. *La Cloche* and *Le Rappel,* November 7, 1872.
53. *Le Figaro,* November 7, 1872.
54. Escorting officer's report, see note 50.
55. *Les Aventures,* III, 199.
56. *Paris-Journal,* April 20, 1873.
57. *Les Aventures,* III, 195–98.
58. *Paris-Journal,* November 10, 1872.
59. *Le Constitutionnel,* November 10, 1872.
60. Police Carton B a/1246, January 9, 1873.
61. A.N. 48 AP 1, letter dated January 10, 1873.
62. *Les Aventures,* III, 201.
63. Police Carton B a/1246, Bridoux Report, February 21, 1873.
64. Reclus, *op. cit.,* pp. 109–29, 170–81.
65. Police Carton B a/1246, Bridoux Report, March 23, 1873.
66. *Ibid.,* April 9 and 11, 1873.
67. Joughin, *op. cit.,* I, 71–72; Reclus, *op. cit.,* pp. 183–92.
68. *Les Aventures,* III, 205–07.
69. Police Carton B a/1246, Bridoux Report, June 3, 1873.
70. *Ibid.,* Bridoux Report, July 25, 1873; A.N. 48 AP 1, Rochefort to Destrem, July 19, 1873.

71. *XIXe Siècle,* August 9, 1873, letter from Jean Destrem.

72. Police Carton B a/1246, report of August 11, 1873.

73. *Ibid.,* report of August 13, 1873.

74. Victor Hugo, *Correspondance* (Paris, 1898), II, 361–63, Hugo to Broglie, August 8, 1873.

75. *Les Aventures,* III, 216.

76. Raymond Manevy, *La Presse de la IIIe République* (Paris, 1955), pp. 66–68; and Roubaud, *op. cit.,* pp. 82–89.

77. Police Carton B a/1246, Bridoux Report, June 29, 1873.

78. *Ibid.,* reports from Ste. Catherine, September 26, 1873; and A.N. 48 AP 1, Rochefort to Destrem, September 29, 1873.

79. *Les Aventures,* III, 217–53.

80. Police Carton B a/1246, reports of September 26 and 27, 1873.

81. *Les Aventures,* III, 143–44.

82. *Ibid.,* 263–88.

83. A.N. 48 AP 1, Rochefort to Destrem, February 28, 1874.

84. *Les Aventures,* III, 289–319.

85. *Le Temps,* June 11, 1874.

86. Letter from Achille Ballière, *Le Précurseur* (Geneva), February 9, 1878; *see also* letter of Alfred Wallerstein *ibid.,* and Achille Ballière, *Les Aventures du Marquis de Rochefort et de l'auteur dans les prisons françaises* (Paris, 1905), pp. 54, 93–98.

87. *Les Aventures,* III, 326–44.

88. Police Carton B a/1246.

89. *Ibid.,* telegram from French consul in Sydney.

90. *Les Aventures,* IV, 3–42.

91. *New York Herald,* June 6, 1874.

92. Police Carton B a/1246, report of June 20, 1874.

93. Joughin, *op. cit.,* I, 87.

94. *Les Aventures,* IV, 47–49; and Police Carton B a/1246.

95. Police Carton B a/1247, Rochefort to Gabriel Ranvier, June 20, 1874.

96. *Ibid.,* Blackford Report, August 24, 1874; also reports of June 20 and July 6, 1874.

97. Reclus, *op. cit.,* pp. 203–18, 231–34.

98. Police Carton B a/1246.

99. A.N. 48 AP 1, Rochefort to Destrem, September 2, 1874.

100. *Les Aventures,* IV, 52–53.

CHAPTER V

1. Police Dossier E a/14, Rochefort's *Carnet.*

2. *Les Presses,* June 10, 1874.

3. *Les Aventures,* IV, 56–58.

4. Police Carton B a/1246, reports of July 31, 1874, and August 4, 1874.

5. *Les Aventures,* IV, 55.

6. *Ibid.,* IV, 65; and Police Carton B a/1246, dispatches of September 12 and 15, 1874.

7. Police Carton B a/1246, Brussels Report, July 6, 1874.

8. *Paris-Journal,* September 24, 1871.

9. *Les Aventures,* IV, 67.

10. Gerstle Mack, *Gustave Courbet* (New York, 1951), pp. 304–28.

11. *Les Aventures,* I, 98.

12. Police Carton B a/1246, report of September 25, 1874.

13. Undated letter in the author's private collection.

14. Maurice Reclus, *L'Avènement de la IIIe République, 1871–1875* (Paris, 1930), p. 237.

15. *Ibid.,* p. 238.

16. *Les Aventures,* IV, 106.

17. *La Lanterne,* #35, February 25, 1875.

18. *Ibid.,* #44, May 1, 1875.

19. *Ibid.,* #47, May 22, 1875.

20. Police Carton B a/1246, report dated June, 1875.

21. A.N. 48 AP 1, Rochefort to Destrem, March 16 and 23, 1875.

22. *La Lanterne,* #45, May 8, 1875.

23. *Ibid.,* #54, July 10, 1875.

24. Maurice Garçon, *Histoire de la justice sous la IIIe République* (Paris, 1957), I, 137–42.

25. Police Carton B a/1247, copy of intercepted letter from Rochefort to Barbieux of *Le Rappel,* undated; and *Les Aventures,* IV, 104.

26. Police Carton B a/1247.

27. Jean T. Joughin, *The Paris Commune in French Politics, 1871–1880* (Baltimore, Md., 1955), I, 54–74; also Guy Chapman, *The Third Republic of France: The First Phase 1872–1894* (London, 1962), p. 73.

28. Joughin, *op. cit.,* I, 88–91.

29. Police Carton B a/1247, meeting on January 3–5, 1875, report dated January 21, 1875.

30. Police Carton B a/1247, January 6, 1876.

31. Joughin, *op. cit.,* I, 92–100.

32. Police Carton B a/1247, note a number of reports dated early in 1876; and *Les Aventures,* IV, 121.

33. *Les Droits de l'Homme,* February 11, 1876.

34. Police Carton B a/1247, Ludovic Report, May, 1876.

35. *Les Droits de l'Homme,* May 24, 1876.

36. Police Carton B a/1246, inventory of Rochefort sentences made in June, 1874.

37. Joughin, *op. cit.,* I, 117–18.

38. *Les Droits de l'Homme,* July 31, 1876.

39. Joughin, *op. cit.,* I, 126.

40. *Ibid.,* I, 129–30.

41. *Les Aventures,* IV, 124.

42. Garçon, *op. cit.,* I, 148.

43. Joughin, *op. cit.,* I, 132.

44. Police Carton B a/1247, telegram, Sigismond Lacroix to Rochefort, February 1, 1877.

45. *Les Aventures,* IV, 174.

46. Police Carton B a/1247, Lombard's Report, June 25, 1876, and Ministry of the Interior memorandum, June 29, 1876.

47. Chapman, *op. cit.,* pp. 167–75.

48. *Les Aventures,* IV, 112.

49. A.N. 48 AP 1, letters from Rochefort to Destrem, April, 1877.

50. Police Carton B a/1247; and *Le Rappel,* May 7, 1877.

51. *Les Aventures,* IV, 168–70.

52. Police Carton B a/1247.

53. *La Défense,* May 31, 1877.

54. *Le Figaro,* July 27, 1877.

55. *Le Pays,* August 3, 1877.

56. Police Carton B a/1247, reports of October 29 and 30, 1877.

57. *Le Réveil,* November 1, 1877.

58. *Le Peuple,* January 5, 1878.

59. *Les Aventures,* IV, 142–43; and Garçon, *op. cit.,* I, 103.

60. Joughin, *op. cit.,* I, 136–43.

61. *Ibid.,* 143–47.

62. *Le Républicain,* January 7, 1878.

63. Police Carton B a/1247, Agent #5, January 6, 1878.

64. *Ibid.,* Ludovic Report, January 7, 1878; and *Le Pays,* January 20, 1878.

65. *Les Aventures,* IV, 104–05.

66. *Le Gaulois,* April 28, 1878.

67. Police Carton B a/1249, report written February 12, 1890.

68. Police Carton B a/1247, Agent #5, December 11, 1878.

69. Police Carton B a/1249, February 12, 1890.

70. *Le Réveil,* February 12, 1878.

71. *Le Pays,* February 16, 1878.

72. *Le Rappel,* July 21, 1878.

73. *La Marseillaise,* January 14, 1879.

74. *Le Rappel,* January 17, 1879.

75. *La Marseillaise,* April 6, 1879.

76. Police Carton B a/1248, report dated September 2, 1879.

77. Joughin, *op. cit.,* I, 182–93.

78. *Les Aventures,* IV, 183–84.

79. *Le Pays,* February 20, 1879.

80. Joughin, *op. cit.,* I, 200–26.

81. A.N. 48 AP 1, Rochefort to Destrem, March 19, 1879; on Arthur Ranc, *see* Garçon, *op. cit.,* I, 41.

82. *Le Pays,* May 8, 1880.

83. *La Marseillaise,* September 14, 1878.

84. Police Carton B a/1248, reports during August, 1879.

85. *La Marseillaise,* October 20, 1879.

86. Police Carton B a/1248, telegram, October 20, 1879.

87. Copy in *ibid.*

88. *Ibid.,* reports of October 8 and December 22, 1879.

89. A.N. 48 AP 1, Rochefort to Destrem, December, 1879 and December 12, 1879; and Octave to Rochefort, June 10, 1880, and Octave to Destrem, June 26, 1880.

90. *Le Mot d'Ordre,* May 27, 1880.

91. *Le Gaulois,* May 30, 1880, for instance.

92. Police Carton B a/1249, Koechlin Dossier; and *Le Gaulois,* June 4, 1880.

93. *Le Nouveau Journal Républicain,* June 5, 1880.

94. *L'Evenement,* June 5, 1880.

95. *Le Courrier de Lyon,* June 5, 1880.

96. *La Décentralisation,* June 5, 1880.

97. A.N. BB. 24/824, Dossier S.76–6039.

98. Chapman, *op. cit.,* pp. 205–06.

99. Jacques Chastenet, *Histoire de la Troisième République,* II (Paris, 1952–1963), 66–67.

CHAPTER VI

1. Edmond and Jules de Goncourt, *Journal,* VI (Paris, 1891–1907), p. 91.

2. *Les Aventures,* IV, 185.

3. Police Carton B a/1248, report dated July 10, 1880.

4. *Ibid.,* Ludovic Report, July 14, 1880.

5. *Ibid.,* from a group of police reports.

6. *Le Figaro* and *Le Constitutionnel,* July 13, 1880.

7. Police Carton B a/1248, various reports on July 12, 1880.

8. *Ibid.;* and *Les Aventures,* IV, 192.

9. *L'Intransigeant,* July 14, 1880.

10. Police Carton B a/1248, Agent Denis, July 16, 1880.

11. *Ibid.,* Agent Howe, July 28, 1880.

12. *L'Intransigeant,* July 27, 1880.

13. Adrien Dansette, *Le Boulangisme* (Paris, 1946), p. 261.

14. Guy Chapman, *The Third Republic of France: The First Phase 1872–1894* (London, 1962), pp. 339–40.

15. *Le Progrès,* July 30, 1880.

16. Examples in Police Carton B a/1248.

17. Police Carton B a/1248, Agent 307, August 27, 1880.

18. *L'Intransigeant,* August 25, 1880.

19. Police Carton B a/1248, Agent 307, September 7, 1880.

20. *Les Contemporains,* #2, n.d., by Félicien Champsaur.

21. *Les Aventures,* IV, 225.

22. Carton B a/1248, a number of police reports that are unusually consistent. Note especially those by Agent A.B., November 7, 1880, and Agent Howe, November 15, 1880.

23. Maurice Garçon, *Histoire de la justice sous la III*^e *République* (Paris, 1957), III, 219–21.

24. *Les Aventures,* IV, 209–12.

25. Garçon, *op. cit.,* III, 223–24; and *Le Temps,* November 29, 1880.

26. Police Carton B a/1248, Howe Reports, November 24 and 28, 1880.

27. *Ibid.,* report of December 24, 1880; and Garçon, *op. cit.,* III, 225–26.

28. *Les Aventures,* IV, 216.

29. *Le National,* December 9, 1880.

30. *Ibid.,* December 10, 1880.

31. *L'Intransigeant,* December 11, 1880.

32. *Le Voltaire,* December 12, 1880.

33. *L'Intransigeant,* December 13, 1880.

34. *La Civilisation,* December 13, 1880.
35. *Le Voltaire,* December 14, 1880.
36. *Ibid.,* December 13, 1880.
37. *L'Intransigeant,* December 18, 1880.
38. Police Carton B a/1248, copy of letter, December 14, 1880.
39. *Le National,* December 14, 1880.
40. *La République française,* December 16, 1880.
41. *La Marseillaise,* December 17, 1880.
42. Police Carton B a/1248, report dated December 19, 1880.
43. *L'Etoile française,* December 19, 1880.
44. *Les Aventures,* IV, 226–28; and *Le Temps,* December 16, 1880.
45. Police Carton B a/1248.
46. *Ibid.,* B a/1246, Officer Collas' Reports, October 17 and 18, 1872.
47. *Ibid.,* B a/1248, Howe's report, November 21, 1880.
48. *Ibid.,* December 16, 1880.
49. *Les Aventures,* IV, 234–38.
50. *L'Intransigeant,* March 15, 1881.
51. *Les Aventures,* IV, 242.
52. Irene Collins, *The Government and the Newspaper Press in France, 1814–1881* (London, 1959), pp. 181–83.
53. Chapman, *op. cit.,* p. 216.
54. The Tunisian question is well handled in Chapman, *op. cit.,* pp. 212–13; and in Jacques Chastenet, *Histoire de la Troisième République,* II (Paris, 1952–1963), 78–96.
55. *L'Intransigeant,* July 12, 1881.
56. *Ibid.,* September 27, 1881.
57. Police Carton B a/1249, report dated September 25, 1881.
58. Chastenet, *op. cit.,* II, 89.
59. Police Carton B a/1249; and *Gazette des Tribunaux,* December 14, 1881.
60. Police Carton B a/1249, reports of December 17 and 19, 1881.
61. *Ibid.,* reports of December 29, 1881, and January 25 and June 29, 1882.
62. Goncourt, *op. cit.,* VI, 97–98.
63. Police Carton B a/1249, various reports by Howe, spring of 1882.
64. *Les Aventures,* IV, 206.
65. *Ibid.,* 196.
66. Chastenet, *op. cit.,* II, 94–103.
67. Jean Bouvier, *Le Krach de L'Union Générale (1878–1885)* (Paris, 1960), p. 2.
68. *Ibid.,* p. 1; Chastenet, *op. cit.,* II, 107–09; Garçon, *op. cit.,* II, 121–24; and Frederic Morton, *The Rothschilds* (New York, 1963), p. 187.
69. Garçon, *op. cit.,* II, 124–28.
70. *Les Aventures,* IV, 267.
71. Chastenet, *op. cit.,* II, 108–10.
72. Police Carton B a/1249, January 11, 1883.
73. *Ibid.,* June 27, 1883.
74. John F. Cady, *The Roots of French Imperialism in Eastern Asia* (Ithaca, N.Y., 1954), pp. 1–17.
75. *Les Aventures,* IV, 309–10.
76. *L'Intransigeant,* December 26, 1882.
77. *Les Aventures,* IV, 313.
78. Chastenet, *op. cit.,* II, 146.
79. *L'Intransigeant,* June 27, 1884.
80. *Les Aventures,* IV, 341–42.
81. Chastenet, *op. cit.,* II, 160–65.
82. Police Carton B a/1249, Howe's Report, March 1, 1884.
83. *Le Cri du Peuple,* March 15, 1884.
84. *L'Intransigeant,* March 17, 1884.
85. Police Carton B a/1249, Howe's Report, March 18, 1884.
86. *Ibid.,* September 8, 1883.
87. *Ibid.,* January 10, 1884.
88. *Ibid.,* June 13, 1884.
89. *Ibid.,* September 11, 1884.
90. *Ibid.,* October 10, 1884.
91. *L'Intransigeant,* August 20, 1885.
92. *Ibid.,* September 3, 1883.
93. *Ibid.,* September 12, 1883.

CHAPTER VII

1. *Les Aventures,* IV, 358–60.
2. Police Carton B a/1249, Agent 4, February 10, 1886.
3. *Les Aventures,* IV, 361.
4. Jacques Chastenet, *Histoire de la Troisième République* (Paris, 1952–1963), II, 175.
5. Police Carton B a/1249, Howe's Report, March 18, 1884.
6. *Le Matin,* February 7, 1886. The vote was the previous day.
7. *L'Intransigeant,* February 10, 1886.
8. Police Carton B a/1249, Auger speech, March 18, 1886.
9. Jean-Paul Sartre, *Anti-Semite and Jew* (New York, 1962), p. 13.
10. *Les Aventures,* II, 84.
11. *Ibid.,* 249–50.
12. *La Nation,* April 23, 1886.
13. *Les Aventures,* IV, 380.
14. Chastenet, *op. cit.,* II, 181; and Adrien Dansette, *Le Boulangisme* (Paris, 1964), pp. 30–31.
15. Dansette, *op. cit.,* p. 23.
16. D. W. Brogan, *France Under the Republic: the Development of Modern France (1870–1939)* (New York and London, 1940), pp. 184–85.
17. Chastenet, *op. cit.,* II, 179–80.
18. Dansette, *op. cit.,* p. 48.
19. *Les Aventures,* V, 11.
20. Dansette, *op. cit.,* pp. 54–55; and Maurice Garçon, *Histoire de la justice sous la IIIᵉ République* (Paris, 1957), I, 161.
21. *Les Aventures,* V, 24–33.
22. Dansette, *op. cit.,* 63–64.
23. *Ibid.,* p. 83.
24. *L'Intransigeant,* December 28, 1886.
25. Chastenet, *op. cit.,* II, 184.
26. Guy Chapman, *The Third Republic of France: The First Phase 1872–1894* (London, 1962), p. 269.
27. *L'Intransigeant,* February 15, 1887.
28. Dansette, *op. cit.,* p. 75.
29. *Les Aventures,* V, 40–42.
30. Brogan, *op. cit.,* 188–90; Chastenet, *op. cit.,* II, 186–87; and Dansette, *op. cit.,* pp. 77–80.
31. Chapman, *op. cit.,* p. 272.
32. *Les Aventures,* V, 54.
33. Dansette, *op. cit.,* pp. 85–88; and Chastenet, *op. cit.,* II, 189.
34. *Les Aventures,* V, 59.
35. Dansette, *op. cit.,* pp. 95–102; and Chapman, *op. cit.,* pp. 273–74.
36. *Les Aventures,* V, 56–57.
37. *L'Intransigeant,* May 14, 1887.
38. *Paris,* May 17, 1887. The original copy of Joffrin's letter was sent to Rochefort's former lawyer, Destrem, then an editor of *Le Rappel,* with a request to publish it. See A.N. 48 AP 1.
39. *Paris,* May 17, 1887.
40. *La République française,* May 19, 1887.
41. *Le Prolétariat,* May 21, 1887.
42. *La Petite Presse,* July 17, 1887; and *Le Voltaire,* July 21, 1887.
43. *L'Intransigeant,* July 23, 1887.
44. *Les Aventures,* V, 79–85; and Dansette, *op. cit.,* pp. 104–06.
45. Garçon, *op. cit.,* II, 69–70.
46. *Les Aventures,* V, 87; and Chastenet, *op. cit.,* II, 194.
47. Dansette, *op. cit.,* p. 110; and Garçon, *op. cit.,* II, 71–75.
48. *Les Aventures,* V, 62–64.
49. Dansette, *op. cit.,* p. 112; and Brogan, *op. cit.,* p. 196.
50. *Les Aventures,* V, 103–06; and Dansette, *op. cit.,* pp. 114–19.
51. Brogan, *op. cit.,* pp. 197–98.
52. Chastenet, *op. cit.,* II, 197.
53. Garçon, *op. cit.,* II, 76–79.
54. Dansette, *op. cit.,* p. 368.
55. *Ibid.,* p. 121.
56. *Ibid.,* pp. 123–26; and Brogan, *op. cit.,* pp. 199–200.

57. *Les Aventures,* V, 118–19.
58. *Le Prolétariat,* March 3, 1888.
59. Chapman, *op. cit.,* p. 280; and *Les Aventures,* V, 120.
60. Chastenet, *op. cit.,* II, 201–02.
61. *Ibid.,* 202.
62. *Ibid.,* 204–05.
63. *La Justice,* May 16, 1888.
64. *Le Parti National,* June 3, 1888.
65. *La Justice,* June 26, 1888.
66. *L'Intransigeant,* June 29, 1888.
67. Garçon, *op. cit.,* I, 165.
68. *Les Aventures,* V, 129.
69. Chastenet, *op. cit.,* II, 206.
70. *Les Aventures,* V, 133–37.
71. Chapman, *op. cit.,* pp. 285–86.
72. *Les Aventures,* V, 146.
73. Harvey Goldberg, *The Life of Jean Jaurès* (Madison, Wisc., 1962), pp. 51–54.
74. *Le Parti Ouvrier,* December 8 and 14, 1888; *Le Peuple,* December 9, 1888; and *Le Radical,* December 10, 1888.
75. *Le Parti Ouvrier,* January 11, 1889.
76. *Enquête parlementaire sur le Gouvernement de la Défense Nationale,* Dépositions des Témoins, M. Dréo, II, 62.
77. *La Bataille,* December 27, 1888.
78. *La France,* January 15, 1889; and Police Carton B a/1250, January 14, 1889.
79. *La Bataille,* January 20, 24, 25, 26, and 27, 1889.
80. *Les Aventures,* V, 154–56; Chastenet, *op. cit.,* II, 207–08; and Garçon, *op. cit.,* I, 166.
81. Frank Harris, *My Life and Loves* (New York, 1963), p. 478.
82. *Les Aventures,* V, 162; and Chastenet, *op. cit.,* II, 209.
83. Brogan, *op. cit.,* p. 207.
84. Harris, *op. cit.,* p. 481.
85. *Les Aventures,* V, 161.
86. Chastenet, *op. cit.,* II, 209.
87. *Ibid.,* 210–11.
88. *Le Rappel,* October 25, 1896.

89. Jean Variot, *Propos de Georges Sorel* (Paris, 1935), pp. 130–31.
90. Police Carton B a/1250, report dated March 1, 1889.
91. Chastenet, *op. cit.,* II, 212; Dansette, *op. cit.,* p. 266; and *The New York Times* (Paris ed.), March 18, 1889.
92. Dansette, *op. cit.,* pp. 273–74.
93. Chastenet, *op. cit.,* II, 213.
94. Dansette, *op. cit.,* p. 293.
95. *Les Aventures,* V, 167–70.
96. *Ibid.,* 177–80.
97. Chastenet, *op. cit.,* II, 213.
98. Dansette, *op. cit.,* pp. 297–98.

CHAPTER VIII

1. Jules Renard, *Le Journal de Jules Renard, 1887–1910,* I (Paris, 1927), pp. 243–44.
2. Maurice Garçon, *Histoire de la justice sous la IIIe République,* I (Paris, 1957), pp. 167–69.
3. Adrien Dansette, *Le Boulangisme* (Paris, 1946), pp. 307–08.
4. *L'Intransigeant,* April 12, 1889.
5. *Ibid.,* April 15, 1889.
6. *Ibid.,* April 19, 1889.
7. Police Carton B a/1250, Arrest Decree from High Court of Justice, Palace of the Luxembourg, April 30, 1889.
8. *Les Aventures,* V, 187.
9. *Le Matin,* May 20, 1889; *Le Mot d'Ordre,* May 20, 1889; and *La Petite République,* May 22, 1889.
10. *L'Intransigeant,* July 18, 1889; and Garçon, *op. cit.,* I, 169–70.
11. Garçon, *op. cit.,* I, 171.
12. *Le Gaulois,* July 19, 1889.
13. *L'Intransigeant,* July 30, 1889.
14. Police Carton B a/1250, report of August 9, 1889.
15. *Le Gaulois,* July 19, 1889.
16. Garçon, *op. cit.,* I, 172.
17. *La Liberté,* August 18, 1889.
18. Police Carton B a/1246, Bridoux

Reports of February 21 and March 14, 1873.

19. *L'Estafette,* November 24, 1881.
20. Police Carton B a/1249, report of November 5, 1881.
21. Police Carton B a/1250, report of April 30, 1889.
22. *XIXe Siècle,* May 2, 1889.
23. Police Dossier E a/55–7.
24. Though he was officially Parti National, Rochefort's campaign statements were Republican in spirit. See *L'Intransigeant,* September 12, 1889. Election tally in Police Carton B a/1250.
25. Dansette, *op. cit.,* p. 329.
26. Jacques Chastenet, *Histoire de la Troisième République,* II (Paris, 1952–1963), 243–45.
27. *L'Éclair,* October 2, 1889.
28. Police Carton B a/1250, report of October 22, 1889; and *Les Aventures,* V, 200–02.
29. *XIXe Siècle,* November 4, 1889; and *Le Voltaire,* November 5, 1889.
30. *XIXe Siècle,* May 27, 1890.
31. Dansette, *op. cit.,* pp. 347–48; and Guy Chapman, *The Third Republic of France: The First Phase 1872–1894* (London, 1962), p. 290.
32. *Le Figaro,* September 6, 1890.
33. Police Carton B a/1250.
34. *Ibid.*
35. *XIXe Siècle,* September 4, 1890.
36. Police Carton B a/1250.
37. *L'Intransigeant,* September 12, 1890; and *Les Aventures,* V, 216.
38. *L'Intransigeant,* September 13, 1890; and *Les Aventures,* V, 217.
39. *Les Aventures,* V, 221–22.
40. *Ibid.,* 223.
41. *Ibid.,* 223–26.
42. *L'Intransigeant,* October 3, 1892.
43. Police Carton B a/1250, reports of January 28 and March 8, 1892.
44. *L'Intransigeant,* January 21, 1886.
45. Chastenet, *op. cit.,* II, 309.
46. Jean Bouvier, *Les Deux Scandales de Panama* (Paris, 1964), p. 8.

47. Chapman, *op. cit.,* pp. 306–07.
48. Bouvier, *op. cit.,* p. 116.
49. Garçon, *op. cit.,* II, 53–55.
50. *Ibid.,* 55–57.
51. Bouvier, *op. cit.,* p. 118.
52. Garçon, *op. cit.,* II, 58.
53. *Ibid.,* 56.
54. *L'Intransigeant,* January 21, April 27, and July 12, 1886.
55. *La Petite République,* June 9, 1898.
56. Chastenet, *op. cit.,* II, 310–11.
57. Garçon, *op. cit.,* II, 61.
58. Chastenet, *op. cit.,* II, 314–15.
59. *Ibid.,* 315–16.
60. J. Hampden Jackson, *Clemenceau and the Third Republic* (London, 1946), pp. 65–68.
61. Garçon, *op. cit.,* II, 63.
62. *Ibid.,* II, 62; and Chastenet, *op. cit.,* II, 316–17.
63. Garçon, *op. cit.,* II, 64.
64. *Les Aventures,* V, 266–68.
65. *La Patrie,* January 10, 1893.
66. *L'Intransigeant,* February 6, 1893.
67. *La France,* February 13, 1893.
68. Garçon, *op. cit.,* II, 64–65.
69. Chastenet, *op. cit.,* II, 302–04, 322–23.
70. Police Carton B a/1250, Agent Félix, November 4, 1892.
71. *Le Gaulois,* January 16, 1893.
72. Police Carton B a/1250, Agent Z's Report, November 5, 1892; and Agent Abel's Report, January 25, 1893.
73. *Ibid.,* municipal elections tally, April 16, 1893.
74. Chastenet, *op. cit.,* II, 324–25; and Chapman, *op. cit.,* pp. 323–24.
75. Chastenet, *op. cit.,* III, 57–59.
76. Police Carton B a/1250, Rochefort to Degeorge, March 22, 1894.
77. *L'Intransigeant,* May 3, 1894.
78. *Les Aventures,* V, 306.
79. Police Carton B a/1250, Agent Léon's Report, June 29, 1894.
80. Garçon, *op. cit.,* I, 238; and Chastenet, *op. cit.,* III, 63.

81. *Les Aventures,* V, 294.
82. *Ibid.,* 296.
83. Police Carton B a/1250, Agent Léon's Report, November 11, 1894.
84. *Les Aventures,* V, 316–17.
85. *Ibid.,* 322–23; and Chastenet, *op. cit.,* III, 75–76.
86. *L'Intransigeant,* February 4, 1895; and *Les Aventures,* V, 323–24.
87. Dansette, *op. cit.,* pp. 363–64.
88. *L'Intransigeant,* February 12, 1895.
89. Police Carton B a/1250.
90. *Ibid.,* Agent Léon's Report, February 2, 1895.
91. *La Cocarde,* September 3, 1893.
92. Othon Guerlac, *Trois apôtres: Drumont, Rochefort, Séverine* (Paris, 1896), pp. 17–19.

CHAPTER IX

1. *L'Intransigeant,* December 3, 1893.
2. *Ibid.,* March 20, 1895.
3. *Ibid.,* March 22, 1897.
4. Jules Renard, *Le Journal de Jules Renard, 1887–1910,* II (Paris, 1927), p. 462.
5. Police Carton B a/1252, report of November 7, 1896(?), from Geneva.
6. Police Carton B a/1251, Félix's Report, October 8, 1896.
7. *La Paix,* October 13, 1896.
8. *Les Débats,* February 6, 1897.
9. *Le Parti Ouvrier,* September 11, 1896.
10. *Le Signal,* March 4, 1896.
11. *Le Rappel,* August 8, 1896.
12. Police Carton B a/1251, Aspic's Report, January 25, 1896.
13. *La Libre parole,* January 25, 1896.
14. *L'Intransigeant,* January 27, 1896.
15. *La Libre Parole,* April 13, 1897.
16. Police Carton B a/1251, report of January 9, 1898.
17. Police Carton B a/1252, marriage dated September 22, 1897.
18. *Les Débats,* December 22, 1896.
19. *Le Peuple français,* December 22, 1896.
20. *L'Aurore,* June 8, 1898.
21. Police Carton B a/1251, report of January 16, 1897; and Guy Chapman, *The Dreyfus Case, a Reassessment* (New York, 1955), p. 152.
22. Denis W. Brogan, *France Under the Republic: the Development of Modern France, 1870–1939* (New York and London, 1940), p. 329.
23. *Ibid.,* pp. 305–10.
24. Chapman, *op. cit.,* pp. 101–04.
25. *Les Aventures,* V, 318–20.
26. Chapman, *op. cit.,* p. 119.
27. *Ibid.,* pp. 135–36.
28. Nicholas Halasz, *Captain Dreyfus* (New York, 1955), pp. 104–11.
29. *L'Intransigeant,* November 3, 1897.
30. Police Carton B a/1251, report of December 1, 1897.
31. *L'Intransigeant,* December 25, 26 and 27, 1897.
32. *Le Matin,* January 1, 1898.
33. Police Carton B a/1251, report of February 9, 1898.
34. *L'Intransigeant,* February 11, 1898.
35. Brogan, *op. cit.,* pp. 340–43.
36. Edward Whiting Fox, "The Third Force, 1897–1939," in E. M. Earle, ed., *Modern France* (Princeton, 1951), p. 132.
37. Jacques Chastenet, *Histoire de la Troisième République,* III (Paris, 1952–1963), p. 122.
38. *L'Intransigeant,* May 4, 1898.
39. *L'Aurore,* May 5, 1898.
40. *La Petite République,* June 4, 1898.
41. *L'Aurore,* June 5, 1898.
42. *La Paix,* June 5, 1898; *Le Radical,* June 6, 1898, also joined the general Socialist condemnation.
43. *La Libre Parole,* June 4, 1898.
44. Police Carton B a/1251, June 11, 1898.

45. *L'Aurore,* June 12, 1898.

46. *L'Intransigeant,* June 13, 1898.

47. *La Petite République,* June 15, 1898.

48. *Les Droits de l'Homme,* June 19, 1898.

49. *L'Intransigeant,* July 3, 1898.

50. Brogan, *op. cit.,* pp. 335–39.

51. *L'Intransigeant,* September 1, 1898.

52. *Ibid.,* September 3, 1898.

53. Brogan, *op. cit.,* p. 339; and Denis W. Brogan, *French Personalities and Problems* (New York, 1947), pp. 54–55.

54. Eugen J. Weber. *The Action Française* (Stanford and Paris, 1962), pp. 19–29.

55. *L'Intransigeant,* October 16, 1898.

56. *Le Radical,* October 16, 1898.

57. *L'Aurore,* October 17, 1898.

58. *Ibid.,* October 19, 1898.

59. *L'Intransigeant,* February 18, 1899.

60. Police Carton B a/1252, reports from December 24, 1898–February 15, 1899.

61. Maurice Garçon, *Histoire de la justice sous la IIIe République,* I (Paris, 1957), p. 175.

62. *L'Intransigeant,* June 4, 1899.

63. Denis W. Brogan, *France Under the Republic: the Development of Modern France, 1870–1939* (New York and London, 1940), pp. 349–

56; and Chastenet, *op. cit.,* III, 168–72.

64. *L'Intransigeant,* February 16, 1900.

65. *La Libre Parole,* January 4, 1907.

66. Léon Blum, *L'Oeuvre de Léon Blum (1891–1905)* (Paris, 1954), pp. 499–500.

67. Weber, *op. cit.,* p. 41.

68. Police Carton B a/1252.

69. Weber, *op. cit.,* p. 68.

70. Léon A. Daudet, *Flammes: Polémique et polémistes* (Paris, 1930), pp. 156–57.

71. *Ibid.*

72. Copy of unpublished letter owned by Mme. Joron of Vaucresson, n.d. but evidently 1901.

73. Original manuscript in the author's collection.

74. Noële Roubaud, *Henri Rochefort Intime* (Paris, 1954), pp. 142, 150, 159, 173.

75. Joron Collection, Rochefort to Mme. Tavernier, March 26, 1901, and a letter written about six months before the elections of 1902.

76. *Ibid.,* D. N. Chérot to Mme. Tavernier, March 28, 1903.

77. *Ibid.,* April 5, 1903.

78. Frank Harris, *My Life and Loves* (New York, 1963), p. 1013.

79. Police Carton B a/1252.

80. *La Patrie,* July 7, 1913.

81. Roubaud, *op. cit.,* p. 179.

BIBLIOGRAPHY

ARCHIVE SOURCES

Archives de la préfécture de police. Paris. Series B a/1245, 1246, 1247, 1248, 1249, 1250, 1251, and 1252. These numbers correspond to those on the file cartons, within each of which are a varying number of dossiers on Rochefort arranged by year. Series E a/14, D a/21, E a/55-7, and E a/14-I are minor dossiers on Rochefort, his father, and his son, Henri.

Archives nationales. Paris. Carton 48 AP 1. Personal papers of Rochefort donated by the lawyer Jean Destrem in 1917. They were originally catalogued as Cartons AB XIX 616-620, but have recently been renumbered. Series BB. 24/830 Dossier 719-S.77 and 24/824, Dossier S.76-6039 contain information on Mourot and Trinquet.

Archives de la Charente Maritime. La Rochelle. The *registres d'écrou* for Fort Boyard and Saint-Martin de Ré are here. Otherwise, these archives have nothing on Rochefort.

Archives de la Seine. Paris. Little but autographs. Series D.3. AZ. 215 (Z⁵) and D.4. AZ. 495 (VR²).

Bibliothèque nationale. Paris. Departement des Manuscrits: Nouvelles Acquisitions françaises. A disappointing smattering of documents, mostly autographs. There remains also a fragment of the manuscript for *Les Aventures de ma vie* and some originals of articles published in *L'Intransigeant* from 1893 to 1897.

Private collection of Madame Maurice Joron of Vaucresson. A small number of personal letters dating from 1899 to 1907.

While the *Archives de la préfécture de police* in Paris contain extensive and valuable papers on Rochefort, it is the only collection of any size or import remaining. The rest is fragmentary and scattered, and the reader will soon realize why. To begin with, Rochefort's home in Paris was evidently ransacked during the last days of the Commune in 1871. Later, he made some attempt to recover family materials, but to no apparent avail. Second, a career repeatedly studded with periods of prison and exile is not conducive to the orderly filing and preservation of papers. Third, his journalistic career was so long ago that most of the newspapers and their records have long since ceased to exist; and he retired from *L'Intransigeant* (now *Paris-Presse*) in 1907, where he is now all but forgotten. Finally, he was on bad terms with his family during most of his life, a fact that precluded correspondence; and his three children all lived abroad. After his death in 1913, no heir ever came forward to claim his royalties. Were it not for the police, therefore, who made it their business to keep a close check on him, or for the fact that he was a prolific journalist, the sources would be too meager for an extensive study of Rochefort.

The use of police records, while indispensable in this case, offers a number of problems of which the historian must be continually aware while reading them. Police agents and informers are known to us only by a code name or number. As the researcher becomes "acquainted" with them, he discovers that some of them have a high degree of reliability: Their sources of information are good, their reports are often confirmed by other observers, and they will occasionally send in a report designed to correct an earlier observation. One also finds evidence of less sophisticated informing—some of it from the unscrupulous individual who feeds his superiors only what he thinks they want to hear; and some of it from men who are particularly susceptible to scandalmongering and who will seriously report the prattle of cranks. It is useful for the historian to have some knowledge of the small talk of his period, but that also increases his burden of sifting the improbable from the probable.

PRINTED SOURCES

Newspaper articles have provided the second great source of information about Rochefort, especially *La Lanterne, La Marseillaise, Le Mot d'Ordre,* and *L'Intransigeant.* And the footnotes will reveal that I have also used the general press extensively. Invaluable too, though riddled with inaccuracies, is Rochefort's memoirs, *Les Aventures de ma vie* (5 vols., Paris, 1896). An English edition was published in two volumes that same year, but I have never seen a copy of it.

Two major collections of government documents relating to the months of crisis in 1870–71 are also important for a study of Rochefort, as those months were decisive for the remainder of his political and journalistic career. As has been pointed out before, both collections reflect the opinions born of military defeat and civil strife; but the testimony therein is valuable: *Enquête parlementaire sur le Gouvernement de la Défense Nationale,* 18 vols., Paris and Versailles, 1872–75; and *Enquête parlementaire sur l'Insurrection du 18 mars,* 3 vols., Versailles, 1872.

Adam, Juliette Mme. Edmond, *Le Siège de Paris, Journal d'une Parisienne.* Paris, 1873. A revised edition, entitled *Mes illusions et nos souffrances pendant le Siège de Paris,* was published in 1906. Letters from Rochefort to the Adams between 1871 and 1874 were published in vols. XCV and XCVI of *La Nouvelle Revue.*

Arago, Etienne, *L'Hôtel de Ville de Paris au 4 septembre et pendant le siège.* Paris, n.d.

Blum, Léon, *L'Oeuvre de Léon Blum (1891–1905)*. Paris, 1954.

Claude, Antoine François, *Mémoires de M. Claude, chef de la police de sûreté sous le Second Empire*. Paris, 1962.

Cresson, Ernest, *Cent Jours du siège à la Préfécture de Police, 2 novembre 1870–11 février 1871*. Paris, 1901.

Daudet, Alphonse, *Quarante ans de Paris, 1857–1897*. Geneva, 1952.

Destrem, Jean, *Rochefort et la Commune*. Paris, 1871. A brief, pamphlet-length apology by Rochefort's lawyer.

Drumont, Édouard, *La Fin d'un monde, étude psychologique et sociale*. Paris, 1889.

———, *La France Juive, Essai d'histoire contemporaine*. 2 vols., Paris, 1886.

Du Camp, Maxime, *Souvenirs d'un demi-siècle*. 2 vols., Paris, 1949.

Favre, Jules, *Gouvernement de la Défense Nationale*. 3 vols., Paris, 1872–76.

Ferry, Jules, *Discours et opinions de Jules Ferry*. 6 vols., Paris, 1895–96.

Flaubert, Gustave, *Correspondance*. 9 vols., Paris, 1926–33.

Flourens, Gustave, *Paris Livré*. Paris, 1871.

Fonvielle, Wilfred de, *Les Dernières causeries de H. Rochefort, annotées, commentées et refutées par Wilfred de Fonvielle*. Brussels, 1871. He was the brother of Ulric de Fonvielle of the Noir affair.

Freycinet, Charles de, *Souvenirs*. 2 vols., Paris, 1911–13.

Gambetta, Léon, *Discours et plaidoyers*, Joseph Reinach, ed., 11 vols., Paris, 1880–85.

Goncourt, Edmond and Jules de, *Journal*. 9 vols., Paris, 1891–1907.

Halévy, Ludovic, *Carnets, 1867–70*. 2 vols., Paris, 1935.

———, *Notes et souvenirs, 1871–72*. Paris, 1889.

Mermeix, *Les Coulisses du Boulangisme revues et augmentées de plusieurs chapitres inédits*. Paris, 1890. The famous exposé actually written by Terrail.

Ollivier, Émile, *L'Empire Libéral, Etudes, Récits, Souvenirs*. 18 vols., Paris, 1895–1918. Volumes XI, XII, and XIII cover the critical years for this study.

———, *Journal 1846–1869*. 2 vols., Paris, 1961.

Proust, Marcel, *By Way of Sainte-Beuve*. London, 1958. Contains some insights into the Dreyfus affair and Léon Daudet.

Ranc, Arthur, *Souvenirs et correspondance, 1831–1908*. Paris, 1913.

Reinach, Joseph, *Le ministere Gambetta: Histoire et doctrine*. Paris, 1884.

Renard, Jules, *Le Journal de Jules Renard, 1887–1910*. 4 vols., Paris, 1927.

Simon, Jules, *Souvenirs du 4 septembre*. Paris, 1874.

Trochu, Le Général, *Pour la Vérité et Pour la Justice*. Paris, 1873.

Vier, Jacques, *Daniel Stern: Lettres républicaines du Second Empire*. Paris, 1951.

Villemessant, J.-H.-C. de, *Mémoires d'un journaliste*. 6 vols., Paris, 1872–78.

Zola, Émile, *La République en marche*. 2 vols., Paris, 1956. Parliamentary chronicles from February 13 to September 16, 1871.

PRINTED WORKS ON HENRI ROCHEFORT

Almèras, Henri d', *Avant la gloire, leurs débuts.* Paris, 1903. Of little value.

Audouard, Mme. Olympe, *Silhouettes parisiennes.* Paris, 1883. A book not to be taken seriously.

Ballière, Achille, *Les Aventures du Marquis de Rochefort et de l'auteur dans les prisons françaises.* Paris, 1905. By one of Rochefort's fellow escapees, written in anger after failing to get Rochefort's support in the elections of 1902.

Bazire, Edmond, *Rochefort.* Paris, 1883. From a series called *Célébrités Contemporaines,* ed. by Jules Claretie. Brief and adulatory.

Bertaut, J., *Figures contemporaines. Chroniquers et polémistes.* Paris, 1906. Insignificant.

Blum, Ernest, *Biographie complète de Henri Rochefort par un ami de dix ans.* Brussels, 1868. Something less than *complète!* A short piece of devoted testimony as to Rochefort's friendliness, egalitarianism, simplicity, and goodness. Altogether touching and unbelievable.

Chalain and Prolo, *Un Français de la décadence.* Paris, 1888. Chitchat.

Daudet, Léon A., *Flammes: Polémique et polémistes.* Paris, 1930. He personally liked Rochefort but knew his political limitations.

Dichard, H., *La Vérité sur M. Henri Rochefort.* Paris, 1868. Slight.

Ducray, Camille, *Henri Rochefort, 1831–1913.* Paris, 1913. The first full-length book published on Rochefort. Popular and insignificant.

Guerlac, Othon, *Trois apôtres: Drumont, Rochefort, Séverine.* Paris, 1896. A brief and slight pamphlet.

Jean-Bernard, *La vie de Paris, 1913.* Paris, 1914. Chapter 27 covers the death of Rochefort.

Pain, Olivier, *Henri Rochefort.* Paris, 1879. Partisan account of their relationship, and of limited value.

Roubaud, Noële, *Henri Rochefort Intime.* Paris, 1954. Based in part on letters written by Rochefort to Noémi Dufaux and her sons and on the published letters to the Edmond Adams published in *La Nouvelle Revue.* It is useful for family details; but the material dealing with Rochefort's career is quite unreliable.

Shortliffe, Glen, *Hugo's Intervention for Henri Rochefort.* s.l., n.d. I have only seen an offprint in the Bibliothèque nationale, but this is evidently from an article originally in *Symposium,* November, 1948. He had the use of the Destrem documents in the Archives nationales; but knowing only a moment of Rochefort's career, Shortliffe took him at his word about the Commune, i.e., that he had taken a moderate stand during the Commune. About Hugo's influence, however, Shortliffe is correct.

Zévaès, Alexandre Bourson, *Henri Rochefort, le pamphlétaire.* Paris, 1946. A sympathetic account by an author who has written extensively on Third Republican topics and people. He saw Rochefort as a patriot, and he avoided some of the touchier topics about the career. I find the book to be superficial as a result, yet it is the best study now available in the French language.

OTHER USEFUL BOOKS AND ARTICLES

Adamov, Arthur, *La Commune de Paris, 18 mars–28 mai 1871, Anthologie.* Paris, 1959.

Bellessort, André, *La Société française sous Napoléon III.* Paris, n.d.

————, *Les intellectuels et l'avènement de la IIIe République.* Paris, 1931.

Billy, André, *Les écrivains de combat.* Nevers, 1931.

Boussel, Patrice, *L'affaire Dreyfus et la presse.* Paris, 1960.

Bouvier, Jean, *Le Krach de L'Union Générale (1878–1885).* Paris, 1960.

————, *Les Deux scandales de Panama.* Paris, 1964.

Brabant, Frank H., *The Beginning of the Third Republic in France: A History of the National Assembly, February-September 1871.* London, 1940.

Brogan, Denis W., *France Under the Republic: the Development of Modern France (1870–1939).* New York and London, 1940.

————, *French Personalities and Problems.* New York, 1947.

Byrnes, Robert F., *Anti-Semitism in Modern France.* New Brunswick, New Jersey, 1950.

————, "The French Publishing Industry and Its Crisis in the 1890's." *Journal of Modern History,* XXIII (September, 1951), 232–42.

Cady, John F., *The Roots of French Imperialism in Eastern Asia.* Ithaca, N.Y., 1954.

Chapman, Guy, *The Dreyfus Case, a Reassessment.* New York, 1955.

————, *The Third Republic of France: The First Phase 1872–1894.* London, 1962.

Charles-Roux, François J., *Alexandre II, Gortchakoff et Napoléon III.* Paris, 1913.

Chastenet, Jacques, *Histoire de la Troisième République.* 7 vols., Paris, 1952–1963.

Choury, Maurice, *Les origines de la Commune, Paris livré.* Paris, 1960.

Clère, Jules, *Les Hommes de la Commune.* Paris, 1871.

Collins, Irene, *The Government and the Newspaper Press in France, 1814–1881.* London, 1959.

Combes, Emile, *Mon Ministère 1902–1905.* Paris, 1956.

Contamine, H., *La Revanche 1871–1914.* Paris, 1957.

Curtis, Michael, "Boulanger: The Original Man on Horseback." History, #3 (1961), pp. 37–70.

————, *Three Against the Third Republic: Sorel, Barrès, and Maurras.* Princeton, 1959.

Dansette, Adrien, *Le Boulangisme.* Paris, 1946.

————, *Les Origines de la Commune de 1871.* Paris, 1944.

Derfler, Leslie, *The Dreyfus Affair: Tragedy of Errors?* Boston, 1963.

Dessal, Marcel, *Charles Delescluze, un révolutionnaire jacobin 1809–1871.* Paris, 1952.

Digeon, Claude, *La crise allemande de la pensée française (1870–1914).* Paris, 1959.

Dommanget, Maurice, *Blanqui et l'opposition révolutionnaire à la fin du Second Empire.* Paris, 1960.

———, *Les Idées politiques et sociales d'Auguste Blanqui.* Paris, 1957.

Du Camp, Maxime, *Les convulsions de Paris.* 4 vols., Paris, 1881.

Dupuy, Aimé, *1870–1871, La guerre, la commune et la presse.* Paris, 1959.

Edgar-Bonnet, George, *Ferdinand de Lesseps après Suez: Le Pionnier de Panama.* Paris, 1959.

Fleury, Comte Maurice, et Sonolet, Louis, *La Société du Second Empire.* 4 vols., Paris, 1911.

Fox, Edward Whiting, "The Third Force, 1897–1939," in E. M. Earle, ed., *Modern France* (Princeton, 1951).

Garçon, Maurice, *Histoire de la justice sous la IIIe République.* 3 vols., Paris, 1957.

Goldberg, Harvey, *The Life of Jean Jaurès.* Madison, Wisc., 1962.

Grèce, Eugénie de, *Pierre-Napoléon Bonaparte 1815–1881.* Paris, 1963.

Guedalla, Philip, *The Two Marshals: Bazaine, Petain.* New York, 1943.

Guillemin, Henri, *Les Origines de la Commune.* 3 vols., Paris, 1960.

Halasz, Nicholas, *Captain Dreyfus.* New York, 1955.

Howard, Michael, *The Franco-Prussian War.* New York, 1962.

Jackson, J. Hampden, *Clemenceau and the Third Republic.* London, 1946.

Jellinek, Frank, *The Paris Commune of 1871.* London, 1937.

Joughin, Jean T., *The Paris Commune in French Politics, 1871–1880.* 2 vols., Baltimore, Md., 1955.

la Gorce, Pierre de, *Histoire du Second Empire.* 7 vols., Paris, 1894–1905.

Laveau, Claude, "Les Communards dans les prisons charentaises." *Bulletin de l'Institut français d'histoire sociale,* #14 (January, 1956), pp. 30–47.

Lawson, F. H., Anton, A. E., and Brown, L. N., *Amos and Walton's Introduction to French Law,* 2nd ed. London, 1963.

Lissagaray, *History of the Commune of 1871,* 2nd. ed. of 1886. New York, 1898.

Lucas-Dubreton, J., *Monsieur Thiers.* Paris, 1948.

Mack, Gerstle, *Gustave Courbet.* New York, 1951.

Maitron, Jean, *Histoire du mouvement anarchiste en France (1880–1914).* Paris, 1951.

Malo, Henri, *Thiers.* Paris, 1932.

Manevy, Raymond, *La Presse de la IIIe République.* Paris, 1955.

———, *La Presse française de Renaudot à Rochefort.* Paris, 1958.

Martin, René, *La vie d'un grand journaliste, Auguste Nefftzer.* Besançon, 1948–53.

Marx, Karl, *The Civil War in France*. London, 1891.

Maurain, J., *Un bourgeois français au XIXᵉ siècle. Baroche*. Paris, 1936.

Maurois, André, *Olympio ou la vie de Victor Hugo*. Paris, 1954.

Minnich, Arthur, Jr., "The Third Force, 1870–1896," in E. M. Earle, ed., *Modern France* (Princeton, 1951).

Mohrt, Michel, *Les Intellectuels devant la Défaite, 1870*. Paris, 1942.

Monteilhet, J., *Les Institutions Militaires de la France 1814–1932*. Paris, 1932.

Osgood, Samuel M., *French Royalism Under the Third and Fourth Republics*. The Hague, 1960.

Paul-Boncour, J., *Entre Deux Guerres: Souvenirs sur la IIIᵉ République*. 2 vols., Paris, 1945.

Plamenatz, John, *The Revolutionary Movement in France, 1815–1871*. London, 1952.

Power, T., *Jules Ferry and the Renaissance of French Imperialism*. New York, 1943.

Powers, Richard H., *Edgar Quinet: A Study in French Patriotism*. Dallas, 1957.

Reclus, Maurice, *L'Avènement de la IIIᵉ République, 1871–1875*. Paris, 1930.

Rihs, Charles, *La Commune de Paris, sa structure et ses doctrines*. Geneva, 1955.

Saint Marc, Pierre, *Émile Ollivier*. Paris, 1950.

Sorel, Georges, *La Révolution Dreyfusienne*. Paris, 1909.

Thomson, David, *Democracy in France*. London, 1946.

Tannenbaum, Edward R., *The Action Française*. New York, 1962.

Verly, Albert, *Le Général Boulanger et la conspiration monarchique*. Paris, 1893.

Viel Castel, Count Horace de, *Memoirs of Count Horace de Viel Castel*. 2 vols., London, 1888.

Weber, Eugen J., *The Action Française*. Stanford and Paris, 1962.

Weill, Georges, *Histoire du mouvement social en France, 1852–1902*. Paris, 1904.

———, *Histoire du parti républicain en France 1814–70*. Paris, 1928.

———, *Le journal, origines, évolution et role de la presse périodique*. Paris, 1936.

Zévaès, Alexandre, *L'Affaire Pierre Bonaparte*. Paris, 1929.

Zeldin, Theodore, *Émile Ollivier and the Liberal Empire of Napoleon III*. Oxford, 1963.

———, *Journal (of Émile Ollivier), 1846–1869*. 2 vols., London, 1961.

———, *The Political System of Napoleon III*. London, 1958.

Index

Illustration Acknowledgments

Credits are given in the same order as the illustrations.

Collection Viollet
Photo Giraudon
Photo Giraudon
Collection Viollet
Yale University, Sterling Library
Radio Times Hulton Picture Library
Radio Times Hulton Picture Library
Collection Viollet
New York Public Library, Prints Division
Radio Times Hulton Picture Library
Photo Giraudon
New York Public Library, Prints Division: From *Album de Siège* by Noé
The New York Public Library, Prints Division
Collection Viollet
New York Public Library
Photo Hachette
Radio Times Hulton Picture Library
New York Public Library
Radio Times Hulton Picture Library
Radio Times Hulton Picture Library
Radio Times Hulton Picture Library
Collection Viollet